MESSAGES TO GROUND ZERO
CHILDREN RESPOND TO SEPTEMBER 11, 2001

Collected by Shelley Harwayne with the New York City Board of Education

Book design by Plainspoke

Heinemann
Portsmouth, NH

HEINEMANN
A DIVISION OF REED ELSEVIER INC.
361 HANOVER STREET
PORTSMOUTH, NH 03801
WWW.HEINEMANN.COM

OFFICES AND AGENTS THROUGHOUT THE WORLD
COPYRIGHT © 2002 NEW YORK CITY BOARD OF EDUCATION

LIBRARY OF CONGRESS CATALOGING-IN-PUBLICATION DATA ON FILE
ISBN: 0-325-00514-1

BOOK DESIGN BY PLAINSPOKE/PORTSMOUTH NH
WWW.PLAINSPOKE.COM

In memory of all the good citizens lost in the terrorist attack on the World Trade Center.

And, in tribute to all the teachers, administrators, support staff and parent volunteers who made sure that the 1.1 million New York City Public School children were out of harm's way on September 11th, 2001.

Out of respect for our young contributors, we've left their pieces
exactly as they wrote them, including the occasional error in convention.

CONTENTS

DEAR READERS,

In your hands, you hold an historic anthology. On the morning of September 11th, 2001 many of our New York City students saw, heard, smelled, and felt things that none of the grown-ups were prepared to explain. Our students, as well as students throughout our country, picked up their pens, pencils, crayons, markers, and paint-brushes and attempted to make sense of this most incomprehensible of acts. Our children attempted to use their words and their art to wrap their arms around the tragedy that befell families in the New York metropolitan area as well as residents of Washington and Pennsylvania, a tragedy that brought heart-wrenching sorrow to citizens throughout our land. Our children also used their writing and art to offer condolence, comfort others and, of course, bear witness.

Since the horrific events of September 11th, 2001, we have spent countless hours reading the writing of children in response to that tragic day and viewing their compelling artwork as well. The vast majority of the pieces was created by students attending New York City public schools. Some were written immediately following the destruction of the Twin Towers, others were written several weeks and even months after the catastrophic event. Some were hastily jotted journal entries, others carefully crafted texts. Some are written in prose, others in poetry. Some pay tribute to emergency workers, others to teachers, neighbors, and family members. Some offer eyewitness accounts, others advice for dealing with loss or suggestions for returning to normalcy. Some are incredibly sad, others unintentionally funny in their childlike naiveté. All, however, were written from young people's points of view and therefore terribly important for everyone to read and remember. It is our sincere hope that our students' words and art will resonate for readers and inspire you to work towards peaceful child-hoods for students the world over.

With great respect for the writers and artists who contributed to this collection and to the teachers and administrators who invited and inspired them to do so.

Sincerely,

HAROLD O. LEVY, *CHANCELLOR*
NEW YORK CITY BOARD OF EDUCATION

SHELLEY HARWAYNE, *SUPERINTENDENT*
COMMUNITY SCHOOL DISTRICT #2

Mom wakes me up. I brush my teeth.

Do my hair and get dressed. Go to school.

Like any other normal day . . .

SEPTEMBER 11, 2001

ELEVENTH OF SEPTEMBER

It was on the eleventh of September
When two planes crashed into the world trade center.
It was a bright and sunny day
When the terrorists decided to have their way.

It was the eleventh of September
Americans will always remember.
The towers fell to ground zero
And America will remember her heroes.

It was a severe attack
But America will fight back.
Americans are united and strong.
And will not stand for what is wrong.

SANDI, GRADE 4
BROOKLYN

WORLD TRADE DOWNFALL

The World Trade Center was a home away from home for thousands. It was a source of power and life and caring. Dreams and jobs was its heart. And thanks to some dysfunctional minds and wicked souls who hijacked aircraft, the Twin Towers are no more.

Sending out cries of terror, the innocent citizens of New York fled from the scene. Police, firefighters, rescue workers and paramedics raced into the danger zone. These everyday heroes responded immediately to this terrible moment.

The explosion of the collapse sounded like millions of haunted ghost trains rumbling full speed ahead through a mountain railroad tunnel. The flames looked like a blazing inferno caused by a strike of zapping lightning. The dust cloud looked like a monster sandstorm in the middle of the Sahara Desert.

WORLD TRADE AFTERMATH

Finally, the swirling cloud of dust died out altogether. There was such a murmur among the crowd surrounding Ground Zero. That was when the extensive search for loved ones began. Children cried for their parents. Co-workers searched for their partners. Workers searched for their bosses.

Dogs were brought in to search the colossal mound of rubble until it was known to have no living bodies contained in the gigantic heap. Slowly the area of rubble is being disposed of. But the memories of the victims and Twin Towers will haunt us forever!

WORLD TRADE RECOVERY

People are now doing everything they can to recover. They have relief funds, memorials and candle lightings. They make badges to remind people not to lose hope. America is strong! Terrorists, whoever you are, wherever you are, beware!

So many songs are sung over America like an echo in a valley. The almighty and forgiving Lord watches over us constantly. God Bless the U.S.A.!

ANDRE, GRADE 3
BROOKLYN

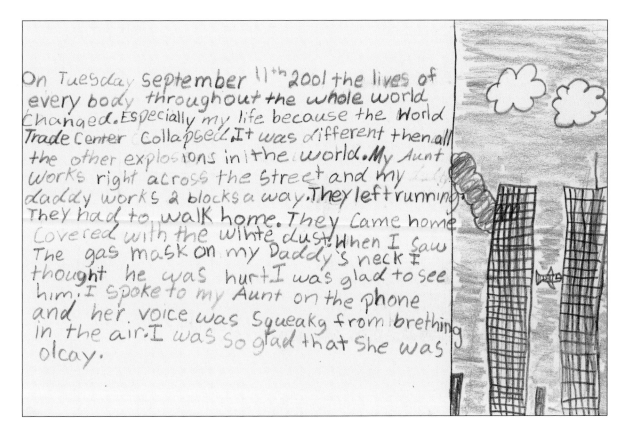

On Tuesday September 11th 2001 the lives of
every body throughout the whole world
changed. Especially my life because the World
Trade Center collapsed. It was different then all
the other explosions in the world. My Aunt
works right across the street and my
daddy works 2 blocks a way. They left running.
They had to walk home. They came home
covered with the white dust. When I saw
The gas mask on my Daddy's neck I
thought he was hurt. I was glad to see
him. I spoke to my Aunt on the phone
and her voice was squeaky from brething
in the air. I was so glad that she was
okay.

REGINA, AGE 8
MANHATTAN

MY POEM OF N.Y.C. TRAGEDY

My heart was torn
As I watched people mourn
I felt such pity for what they did to my city
The ground of Manhattan rumbled
As the Twin Towers crumbled
As this tragedy put a stain on our lives
We will work as a nation
To revenge our devastation
My heart will heal in time
But for now I can't get this off of my mind

VERONICA, GRADE 6
QUEENS

WALI, GRADE 5
BROOKLYN

THE DAY

Everyone started the day like any other.
The usual hustle and bustle of the morning.
People drinking huge mugs of coffee.

Until,

Something unusual happened,
two airplanes crashed into the
World Trade Center.

The whole city froze for a second.

The whole world froze for a second.

Now everything is different.

JACK, GRADE 4
MANHATTAN

MIZUKI, GRADE 6
QUEENS

9-11

On 9-11,
September 11, 2001
New York City
lost its
two front teeth.
For that was the day
the two
Twin Towers
collapsed.

JESSICA, GRADE 5
BROOKLYN

THE WORST HAPPENING

Too many people died.
I'm scared. I cried.
Many people lost their family.
But I was safe and so was my family.
Women, men, and children got hurt under the debris.
Some people died because they couldn't breathe.
Just because two hijacked air planes crashed in to the
Twin Towers
This was done on purpose
And happened in the middle of September.

MIZUKI, GRADE 6
QUEENS

MY thoughts about the World Trade Center... I think that it's very sad because many people died in the World Trade center. Many people are working very hard. The fire fighters, police, and other people are trying to clean it all up. I think that it is not going to be a war becase The Mayor and the President are takeing care of it. These days are almost safe thanks to everyone helping our city.

ILIRIJANA, AGE 8
MANHATTAN

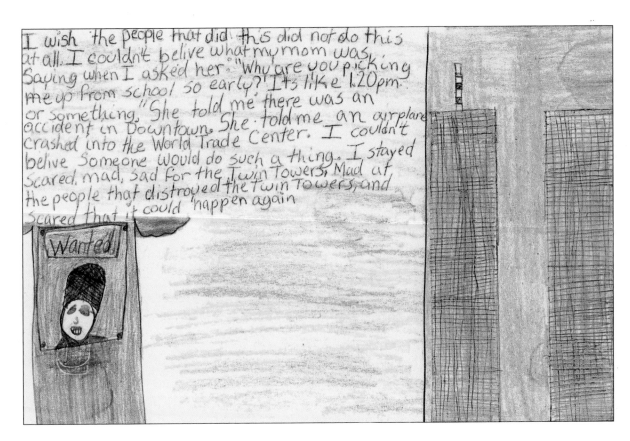

I wish the people that did this did not do this at all. I couldn't belive what my mom was saying when I asked her. "Why are you picking me up from school so early? It's like 1:20 pm. or something." She told me there was an accident in Downtown. She told me an airplane crashed into the World Trade Center. I couldn't belive Someone would do such a thing. I stayed Scared, mad, sad for the Twin Towers, Mad at the people that distroyed the Twin Towers, and Scared that it could happen again

Wanted

NUBIA, AGE 7
MANHATTAN

I rushed to the window to see smoke coming from the World Trade Center.
I saw an explosion coming from the other tower.
There was also an explosion
coming from my heart
when I saw the ball of fire.

SEPTEMBER 11

On September 11, 2001, the whole world came tumbling down. My uncle picked me up from school early in the day. Channel 7 showed the two planes crashing into the Twin Towers. I asked my mother why this happened. She told me that evil men called terrorists were responsible. I asked myself, "Why would anybody want to fly a plane into the buildings?" While I watched TV, I saw people jumping to their deaths one by one. The people on the ground were running away escaping from the crashing buildings. I saw fire and smoke. Then, the buildings came tumbling down.

Many people died. Luckily none of my relatives worked in the buildings.

DEVYONNE, GRADE 3
BRONX

THE ZOOMING PLANE

so much depends

upon

a plane zooming

by

next to a

building

filled with

people

JACK, GRADE 4
MANHATTAN

I'M PROUD TO BE AN AMERICAN

Meaningless touches,
   Icy Stares,
Cold-hearted people,
Millions of glares.
How can they know?
What do they see?
They think they know
What goes on inside of me.
I can't help but ask,
Were they once in my shoes?
Have they too paid their dues?
Have they been different?
Then there was one behind me,
Which was Bin Laden, I could see.
I turned around and boldly said aloud,
"I am an American and I'm proud!"

STEPHANIE, GRADE 8
BROOKLYN

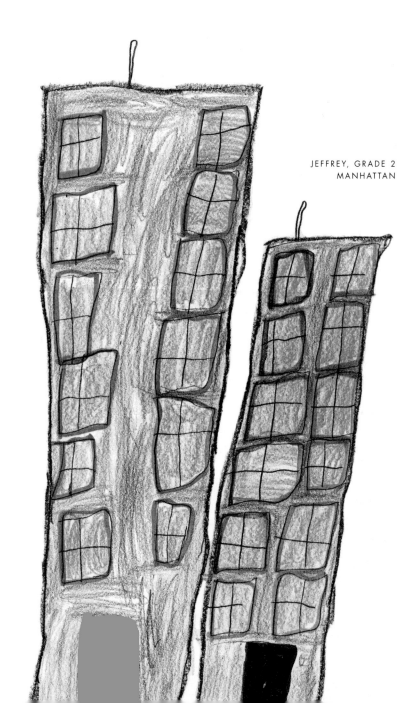

JEFFREY, GRADE 2
MANHATTAN

A DAY OF INFAMY

People's hearts are broken
Their tears could fill an ocean
Children's lives are shattered
Into a smoke of terror
Let us all mourn together

LEOVINA, GRADE 5
BROOKLYN

On September 11th my mom picked me up early from school. She asked if I knew what had happend. I said "Yeah, the trains are not working and the buses are not running." That's not all that had happend. Then were two airplanes and they went straight for the Twin Tower. When it hit there was a hage explosen. The smoke came zooming down. People ran for their lives. The smoke came rushing. Finally it comed down. Finally it was over. But it's not over for New York.

THE UNKNOWN TRAGEDY

Mom wakes me up.
I brush my teeth.
Do my hair and get dressed.
Go to school.
Like any other normal day.
Teacher leaves the room.
Comes back in sorrow.
Kids have no clue of what's going on.
Teacher tells us the World Trade
Center is now gone.
Pentagon also hit but not destroyed.
Kids sad and worried.
School right there and then was
a scared angry place.
Tears wanting to come down.
Kids hoping parents are okay.
School right now is over.
I went home early.
Not with my mom but with my
grandma.
2:30 P.M. my mom comes home.
Sisters happy with joy.
Mom tells the amazing story.
I go home in peace.
But sleep in terror.

DANIELLE, GRADE 5
BROOKLYN

ANGELINA, HIGH SCHOOL
QUEENS

ATTACK ON AMERICA

It was an attack,
an attack on America! Horrifying!
The Twin Towers came falling down,
to Ground Zero!
Hijacked planes crashed
into New York's skyline.
During the infamy
Tons of people
called 911, on a day
that will go down into
the world's history 9/11
We honor all those rescuers,
being courageous,
risking their lives
for the
*U*S*A*
How could they do this,
many people ask
those crazy terrorists
crashing into the Twin Towers
Ending their lives with a blast
But our American life
continues to go on!!
It was a terrible, disastrous
thing that these terrorists did
But America, being the
STRONGEST
country in the world,
Won't let this happen again!

Let Freedom Ring

HELAINE, GRADE 5
BROOKLYN

THE TOWERS

Two buildings in the heart of New York gone with the blink of an eye. You try to remember the last thing you said to him or her today. Tears shed all over. People become heroes, whether they're police officers or men bringing clothing to a shelter. People being put out of homes. Trains, buses and airports are shutdown. Smoke everywhere. Trembling women clutching their children. All the while trying to be brave, slowly trying to accept the fact that they will no longer see or hear their loved ones ever again. Streets covered with smoke, damage and dust. Frantic people running, trying to save themselves. Buildings crumbling down to the ground with people's precious lives going down with them.

In Loving Memory of the Victims,

We Give Our Condolences to Their Families

DANIELLY, GRADE 7
BRONX

HELAINE, GRADE 5
BROOKLYN

THE ATTACK

On a warm tuesday morning we were at school. We practiced our class poem then everone ran to the window to admire to airplan that was flying by. After the plan had passed the window we heard a huge explosion! A while after we had to be dismessd.

I walked out of the school and I watched the enormuse towers burn in flames. My mother and I wasted no time watching and ran up town to get my sister and spend the night in my fathers office. We were on a walkway by the river in a small crowd of people. We were a safe distance from the towers when the first building collapsed. The smoke around the tower curled in then sqeezed out again. Everyone ran. People screamed and burst into tears.

Minutes later the second building collapsed. I could tell on the looks on their faces, almost everyone was going to faint. We got safely away although it was a very terrible tragety.

WESLEY, GRADE 4
MANHATTAN

ON SEPTEMBER 11

On September 11, the twin towers were torn apart.
Along with it went a piece of everyone's heart.
On September 11, a tragedy took place.
The people who did this are a disgrace.
On September 11, terror hit home.
Many people felt sad and alone.
September 11, people cried.
They prayed their loved ones were still alive.

On September 11, many were lost.
Osama Bin Laden must pay the cost!
On September 11, we were unprepared.
Now the attackers are all scared!
On September 11, no one could run.
Now it's America's turn to have some fun!
On September 11, we all shared pain
In our hearts, we only saw rain.
On September 11, we were all changed
None of us will ever be the same!

STEPHANIE, GRADE 7
BRONX

I REMEMBER

The sensation I felt
When our principal
Told us what had happened.

I remember
The look on people's faces
At school
And hearing
People cry.

I remember watching TV
How Bush's words
Had such an impact on me.

I remember
How you could see the towers
The sun glinting off the windows
Feeling almost proud of the towers.

Then finally seeing my mom
Hugging her
Like I hadn't seen her in days.

Watching the news
Seeing the plane crash
And hearing the screams
As the towers
Crashed to the ground

FERNANDO, GRADE 7
MANHATTAN

HEROES

TO THOSE WHO CAME TO THE RESCUE

HEROES

Heroes are . . .
. . . The sunlight
Of a growing plant.
. . . The water
Of a waterfall.
. . . The colors   Heroes can be . . .
Of a rainbow.   . . . Of any race.
. . . The honey   . . . Of any color.
Of a honeybee.   . . . Of any gender.
. . . A part of America.   They are all special in their own way.

Heroes belong to families—
To children,
To wives,
To husbands,
To communities,
To you and I.

The WTC tragedy showed us that the
United States of America is a land of heroes.

LAURA, GRADE 5
QUEENS

DEAR FIREFIGHTERS,

I am very sorry about what took place on September 11th. I am very
fearful but I wanted to be strong for you. I know you would want me
to be. I am going to stay positive as long as you need me. I feel sorry
for you because you have to go to the Twin Towers every day. I know
your feet must ache and your backs pain. My classmates and our entire
school are trying to help. We have collected pennies to donate toward
all your hard work. You are trying to keep Manhattan clean. Sometimes
I get very disappointed in what I hear on the news. I try not to listen
but I can't stop. I hope life gets better for us all.

SHERIKA, GRADE 3
BROOKLYN

HEROES

Superman's NOT a hero, a real one is my Dad.
Papa is a fireman, the best you ever had!
Helping people, saving lives is something done each day.
He does not leap tall buildings, he climbs up all the way.

Spiderman's NOT a hero, a real one is my brother.
He is a policeman and brave like no other!
Helping people, saving lives is something done all year.
He does not throw a magic web, he helps people not to fear.

Wonderwoman's NOT a hero, a real one is my Mom.
As a nurse she is the best, hard-working, kind and calm.
Helping people, saving lives is something done with love.
She doesn't have a magic rope, she has a gentle touch.

Batman's NOT a hero, a real one is my uncle.
As a doctor he's the one you'll want when there is trouble.
Helping people, saving lives is something done with pride.
He doesn't have a Batmobile, an ambulance is his ride.

PowerRangers are NOT heroes, real ones are my cousins.
As hard-hats they went to work numbering in the dozens.
Helping people, saving lives are things they've never done.
They do not have Zap power but moved steel beams by the ton.

ERICA AND TARA, GRADE 5
BROOKLYN

LESLIE, GRADE 8
BRONX

**"I'VE LEARNED—
THAT YOU CAN KEEP GOING LONG
AFTER YOU THINK YOU CAN'T."**

In the World Trade tragedy the firefighters kept going long after we thought they couldn't. They ran inside a burning building to save people and lost their lives. They looked for bodies day and night. They are still standing by each other giving a helping hand. They don't want to stop digging. These are the heroes of New York City.

ISAIAH, GRADE 8
BRONX

PARA LOS BOMBEROS,

Le damos muchas graseas por ayudar a todo el mndo.
Una niña de primer grado de la escuela 84.
Yo soy Genesis.

Dear Firemen,

We give you many thanks for helping the world.
From a girl in first grade at School 84.
I am Genesis.

**"I'VE LEARNED—
THAT HEROES ARE THE PEOPLE WHO DO WHAT
HAS TO BE DONE WHEN IT NEEDS TO BE DONE,
REGARDLESS OF THE CONSEQUENCES."**

Our heroes during the tragedy on Tuesday were the fireman. They went inside the building to help people get out. While doing this they ended up losing their own lives. They risked their lives to help others. They didn't think about what could happen to them. This is why they are called New York's Bravest.

GABRIEL, GRADE 8
BRONX

CATHERINE, GRADE 3
QUEENS

DEAR LOCAL FIREHOUSES,

On September 11, 2001, a terrible tragedy occurred. The Twin Towers was destroyed. But still, you firefighters came to the spot where the World Trade Center once stood and started digging for surviving victims underneath the rubble. You kept on working even though you were dirty, tired, and hungry. You didn't even sleep for a whole day and still you kept right on working and I admire that. That is why you deserve lots of appreciation from different kinds of people. And you certainly deserved my appreciation one hundred percent!

LAWRENCE, MIDDLE SCHOOL
BROOKLYN

QUERIDOS BOMBERS,

Grasa muchas grasas para ayouda a nostos.
Yo Soy Rosalind.

Dear Firemen,

Thank you, thank you very much for helping us.
I am Rosalind.

Sept. 17th

Dear Fireman,

My name is Cadence. I'm
missing an uncle. Please find
him. His name is Gonja. His
Family misses him. We'll keep praying
for him. If he's alive and you
find him tell him "Cadence and
his family miss him". He was
the Best uncle in the world. I
feel like crying.

Love, Cadence

CADENCE, GRADE 4

CANDY, GRADE 4
BROOKLYN

. . . firefighters came to the spot where
the World Trade Center once stood and started digging
for surviving victims underneath the rubble.

You kept on working even though you were

dirty, tired, and hungry

. . . and I admire that.

QUERIDOS BOMBEROS,

Gracias a todos los bomberos pol salvar las getes.
Yo soi Amy.

Dear Firemen,

Thanks to all the firemen for saving people.
I am Amy.

MY HERO

My hero,
My pillow before a fall,
My life preserver in deep water,
My medicine during a cold,
My fuel during a race,
My jacket in cold weather,
My solution to a problem,
My help in time of need,
My family,
My very own firefighter—

My Uncle Phil.

GREGORY, GRADE 5
QUEENS

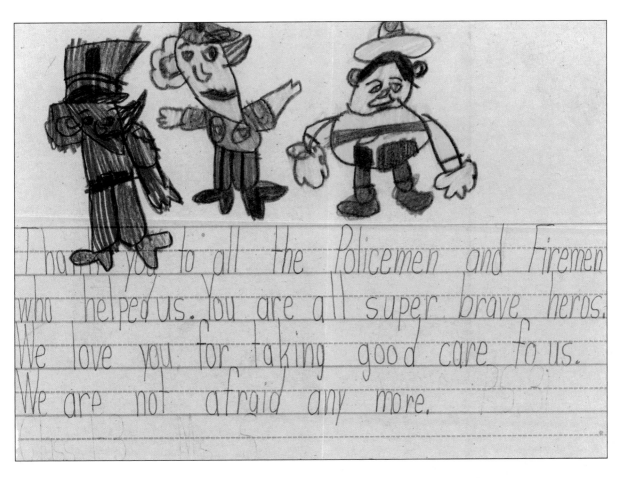

Thank you to all the Policemen and Firemen who helped us. You are all super brave heros. We love you for taking good care fo us. We are not afrgid any more.

ALICE AND KATTY, GRADE 1
BROOKLYN

DEAR FIREFIGHTERS,

Thank you for helping people injured in the World Trade Center. My mom works right next to the World Trade Center and saw what happened. My mom saw when the first plane hit the tower. My friend and I did not know what was going on in the city while we were reading, writing and solving math problems. However, I knew something didn't feel right in my stomach when I saw many kids in my class going home early. When my dad picked me up after school, he told me what happened. I asked him where it happened and he told me in Manhatten.

I will never forget September 11, 2001, and what you did to help us. From my home I see so many people with American flags on their cars and outside their homes. I can't help but think how beautiful the red, white and blue looks. When I look at the news I see how it looks on ground zero, I cry when I think about what happened. My mom had to get all her stuff from her old job so she could bring it to her new job. My mom said her desk was messy. I am sorry that some of your friends did not make it. Sometimes when it is time to go home, you just go. We do not always know the circumstances. You should always believe in someone or something, that usually helps me during tough times. I pray for all of the Firefighters in the world every night. When I am doing math I always say to myself, if my school was in Manhattan next to the World Trade Center what would have happened to us? I am happy to be here.

GABRIELLE, GRADE 3
BROOKLYN

The fireman, Red Cross, policeman,

from all over the United States helped out in the rescue.

When something happens to others we help.

This is why we are called

the United States

of America.

SAMANTHA, GRADE 5
QUEENS

HERO

A fireman is so brave,
for all the lives he tries to save.
There's flames and smoke and blazing fire,
yet toils and doesn't tire.
When people and pets are running out,
firemen rush in without a doubt.
They've worked for days at a site named "Ground Zero."
To me a fireman is truly a "Hero."

JESSICA, GRADE 5
BROOKLYN

My American Hero

My favorite American hero is a fireman, because he is one of New York's bravest. Every time the alarm sounds he knows he is about to risk his own life to rescue people or put out a fire in a burning building. Along with his fellow firefighters, he jumps into a bright red fire truck with lots of sirens to head to a scene unknown. Once he get there, he searches for the fire and the victims. I think that being a fireman is a very tough job. I feel that we should honor the New York Fire Departments, men and women who fight fires everyday.

DONOVAN, GRADE 4
BROOKLYN

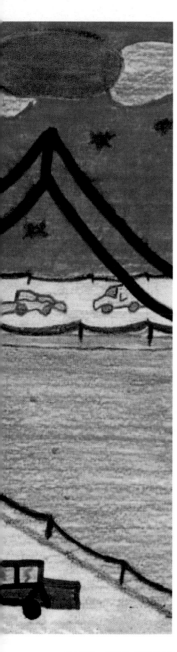

CAROL, HIGH SCHOOL
QUEENS

**"I'VE LEARNED—
THAT IT'S NOT WHAT HAPPENS
TO PEOPLE THAT'S IMPORTANT.
IT'S WHAT YOU DO ABOUT IT."**

We had nothing to do with what happened to people
on Tuesday. Many Americans united to do something
about it. The fireman, Red Cross, policeman, from all
over the United States helped out in the rescue. When
something happens to others we help. This is why we
are called the United States of America.

ANDRE, GRADE 8
BRONX

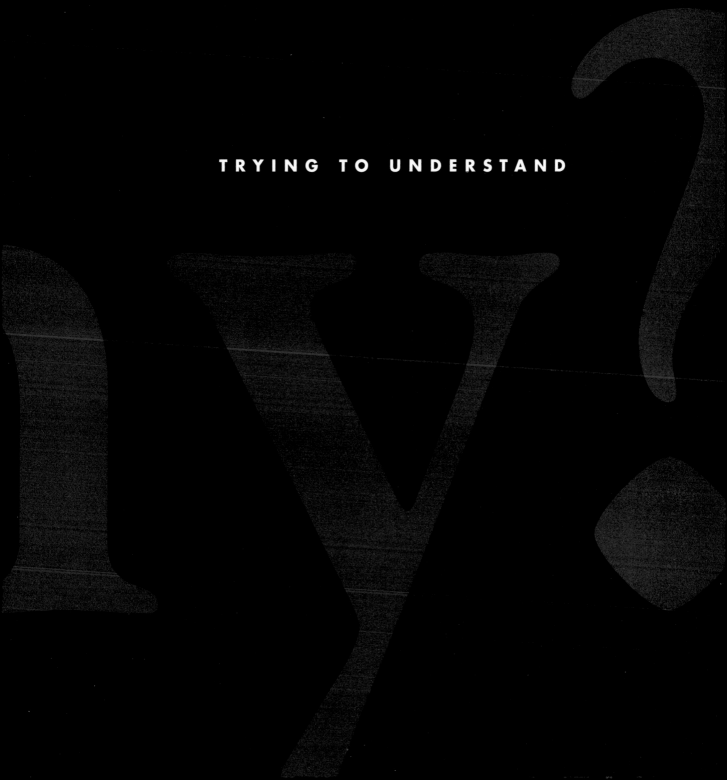

TRYING TO UNDERSTAND

I ASK MYSELF

"Why is there so much hatred and envy?" I asked myself as I saw the pain in my fellow classmates' eyes. I saw tears roll down many faces as they anxiously wondered about their loved ones. It was hard to grasp. I stared at the screen, incredulous. I saw the flaming giants, brothers built with time and effort, crumble in a matter of seconds.

We cannot do this to ourselves, we cannot. Do we all not bleed red? Are we not the same inside? The hearts and minds of the men capable of this atrocious act were twisted and that was perhaps the greatest difference.

So why is there so much hatred and envy, I ask myself. Why?

CRISSY, GRADE 12
QUEENS

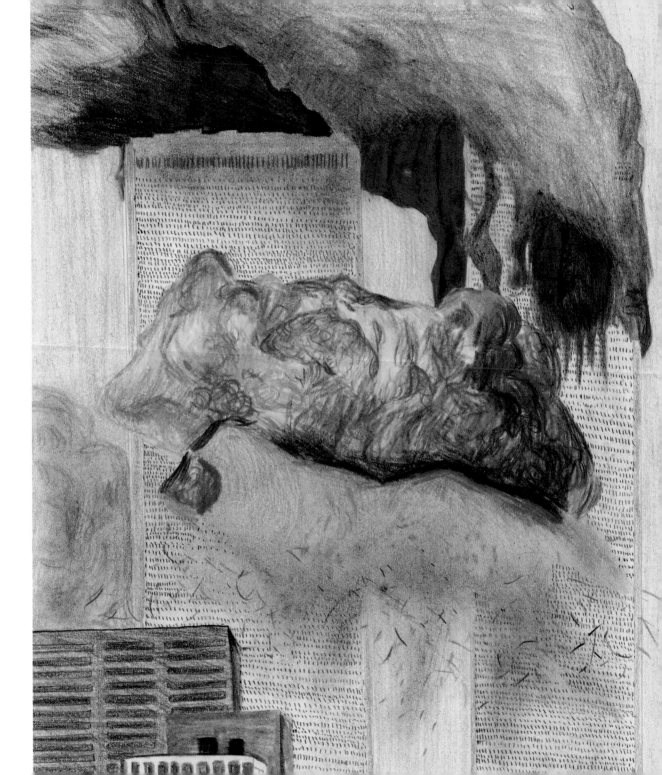

I felt sad about the World Trade Center. It was so sad. Some lost their brother and sister and friends. It wasn't time for them to go All those People to go. That was so so Sad.

KEVIN, AGE 8
MANHATTAN

NECESSARY BLAME

Targets of violence
Reports of harassment against Arabs
Direct opposition to the
principles of the United States
An attack
A priest awakened early
To bottles filled with gasoline and
Flames pouring out
A man
Screamed
He was doing this for his country
The phone at the mission
Ringing with death threats

ALEX, GRADE 7
MANHATTAN

ANSWER MY WHYS

Why must our world be like this?
Why did the twin towers get destroyed?
Why must there be war?
Why didn't the President and the enemies think?
Why not handle this in Mars?
If we knew why,
There would be no such thing as war.

Innocent people, all trying to earn a living,
Why must we be scared?
Why must the world be like this?

JEFFREY, GRADE 8
MANHATTAN

Buildings crumbling down to the ground with

people's precious lives

going down with them.

"I'VE LEARNED—
THAT WE ARE RESPONSIBLE FOR WHAT
WE DO, NO MATTER HOW WE FEEL."

If the terrorist didn't like our way of living they should not have destroyed our buildings and killed so many innocent people. They are responsible for all of our crying and heartaches. They should pay for what they did. They should be punished. They should be executed.

CURTIS, GRADE 8
BRONX

THE DAY

Planes fly over quiet skies bringing news hastily
People watching unaware that death rides through the air

   Planes now crash as fear dances
"Yes, get scared," is what we hear

People run away
People jump off . . . don't stay
People are killed . . . with no good-bye
   When planes fly over quiet skies,

We must now be careful
of those filled with
lies!

KEVIN, GRADE 5
BRONX

WORLD TRADE CENTER

Innocent people staring
in foreign skies, making
their last calls,
saying good bye.

People walking into their
tombs,
different chamber rooms.

Death called those souls
that day
but, "Bin Laden the U.S."
says,
"You Shall Pay!"

NELSON, GRADE 5
BRONX

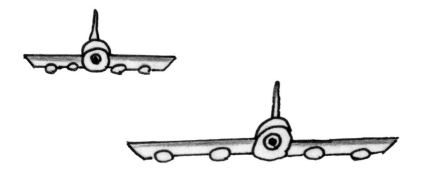

People are killed . . .
with no good-bye

When planes fly over quiet skies

DON'T GO

Mommy please don't go to work today,
I don't feel right, you have to stay.
Honey, you know that I have to go,
There's no way around it, the money is low.
I'll try to call you on my lunch break,
Take some aspirin if your tummy starts to ache.
Okay, Mommy, I'll miss you lots,
Please tell me I'll be in your thoughts.
Don't worry, baby, you will be,
Just rest here and wait for me.
And that was when she left her little son,
With no idea of the importance in 9-1-1.
She stepped into her office on the 92nd floor,
Not knowing she would witness a horrible act of war.
After she was at work for almost an hour,
A hijacked airplane crashed into the tower.
She ran down the stairs as fast as she could,
But realized that it would do no good.
The building was collapsing on top of her,
She tried to get out, but it was all a blur.

Soon she couldn't breathe from all the dust,
But she thought of her son, keep going, she must.
She screamed for help, but her cry was ignored.
She thought of her son, and prayed to the lord.
She tried to hang on, but it was just too much.
She prayed for her son, just one last touch.
She and thousands of others were later found dead.
People across the nation were hurt, countless tears
    were shed.
Whoever did this should be haunted with shame.
The great New York City will never be the same.
A shattered city is all that is left behind.
These acts of hatred have left us blind.
Too blind to see what the world would be,
With peace and love and all people free.
Mommy please, please don't go.
If only she listened to her little hero.

AMANDA, GRADE 8
BROOKLYN

A CHANGING WORLD

There is an old Chinese saying: "We live in interesting times." We used to think that meant a healthy economy, numerous technological advances and a bright future. On the morning of September 11th 2001 however, those interesting times changed.

We were attacked and many innocent people lost their lives. It was unprovoked and it took us completely off guard. The television news channels were in full force, as were the police and fire department. Now the interesting times in which we live are uncertain and frightful. News of anthrax, war and the dead consume our lives. It is not escapable, and it is certainly not over.

Despite all this, we continue. Our leaders have asked us to do what we normally do. Go to school, shop, take someone out or play a sport. No one thought the day would come when we would be asked to go on with our lives as usual.

The time has come to fight back and we are. By supporting our leaders and each other, we are stronger than ever. We will never forget those who died, nor will we forgive those who took them from us.

MICHAEL, HIGH SCHOOL
QUEENS

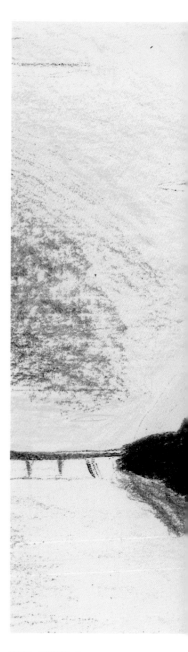

ERIC, GRADE 9
QUEENS

Whoever did this should be haunted with shame.

The great New York City
will never be the same.

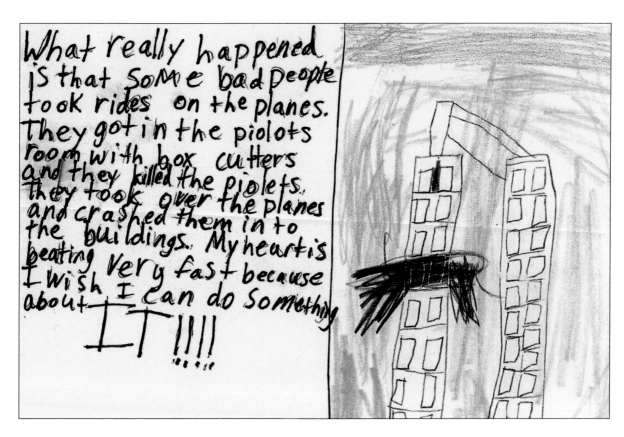

What really happened is that some bad people took rides on the planes. They got in the piolots room with box cutters and they killed the piolets. they took over the planes and crashed them in to the buildings. My heart is beating very fast because I wish I can do something about IT!!!!

MIKE, AGE 7
MANHATTAN

THE WEAPON

People keep saying, "its like a movie, like a book".
No not at all like a movie or a book.
This is what it looks like when an actual plane with
actual people hits skyscraper.
This is the truth.
This was men armed only with knives and box cutters
Relying on simple speed to accomplish their goal.
All you had to do was be willing to die and these guys were.
It could happen again

JAKE, GRADE 7
MANHATTAN

WE BEND BUT WE CANNOT BREAK

This time, no
New Yorker
Escaped the agony inflicted by the terrorists
     who hijacked the passenger planes
and turned them into human
Missiles
If nothing else, every living soul breathed the
     air befouled by fire and smoke and
yes,
Seared
     Human
          Flesh.
Now everyone knew the acrid smell of
Death.
Now they knew fear
Proud pillars of culture seemed
     momentarily irrelevant.
But while the city
B
  E
    N
      T, it did not fold.
Not for a second.

By its nature, true heroism is in the province of few.
Ordinary
New Yorkers
Responded to catastrophe with *grace* and small kindnesses
Passengers collided on the subway and exchanged
     understanding glances
instead of four-letter insults
One procession of 156
Hearses
S t r e t c h e d for almost a mile.
This time, the
Hearses
Could extend to the
horizon
Everyone has been painfully reminded that
Manhattan
Is an island.
When disaster strikes there is no easy way out!

CARA, GRADE 7
MANHATTAN

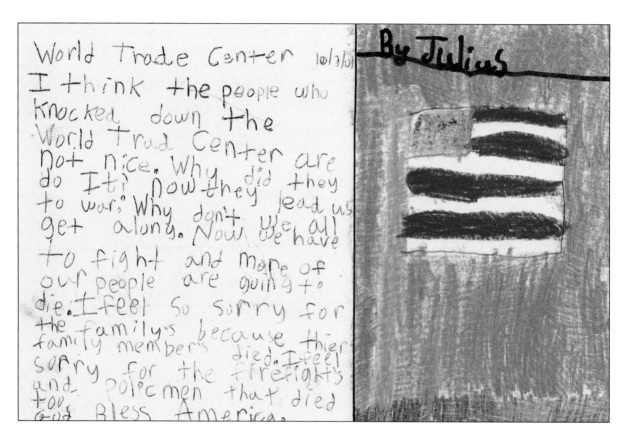

World Trade Center 10/3/01

I think the people who knocked down the World Trade Center are not nice. Why did they do It? Now they lead us to war? Why don't we all get along. Now we have to fight and more of our people are going to die. I feel so sorry for the family's because thier family members died. I feel sorry for the firefights and policemen that died too. God Bless America.

By Julius

JULIUS, AGE 8
MANHATTAN

SHOULD I HAVE KILLED
OSAMA BIN LADEN?

I have a very vivid imaginary life. In that world, I love to fly in my jet, to drive fast cars on racetracks, to lick on a lollypop that never runs out.

Since September 11th, I have been imagining that the world never changed, that the World Trade Center never collapsed, that there were no hijackers in the air, that little kids and grandmas did not die in the fire.

In my imaginary world, I am free to travel in time. I'm face to face with Osama Bin Laden and we're both children. I also have the power to see into the future and see the evil he will bring to the world. I look into his eyes and try to ask him, "Do you need help? Do you need love?" I try to figure out who has offended him so much that he could never forget and never forgive. I have the chance to kill him so the firefighters could go home on September 11th, so their kids would not be orphans, so there would be no cloud above Manhattan. I cannot, though. I know there will always be someone else who will try to bring evil to the world, and I am not an evil person who can kill another.

I know all about evil. I lived it in Moscow, Russia where people were evil and hated those who were different just because of their background. That hate brought death. I smelled death around me. I hid under the bed when the tanks were shooting and the helicopter was hanging above my roof. I know all too well how that terror made me stutter.

On September 11th, I knew I was not imagining anything. I knew it was a war. But this war was different. This war was worse than any other. This war reminded me of when I was in California with my uncle on July 4. I heard the fire works and thought that war started. But I was wrong. My uncle said there are no wars in America. But now I realize he was wrong.

KEVIN, GRADE 5
MANHATTAN

POEM

There were people running up Broadway
I don't know how I can help
All I saw were scared faces
I don't know how I can help
Many were talking to each other, "What is the next target?"
I don't know how I can help
I smelled the panic
I don't know how I can help
Raging fires, broken windows in apartments
I don't know how I can help
Dust on cars, smashed, wrecked trucks, sound of sirens
I don't know how I can help...

EDWIN, GRADE 7
MANHATTAN

WHY?

People's lives are destroyed
They are more than annoyed
A heap of garbage everywhere
Look at the terrorists, they don't care
The terrorists might be here today
We must destroy them, they must pay
They have hurt us in more than one way

LEOVINA, GRADE 5
BROOKLYN

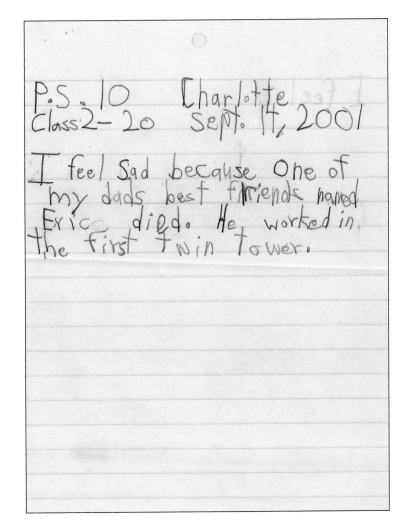

P.S. 10   Charlotte
Class 2-20   Sept. 14, 2001

I feel sad because one of
my dads best friends named
Erice died. He worked in
the first twin tower.

CHARLOTTE, GRADE 2
QUEENS

CRASH

Crash
Terrorists Crashed
Killed Themselves
To Kill Other People
Very Cruel
New War Begins
Very Scary
Like A Movie
People Run
People Die
Smoke
Debris
Darkness

BRANDON, GRADE 5
BROOKLYN

THERE WAS . . .

There was the underlying
sense of fear and disbelief as
I looked outside my building
at the burning, once
splendid World Trade Center,
smelling the acrid smoke
pouring from within the very
heart of the structure,
feeling my mouth open in
disbelief as, with a sonic
boom, the once magnificent
edifice collapsed, leaving an
exceedingly pungent taste
in my mouth.

KATE, GRADE 7
MANHATTAN

"I'VE LEARNED—
THAT YOUR LIFE CAN BE CHANGED IN
A MATTER OF MINUTES, BY PEOPLE WHO
DON'T EVEN KNOW YOU."

We didn't know who the terrorists were and they managed to change our lives. People are mourning and others are praying. People that never went to church before are going to church now. The terrorists really woke the United States up. Many people lost their lives. So many people lost their loved ones. A large number of people lost their jobs. Our buildings, The World Trade Center, and the Pentagon were destroyed. We didn't even know these people and look at how we are affected by this tragedy.

JOHN, GRADE 8
BRONX

**"I'VE LEARNED—
THAT THE PEOPLE YOU CARE ABOUT
MOST IN LIFE ARE TAKEN FROM YOU
TOO SOON."**

In the World Trade Center tragedy many people got killed. These people had families. They had children. It isn't fair that they died the way they did. Their families feel bad. They should not have died that way.

SHELINA, GRADE 8
BRONX

GRACE
QUEENS

Thinking of a Blessing

Thinking of days gone by
where people were happy
and didn't cry

Thinking of flowers
blowing in the wind

Thinking of the children
I don't know where to begin

Thinking of the tragedy
of America the great
Thinking of the people
waiting at the golden gate

Thinking of a blessing
to think and to say
Thinking of that
very sad day

JULIAN
LEOMINSTER, MASSACHUSETTS

VIEWS FROM A CHILD, AGE 4

Why is mommy so sad today?
She won't play with me
Where did those tall buildings from the window go?
Mommy hasn't stopped watching TV
The same scary movie has been on all day
It's about buildings falling down
Mommy is crying
Daddy hasn't come home from work yet
Why is mommy so sad today?

KAREN, GRADE 7
MANHATTAN

SEAMLESS MONUMENT

The grimy dust covered streets
full of people.
Dark confusion is hidden
in every corner,
waiting to jump out
on the next person it sees.
There is no yelling.
Quiet.

People streaming across streets.
People of different colors, different races.
People just walking away.
People getting away from the world
behind them.
Away from a world they don't want to know
about.
Away from tragedies they don't want to face.

SOPHIE, GRADE 5
MANHATTAN

JONATHAN, GRADE 8
QUEENS

I DON'T KNOW

Why did so many people have to die?
I don't know.

Candles lit in Union Square for each of their souls, canvasing
the area to give their families some hope.
I don't know.

A school day turned into a nightmare.
I don't know.

A trip home turned into chaos and confusion.
I don't know.

I look down Third Avenue, and in place of the Twin Towers,
I see a huge dark plume of smoke, smearing the sky with grey.
I don't know.

There's an eerie silence in my neighborhood, and then, once
in a while the shattering sound of a siren—where is it going?
I don't know.

Why did so many people have to die?
I don't know.

ADRIA, GRADE 7
MANHATTAN

...I heard the fire works and thought war had started.

My uncle said there are no wars in America.
But now I realize
he was wrong.

ANTONIO, GRADE 9
QUEENS

METAL GRASS

Torn metal, twisted and bent,
Like something out of a bad dream.
Fire and smoke; people tearing through the barrier,
Of ash and iron.
Dust, like morning dew, settling upon everything in sight,
Debris, piled high on the ground.
A field of metal grass,
The blades stretching upward and in every direction possible,
The people like ants, searching through the grass,
For others like them who have fallen.
Tears fall and truths are realized,
Coming to terms with disaster is never easy,
Especially when you're so small,
Like an ant in a field of metal grass.

DAVID, GRADE 10
MANHATTAN

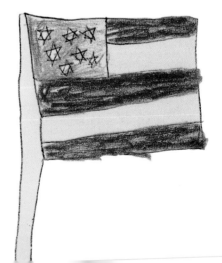

9.11 TRAGEDY

In the land
of the free
and the home
of the brave,
    Everybody's
perplexed and indignant.
Who did this?
What happened?
Why did it happened?
    Everybody
offended and in outrage.
    Everybody
so preoccupied
of this matter,
so unforwarned
and so unfortunate.
    Everybody
in panic and chaos.

Everybody
in devastation and in tears,
so heavyhearted and mournful.
    Everybody
shaking their heads
not believing anything they saw.
    The only face
in this scene that is joyful
is the face of
the terrorist
the face of
evil and
the face of
Osama Bin Laden.

AMANDA, GRADE 5
MANHATTAN

Where were you?

HENRY'S DAY

As I was dropped off by my mother at the Middle School, I sensed that nothing could possibly go wrong. I was being switched into my favorite class today, and had all my work done in advance as well. Yes, today was a great day.

My mother hugged me and I said goodbye to her. I bolted up the stairs, excited and elated to be in this new class. When I reached the 4th floor, I walked into my new classroom. Our teacher, Mr. Henn, said, "Good morning, class." And we replied, as always, in a dull tone, "Good morning, Mr. Henn." He picked up a piece of chalk and proceeded to write the date and his name on the board, so it read: Mr. Henn, September 11th, 2001. He turned to face us and opened his mouth to say something, but was cut off by the sound of the bell. I picked up my books and went down to music.

As I walked into the music room, I felt the bustling of kids moving this way and that. After walking through a sea of kids, instruments, and music stands, I finally reached the instrument room. I took out my trumpet, X14, and began to warm up. Mr. Pitt, our music teacher, tapped his conducting wand twice on a stand, and raised his hands for us to cease playing. As he began to talk about playing music, and the old teachers he once had, the phone rang.

In all of my school years I am yet to get a call summoning me to the office. But this one was for me. I was instructed to go directly to the office and to bring my books and to put my instrument away. After doing so, I ran up the stairs the same way I had in the morning, except this time in a nervous, jolting way. As I walked through the empty, quiet hallways, questions raced through my head. What had I done wrong? Are they switching me again? I searched my head and could find no reason for this call. Then I walked in the office to find my mother, standing there. A small tear was rolling down her cheek. I asked her what had happened, and then I was told the news.

As I climbed into the large car, I found my brother there, with a frown on his always-smiling face. As I pulled the door shut, I felt an unsteady silence in the car. Such a silence had never existed in our car before, and this added to my shock and sadness. My eyes welled up with tears and I began to cry, but with no noise involved, it was just simply tears.

As we were driving on to pick up my sister at her school, I heard a shocking statement that made me ponder upon whether this tragedy was a reality.

I cupped my hand over my mouth and my ears just couldn't transfer it to my brain. No more than 20-30 minutes later, the next tower collapsed, leaving only a pile ten stories high of murder, death, and twisted metal. I could hear screams of a reporter, of her interviewee, running from the flying smoke and rubble. I covered my ears as if it was right outside of the car window.

I couldn't believe it. The same towers that beautified the skyline we were famous for. The same towers I would hang out with my friends in. The same towers that I would smile at seeing at each morning. I felt horrified. I felt saddened. But most of all, I felt stripped of the same towers that belonged to my view.

HENRY, GRADE 7
MANHATTAN

"We have just received news that two planes have crashed into the World Trade Center. We think these are terrorist attacks. The first airplane hit the building at approximately 8:30am. Only 18 minutes later, a similar plane hit the second building. If you have family members that work in, or near the World Trade Center, please stay behind in the auditorium."

At 9:45am I heard this announcement in a school assembly. At first, I couldn't comprehend what I just heard. Everything I was listening to seemed to be so fuzzy. All of the students just sat there. Everyone was totally dumbfounded including me. This just didn't seem possible. How could our tall, proud standing buildings ever be demolished? We walked back to our classes silently. I don't think that anyone really knew what to say.

I only really realized the seriousness and the reality of it all when I got home. I saw the images on my television and was in awe. I saw the explosions, and the buildings crumble to the ground. I could feel my heart beating faster and faster. I saw people jump and run for their lives as the two tall structures were enveloped in flames. The debris, paper, and smoke littered the sky. It was somewhat like a Bruce Willis film. With the cheesy plot and all of the big explosions. I could see Bruce Willis coming out of the building with a sexy woman in his arms yelling out something like "Whoa! What a crazy day at work." You know something really bad like that and then the movie would end: but this, this was reality. It was right there in front of me. No, this was true. There were no cameras or stunt men. These were true fires, real people. And Real Lives.

My family and I watched late into the night. And I played the images over and over again in my mind. The only thing that I was truly thinking to myself was "What if I was there?" And that's all I thought about through the night "What if I was there, what if?"

The next day I turned my thoughts over in my mind. How much damage would something like this cost us? Will we rebuild the twin towers?...What is the death toll?

Today I realized how many lives were damaged and lost. Along with the thousands of people that were killed there were even more lives destroyed. All of the families that have lost loved ones were devastated. In a way, part of them had died along with the others too.

I think, who could have done such a inhumane and barbaric thing? Why would anyone want to kill so many people? Who would want to strike so much fear into so many?

Although people were hurt, we can rebuild. Possibly not buildings, but our spirit. I've heard of hundreds of people flying their American flags high in the air. People giving blood and standing in long lines to give goods to the injured. Even small acts of kindness, like leaving flowers for the deceased, shows that America will never be broken. I thank all the Firemen and Policemen for risking your own lives for the sake of ours. You are wonderful, fearless, people that have dedicated your lives to helping others. I'm sorry about some of your friends and co-workers that have passed away in the last five days. God bless you and keep on fighting.

YOU ARE AMERICA'S TRUE HEROES...

MAXINE, GRADE 7
MANHATTAN

TALIA'S DAY

September 11th started out as a normal day, but it wouldn't stay that way for long. I was in my third period class, Creative Writing when I heard the PA system say my name. "Talia, please report to the main office, Talia," it said, sounding staticky and crackled.

What was I being called down for? Lately I had been hearing a lot of names called down over the PA system, but why me? I walked to the office, my pass clutched in my hand. When I got there, it was mass confusion.

A mob of parents was crowded around the office doors. One woman was yelling hysterically. The principal had to get the security guard to calm her down. I tried to get an adult's attention, but everyone was yelling.

"Um, my name is Talia," I told one teacher. "I heard my name over the loudspeaker. What am I supposed to do?" Suddenly, all these people were staring down at me. "What is going on?" I asked. "Oh, Talia, honey. We just needed to tell you that your dad is okay. Okay? Your dad is okay. Whatever you hear about bad things happening at the World Trade Center, your dad is okay." Then they dashed off somewhere, leaving me there, amid the mass confusion. What was going on?

The rest of the day rushed by. As the clock ticked, I was learning more and more about what had happened. Kids whispered: Did you hear what happened? What? A plane crashed into the World Trade Center. A plane? A plane. One kid kept annoying me by asking "Is your dad okay? Are you really sure your dad is okay?" I didn't get any definite information until I asked a teacher in the lunchroom what was going on. "A plane hit the Twin Towers and they collapsed." Collapsed? It wasn't possible!

As the day went by, names were being called every 5 seconds. At the end of the school day, an announcement told us all buses were cancelled. How would I get home?

So everyone sat in the auditorium while parents came to pick up their children. The auditorium was crazy, people were yelling. I had a pounding headache that hurt like anything. Each time the microphone was picked up to announce names, I hoped that my name would be next.

After having waited for what seemed like a year, my mom and dad came. I hugged both of them, happy to see them. My dad told me his story. He had gone to vote that morning, so he showed up later for work. He was in the concourse of the Trade Center, when he saw people running out. He knew what to do. He headed for the exit, not stopping for anything. When he got out, he ran a block without stopping. When he looked back, he saw that the building was on fire.

When I got home, I turned on the TV. Tapes of the crash were being played over and over again. I turned it off. So, it was true. The Twin Towers really were gone. I couldn't believe it; it was unbelievable. All these people dead, and the World Trade Center gone? I thought of my dad and how lucky I was that I still had him. I knew that there were plenty of moms and dads there whose children weren't so lucky. I knew these times would be hard for my dad, who had so many friends in the World Trade Center.

That night I walked up to my roof and looked at the place the World Trade Center used to be, and I remembered my dad's office in Tower 1. I remembered it as the place I would go to on those days when I was off from school. I would ride on the A train to the World Trade Center. I would walk beside my dad, matching his stride, into the grand lobby, with its high ceiling and chandeliers. I remembered my ears popping on that long ride up to the 65th floor. I remembered my dad's friends, and their daughters. I remembered Britney and I planned (and carried out) two parties to liven up the dull business going on. Each party had balloons, invitations and snacks. I remembered those kind people, Cecilia, Nancy and Debbie. I remembered playing with the copy machine and making a gazillion copies of everything I could copy, including my shoe. I remembered all these wonderful things. Now, this building full of all these good memories is gone.

There is a hole in that skyline, a skyline changed forever. When I was in second grade, I went with my class up to the observation deck on Tower 2 and met my dad there. We sketched what we could see of New York. This year my brother is a second grader. He won't be able to do that. There's a hole in the skyline.

TALIA, GRADE 6
BROOKLYN

MAY'S DAY

It started out like a regular school day but it wasn't. It was September 11. No one in the U.S. knew of the terrible tragedy that was coming.

My dad droped me off in front of my school and left. I walked over to my class. Jeanne picked us up and we walked to room 301 on the third floor. Then Amille said "The twin towers are on fire."

Everyone in my class went to look. We all thought it was a joke or something but we were wrong. Then we heard Anna on the intercom, "parents that hear this please take you're kids home." Two seconds latter we hear Annas voice again "All classes facing the south side please close you're shaids." Then Anna said "Jeannes class and Pat C.'s class and Kellys class please go to the lunch room. Miki's class go to the auditorium. K-1 classes go to the gym and 2-3 classes go to the lunch room along with the 5th grade." Then I saw my best friends dad I asked if I could call home and go with him my teacher said okay I went with him to the front door of the lunch room when Clare (Johns wife) came with Francie: she went to look for Rosie. My old teacher Dana came over and said she would go look for Rosie. When Clare and Dana returned Wendy (Julias mom) came by and said she would take me home. I went to call home in the ofice with the asst. princeapal. My dad answered the phone and he said that I could go home with Wendy. We started walking to the subway but Wendy desied not to. We were going to walk over the bridge.

We were 20 feet past the first tower on the bridge when the first tower fell people screamd, cursed and one person fainted then there was a human stampied. My legs wouldn't stop.

When I got home my dad ran down the stairs and opened the door he squshed me. Then I ran up stairs and my mom huged me.

My friends mom invited us over to her house if we wanted to be with some people. I went over and 15 minutes later my mom and dad came over.

MAY, GRADE 4
MANHATTAN

ANDY'S DAY

I rushed to the window to see smoke coming from one of the World Trade Centers. I saw an explosion coming from the other tower. There was also an explosion coming from my heart when I saw a ball of fire. It was because I realized that my sister's school was 6 blocks away from there.

My stomach was a pit of darkness with smoke coming from it. A pit of fear, of disaster. I stared at the building. Andrea had a short discussion about it. I wasn't paying any attention. I couldn't. When the discussion was done Andrea told Kelsie she could call her parents. I knew that I wanted to call too so I hastily asked Andrea if I could call too. I went to the room people were calling in. Girls came in some crying. But I couldn't cry, I was a boy. "I couldn't do that," I said to myself quietly. They were hugging each other. They asked if I wanted to go next, I said "No." I will be strong, I thought shivering. I tapped my foot fast. I thought I was going to cry. I wiped my eyes. "No." I thought, "No." They said it was my turn. I told my student teacher my home number. She couldn't get through. My brain hurt. It was like someone was pounding on my skull. I told her my mom's work number. She dialed. It didn't work. I knew it. I was going to cry. She tried again. It got through. I said "Hi." Then I asked her if Josie's okay. "Josie's fine. She tried to go to school but they made her go back home." I sighed, said good-bye, and silently got off the phone.

The pounding stopped
The crying stopped
everything stopped

That was part of the morning
of tuesday september 11th 2001

ANDY, GRADE 5
MANHATTAN

reaching

LETTERS TO NEW YORK

Liebekinder
ichweis wi ir euch
fült.ich hab meterLebt
en Kosowo krig.
denke aneuch

vonEdison

DEAR CHILDREN,

I know how you feel. I have been in Kosovo war.
I think of you!

EDISON

Dear Students in New York,

I'm sorry that there was a disaster. I hope some of your family members weren't in the building. I'm thinking of you even though I don't know you.

Sincerely,
The Kids
From an Elementry School
From Oregon.

PEace Builders

DEAR STUDENT OF P.S. 89,

Hi my name is Ashley and I'm nine years old. I live in Sheboyagn, Wisconsin. I have a big brother, and a stinky Scottie dog her name is Shay. My brother, Grant has a dumb black cat name Salem. Once my brother and I were raiding the spice cabinet and we came across some cocoa. So I tryied it. It was nasty and I looked like a cocoa-breathing dragon! Of course my brother was laughing his head off. Then I was spraying water in my mouth from the sprayer that's from the sink. It was all funny and everything except we had a huge mess to clean up before mom came home. The funny thing is that my mom still doesn't know about it! I got my stories of bad stuff but not as bad as you have it. I know how it is to lose a loved one. I lost my great-grandpa a long time ago. Even though I still remember some of his funeral. But it isn't as bad as losing your mom or dad or even both.

I'm very, very, very sorry about what happened. It must have been scary when it happened. I know it isn't fair but we are seeking revenge from the Talaban.

You can write back if you want to (just if you want). I hope this letter helps you forget about it.

ASHLEY, AGE 9
SHEBOYGAN, WISCONSIN

I am so sorry for what happened.

It was very scary here in Ohio so it must have been

very, very, scary

in New York.

Queridos Amigas,
Me siento mal te
lo que pasó. Ya
escribí um poema.

"¡No, No! ayuden a
las bomberos!"
lágrimas pegando el
piso "ayuden, ayuden"
todas desesperadas.
Un milagro, un milagro
salieron a salvo."

¿Cómo te sientes,?
    Tu amigo,
            adrian

Dear Students of Public School #234,   10/2/01

Don't worry every thing is going to be fine.
I'd be petty sad to if I had to move to another
school but don't worry you'll get use to it. Just
look in the bright side, soon you'll go back to your
real school. YOU ARE BRAVE! For right now just
try to get comfortable in your new school. Patience
gets it reward. Nothing really changed just welcome your
selfs.

Sincerly,
Jose

DEAR FRIENDS,

I am sorry about what happened. I have written a poem.

"No! No! Help the firemen!"
Tears are hitting the floor. "Help them, help them," in desperation.
A miracle, a miracle, they got out safely.

How do you feel?

ADRIAN
GLENDALE, ARIZONA

Dear President Bush

I wish the president,
all the wishes on all the stars
in the sky that ~~that~~ we will
stand tall forever

Love
Hanna

Dear Student,
My name is Erin and I am a fifth Grader at Darby Creek Elementary.
I am so sorry for what happened. It was very scary here in Ohio so it must have been very, very, scary in New York. If you ever get scared or sad think about lollipops, it makes you feel happy.

from,
Erin

P.S. If you have time write back. Maybe we could be pen or pencil pals! My School adress is the one right below if you want to write back.

ERIN, GRADE 5
OHIO

I got these two bunnies
for Easter. I gave them
love and snuggles and they made
me feel safe. Now I give them
to you so you're happy. I hope ~~th~~
they help you feel safe, too.

Tyler's Gift.

Dear 5th grader,
    I am very sorry about the tragedy that happend. I'll bet you are very worried. I might be able to help you and make you feel better.
    Well, what makes me feel better is my imaginary friend Darien. I met him Sep.1,2001. He makes me feel better because I tell him everything. Sometimes, when you tell people how you feel, you feel abt better.
    If you don't want an imaginary friend, you could try and do something like jumproping, watching tv, play video games...Ect. Take your mind off of it.
    Or you can be my pen pal and write to me about how you feel (happy, sad, mad). I promise I won't laugh. I hope the teddy bear you have or get is considered a hug from me to make you feel better!
    I hope you write back soon!
        Your new pen pal,
        Stephanie

STEPHANIE, GRADE 5
SARASOTA, FLORIDA

DEAR MAYOR GUILIANI,

The recent tragedy that occurred in New York City with the World Trade Center and Twin Towers made me think. Why don't we make a memorial like the Vietnam Veterans Memorial in Washington D.C., designed by Maya Lin? These heroes and innocent defenseless people who died deserve to be recognized and remembered. This tragedy united the nation but in a couple of years people tend to forget. This is not something we should forget. We need to show the victims and the families that they'll never be forgotten.

CRYSTAL, GRADE 7
BRONX

STUDENTS OF NEW YORK...

We are members of the Thompson Valley High School Link Crew in Loveland, Colorado. We work as a team to unite our school and wish to contribute in uniting our nation, as well. We wish to send our deepest thoughts and prayers to you in the toughest of times. An attack which was supposed to tear us apart only made us stronger and more bonded as a nation. We wish you the very best of luck in all you do and would love to keep in touch!

THOMPSON VALLEY HIGH SCHOOL LINK CREW
LOVELAND, COLORADO

I will brighten up American's hearts from the worst of times to the better

STEPHANIE, HIGH SCHOOL
QUEENS

We wish to send our deepest thoughts
and prayers to you in the toughest of times.

An attack which was supposed to tear us apart
only made us stronger and more
bonded as a nation.

Americain air line

DEAR FELLOW STUDENTS

My name is Chad. I am 10 years old. I like drawing and swimming. My favorite shows are pokemon, digimon, dragonballz, and medabots. We have twenty-five kids in our class. There are fifteen boys and ten girls.

I am real sorry for what happened to the World Trade Centre. I hope you haven't lost any parents or relatives. I hope this letter cheers you up because I am sending a picture with this letter.

CHAD
WINNIPEG, MANITOBA
CANADA

hope

peace, love, understanding

A WORLD WORTH CREATING?

Imagine a world that's all the same
Of one color, one race, and even one name.
Where March is like May and day is like night,
And content is like angry and prideness like fright.
A world full of people, but no one to speak
Because no thoughts are special, nor feelings unique.

Is that a world that's worth creating?
Where day by day our lives keep fading
Our differences make us who we really are
So let's stop the fighting and let's stop the war!

EMERITA, GRADE 8
BROOKLYN

The birds singing light and freedom the flag waving proud, the wind blows my hair while our flag is still there. My hopes are up we are one nation always strong nothing can break us, as we are always shiney, always.

WENDY, GRADE 7
MANHATTAN

"I'VE LEARNED— THAT IT'S NOT WHAT YOU HAVE IN YOUR LIFE BUT WHO YOU HAVE IN YOUR LIFE THAT COUNTS."

I may not have what others have but I have a family that loves me. The Twin Towers may have fallen, and the few that survived are the lucky ones. They may not have a job to go to but they have their lives. They have a family to go home to.

CRYSTAL, GRADE 8
BRONX

PAST GOES THROUGH THE DEBRIS

The phone rang at Alex Bandon's West Village apartment
At 6:45 A.M.
Two days after the attack.
It was an ex-boyfriend,
A man she had dated a decade ago,
Calling from Edinburgh to check on her.
"He was a footnote in my life," Miss Bandon said.

The chain of events set off by loss of life
On September 11
Emphasized for many people
How fragile are the bonds that connect
Human beings to one another.

Jordan Walsh, a lawyer in Los Angeles,
Said he was unable to sleep
Ticking through a mental rolodex
Of friends in New York.

A producer from ABC News
Said she received a call from a woman
Who abruptly cut off their relationship 10 years earlier.

The phone rings, and the voice is sometimes reassuring,
Sometimes draining.
After a calamity the past always calls.

MAX, HIGH SCHOOL
MANHATTAN

After the September 11th attacks in New York and Washington D.C. the United States of America has really pulled together. That really gave me a good vision in my head that we really could all get along. People should always show kindness like how they are showing kindness now.

I think every one in America should thank the emergency workers for helping with this crisis. The generosity of Americans not just New Yorkers makes me feel good to be an American. It makes me feel good because I know that people wouldn't be unwilling to help if such a thing were to happen again. Instead of Americans feuding, fighting and hating each other because of their race or religion they are helping one another. So to conclude this essay all I have to say is . . .

GOD BLESS AMERICA

TENIESHA, GRADE 4
BROOKLYN

I dont want anymore
terrorists in the world.
I want everybody to love
one another, and be peaceful.
I don't feel good about it because
it could have been this shool
Who knows? It could have happened,
I do not want to feel this way.

TAYLOR, GRADE 2
BROOKLYN

**"I'VE LEARNED—
THAT YOU SHOULD ALWAYS LEAVE
LOVED ONES WITH LOVING WORDS.
IT MAY BE THE LAST TIME YOU SEE
THEM."**

The people that worked in the World Trade Center
maybe did not get the chance to say goodbye to their
wives, husbands, children, and other family members.
This is why I kiss my mother goodbye everyday before
I leave my home.

STEPHANIE, GRADE 8
BRONX

MEMORIAL

They came from all around
The grieving,
the hurt and
broken
looking for a flicker of hope

Thousands lined the streets
Each was handed a
single
rose
"I'll be up here praying."
A worshipper holds fast
two symbols of her faith

A rosary, and
a USA scarf

They sang "God Bless America"
The notes hung up
in the cathedral

WENDY, GRADE 7
MANHATTAN

I don't want any horror
I want peace
No violence
No terrorism
No unhappiness
No sadness

KYLE, GRADE 2
BROOKLYN

I am angry because the Twin Towers were destroyed. I am angry because they hijacked our planes. I am angry because so many people died. This doesn't give us the right to be angry at people who live here that are from the same country as the terrorists.

MILLIE, GRADE 8
BRONX

Hope is that source of strength,
That feeling that gets you through the day.
. . . It's what helps us overcome
the obstacles that we face.

God Bless America

JAY, GRADE 5
QUEENS

I think it was really sad that the Tuin Towers fell. Osama Bin laden is the man who did this but I think in some other time and some other place he could have been nice! we shouldn't go around hateing people. It doesent make senee. It is not the way God made the world. I think in a way everybody has kindness in their hearts. Mabey he just needed some friends.

ALLIE, GRADE 3
MANHATTAN

AT THE END OF MY STORY

At the end of my story, at the end of me,
I shall overcome life's greatest fears.

At the end of time, at the end of the minute,
I will be with you always, every second.

When the sun won't shine, and the moon is the only light,
Eternity is nothing to how long I promise to stay with you.

Your sky is lonely, your moonlight is a shadow behind you.
Although your sunlight is bright and life goes on and on
Hope is a simple thing that will show the light within.

JACOB, GRADE 4
MANHATTAN

They came from all around

The grieving,
the hurt and broken looking for

a flicker of hope.

SULFIKAR, HIGH SCHOOL
QUEENS

I hope Kara's next door neighbor finds her husband

ALESSIA, GRADE 1
BROOKLYN

HOPE

Hope is a fireman digging through the rubble of the
World Trade Center,
Looking for a fallen brother.
Hope is sitting near a telephone,
Waiting to hear that your loved one didn't take
that plane.
Hope is when you go to the doctor because of that
suspicious lump that you found,
And waiting for him to say that it wasn't cancer.
Hope is waiting to get back a test grade,
After studying for it all night.
Hope is interviewing for a job that you really want,
And waiting to be offered the position.
Hope is when you really like someone,
And you are waiting to find out if they feel the
same way.
Hope is carrying a baby for nine months,
And waiting to hear that you have a healthy child.
Hope is applying to different colleges,
And waiting for them to respond.
Hope is buying a lottery ticket,
And waiting for your numbers to be picked.
Hope is forgetting to do your homework,
And praying that the teacher doesn't pick on you.
Hope is writing to Santa when your 7 years old,
And waking up Christmas day to find all of the presents
that you asked for.

Hope is waiting for rain,
When there is a famine because of drought.
Hope is cheering your favorite team on,
When the odds are against them.
Hope is sitting in a jail cell waiting for a verdict,
When you have been wrongfully accused.
Hope is riding up to Albany,
To demonstrate against the Regents.
Hope is being completely covered in a veil,
And wanting desperately to be allowed to go to school.

Hope is that source of strength,
That feeling that gets you through the day.
It is one of the most basic emotions,
Shared by all, regardless of age.
It's that desire,
Which keeps us from going insane.
It's what gets us up in the morning,
And allows us to fall asleep at night.
It's what helps us overcome the obstacles that we face.
Hope is the gift that keeps us going.

CHARLES, GRADE 10
MANHATTAN

WENDY, GRADE 7
MANHATTAN

MUSLIMS = PEACE

"Muslims for Peace"
"Hate crimes are crimes"
Over 500 Muslim Americans show their solidarity
With those lost in the attack
The people who died were our friends and neighbors;
I want to show my sorrow.
It breaks my heart
Not to see those buildings anymore and
To hear about all those dead people
What happened was a terrible act of terrorism.
Islam does not stand for this.
Terrorism is unIslamic.
Arab language prayers, candles, American flags.
God bless America,
Allah loves America.
Islam is compassion,
Not violence.

VIDA, GRADE 7
MANHATTAN

**"I'VE LEARNED—
THAT WRITING, AS WELL AS TALKING,
CAN EASE EMOTIONAL PAIN."**

I understand better when I write how I am feeling. I get
to reread it over. Then I understand how to solve my
problems easier that way. I can talk about things without fighting or yelling. I work it out instead. Fighting
doesn't solve anything. It makes me feel better.

JAMES, GRADE 8
BRONX

we will NEVER forget

THE TWIN TOWERS

They use to be standing
High and proud
Next to the Hudson River.
They burned to ashes
Covered in rubble
And destroyed in a million pieces.
They once were there,
But now they are gone,
And in everybody's heart we will remember
That the Twin Towers were once there.

JESSICA, GRADE 5
MANHATTAN

MADELINE, HIGH SCHOOL
QUEENS

Twins No more.

Tall, not fancy
Just right and mine.
Look like twins
But don't act the same
Very popular too
Can hold a lot of people
exspecially me.
But now not tall, not fancy,
not just right, not mine.
Don't look like twins no more,
don't act like nothing.
But it is still there
In your head,
It is still there in you.
It stands up for each other
But now it's down.
Don't stand up for each other
No more. But you have to go on.
Stand up for your selves, be strong
Don't forget nothing can stop us!!
Us Americans has to be strong.

By Frank

FRANK, GRADE 4
MANHATTAN

TWIN TOWERS

Tragedy
Inconceivable to see this happen
What will happen next?
No longer here

Tragic to see this happen to children without parents.
Oh my, this must be a dream
We care for people who are injured
Every day we think about the people we lost
Remembering this day forever
Sorrow for the children who lost their parents

MARY, GRADE 6
QUEENS

AN EMPTY GRAY SPACE

I look at the glittering bright skyline and see,
Two big strong buildings looking right back at me.
I smell the man selling pretzels by the big fancy doors
And I hear cell phones ringing on all 110 floors.
Then to my surprise, I go up to the top,
And I share a great dinner, just me and my Pop.

Then my alarm wakes me up with a buzz and a ring,
And I realize I was dreaming all those wonderful things.

The strong towers are gone.
Everything has turned to gray.
Our beautiful towers were taken away.

The terrorists came and the innocent died,
And every American came together and cried.

Nervous, sad, angry, in pain
Everyone stunned from Hawaii to Maine.

But New Yorkers are great and we will rebuild,
And the empty gray space soon one day will be filled.
The strong, powerful buildings that fell to the ground
Will leave a memory that forever will always be around.

HARRISON, GRADE 4
BROOKLYN

On the day of the disaster I was very sad and confused. It was very cruel of who ever did it. Because the World Trade Center was one of the special high rises in New York. I was scared and worried about the people in the World Trade Center. Because to be in an exploding building is very scary. I hope we figure out what to rebuild in it's place because it is now empty. This was a day we will never forget.

The World Trade Center Diaster

KINU, AGE 7
MANHATTAN

My thoughts about the Wourld Trade Center. I think it was sad. The World Trade Center was an important building to the city. The first time I went to the World Trade center it was so tall I thought it was going to fall on me. But my mom and dad told me that it was built strong. I went inside. It was huge and felt cool. We never got to the top. We got to see the Malls on the first floor. It was big and crowed. Since the World Trade center is not there any more I will probably go to the Empire State building I'm not sure because that might be thier next target.

MARK, AGE 8
MANHATTAN

The Little Dim Light

*I was buried in the thick black smoke.
But I saw a little dim light,
In that little dim light, I see all my memories of the
          World Trade Center.
But now those two skyscrapers are gone,
My memories of it will never fade...

Deli

YUAN, GRADE 7
MANHATTAN

THE TWIN TOWERS

The Twin Towers are gone and that's really sad
People lost their lives and that's really bad
You attacked us but once and will never repeat
Everyone's strong now and back on their feet
All the fallen heroes we'll never forget
Who tried to save those who they never met
We all suffer the loss from that tragic day
And hope that the best will come our way
We will never forget all of those that are gone
And they will remain in our hearts from now on

JARED, GRADE 6
QUEENS

But New Yorkers are great and we will rebuild,
And the empty gray space soon one day will be filled.

The strong, powerful buildings
that fell to the ground
Will leave a memory
that forever will always be around.

September 11, 2001
We will never forget.

AMANDA, TERESA AND TANYA, GRADE 6
MANHATTAN

Today I was thinking about something but some how the world trade thing came to mind. I was thinking that it feels like the world trade is stuck to the palm of my hand and I can not get it off. I'm blowing on my hand it starts to budge but comes right back like a boomerang. I tryed to squish it down but it will pop back up like a balloon.

I try to think of other things but every thing seems connected. It's like I'm walking through a maze but every path leads me to the place I'm trying to get away from. I will not forget the World Trade Center. It will travel through my mind and heart always.

SHOMARI, GRADE 5
MANHATTAN

MATTHEW, GRADE 8
BRONX

My thotghs about the World Trade Center:
I never went to the top of the World Trade
Center. I remember my mom took a picutre
of me in the summer. I stood Behind
the World trade Center. I Remember on
Tuesday I could see the World Trade Cent
er from Brooklyn. I Remember when I wen
t on the Path train to Newport Center, New
Jersey and the N and R to Lexington Aveu
ne. I would Remember those Big flags.
September 11th was the Saddiest day in the
United States of America's history.

MARCELINO, AGE 7
MANHATTAN

GOODBYE WORLD TRADE CENTER

The walls of the World Trade Center
Descended down, down, down, into the Underworld
Taking people's lives with it.

Screams of terror
Fill the air
Like a nightmare.
People jumped from windows
Bodies fell into nearby rivers
People wept for family and friends.

Terrorists laughed and celebrated
While our tears flow down our faces
Americans gathered to form an army
Vowing never to forget.

The World Trade Center is gone
Lives are lost
Our spirit for America
Is alive
Oh very well alive
Fighting the battle
We know that we will win.

TIFFANY, GRADE 4
BROOKLYN

MARTHA, HIGH SCHOOL
QUEENS

From my home I see so many people with American flags on their cars and outside their homes.

I can't help but think how beautiful the red, white and blue looks.

The "towers" blew up
on septmber 11# 2001.
We will never forget this
attack on the "World Trade
center" Thousaids of people
died. Some are alive but
many are dead.
Over 300 fire man died.
in the World trade
center. Do they need
blood? Not now. Now
they need us to think
about them. We lit candles
made cards, and put flags
in our windows.

ERNESTO, AGE 9
MANHATTAN

Tall
windows on the world
iron
national icon

tower
on 9-11-01
why
evolution
reconstruction

SAM, GRADE 6
QUEENS

ONE TIME

In a moment of tragedy
We were struck with grief
Such cruelty was beyond belief

In that moment of silence
We sat and stared
Knowing every American was scared

All the families
That lost a love
Turned their eyes to heaven above

Never can we forget
The sadness we felt
The pain with which we dealt

Forever we remember
The emotions we shared
A time when everyone cared.

ADIL, GRADE 8
QUEENS

BECAUSE I SAY SO

5000 x 4,000,000 is 2 . . . ('cuz I say so.)
We don't have a heart . . . ('cuz I say so.)
We can't see . . . ('cuz I say so.)
There are no rocks . . . ('cuz I say so.)
There are no fish in the sea . . . ('cuz I say so.)
There's no such thing as the Titanic . . . ('cuz I say so.)
There are no trees in the world . . . ('cuz I say so.)
The World Trade Center's Twin Towers are still standing . . . ('cuz I say so.)

ANDREW AND MAX
DENVER, COLORADO

DAVID, GRADE 4
MANHATTAN

ACKNOWLEDGMENTS

From the Editor and the NYC Board of Education

Shortly after the tragedy of 9/11/2001, Stephen Jay Gould, in an article in The New York Times, suggested that Americans must keep a "ledger of infinite kindnesses." We have a responsibility, he noted, to reaffirm human decency and "overwhelm the power of any terrorist's act." May the following acknowledgments serve as part of a ledger kept by those of us closely involved with the New York City public schools, the events of September 11th, 2001, and the publication of this book.

First, we'd like to thank our young authors and artists, their parents, teachers, school administrators, and district leaders for contributing these memorable works.

Then, although noted in the dedication of this book, we would like to pay tribute to all New York City educators for making sure that our 1.1 million students were in safe havens the night of September 11th. In particular, we'd like to acknowledge the educators who work in the schools that border the World Trade Center site. That day and in the weeks and months that followed they redefined what it means to be a teacher and to be a principal. A special thank you goes out to the following principals and all members of their school communities:

Patrick Burke, principal of High School of Economics and Finance
Ada Rosario Dolch, principal for High School for Leadership and Public Service
Ellen Foote, principal of IS 89
Ronnie Najjar, principal of PS 89
Alyssa Polack, principal of PS 150, the Tribeca Learning Center
Anna Switzer, principal of PS 234
Stanley Teitel, principal of Stuyvesant High School

Another tribute is extended to teachers throughout the land who invited their students to correspond with our children. In addition to their letters and sketches, many sent banners, quilts, books, school supplies, stuffed animals, and money raised from lemonade stands, cake sales, book fairs, car washes, and penny drives. Your deeds are permanently inscribed in our ledger of infinite kindnesses.

Throughout those horrific autumn weeks and later into the winter months, the Central Board of Education rallied around the schools nearest to Ground Zero. Under the steadfast leadership of Chancellor Harold Levy, the wise counsel of his Deputy Chancellors David Klasfeld, Judith Rizzo, and Tony Shorris, and the devotion and expertise of Chief Executive Burt Sacks, shattered school communities were able to become whole again. School superintendents, representing communities throughout our city are ever grateful to all these gracious leaders for supporting us as we attempted to focus on providing quality instruction for all students amid many mental health and environmental concerns.

Additionally, we must pay tribute to the many individuals who worked their magic in relocating students, comforting family members, supporting teachers, tending to myriad concerns, and enabling makeshift school communities to keep on keeping on with the business of educating children.

Our heartfelt thanks to the following principals whose students, teachers, support staff, and family members rolled out the red carpet for our evacuated school communities:

Lois Weiswasser, principal of PS 41 for sheltering many children on September 11th and for housing PS 234 for several weeks thereafter

Lisa Siegman, principal of PS 3 and Jacky Grossman, principal of Greenwich Village Middle School, for sheltering many children on September 11th and for housing PS 89 and PS 150 for several weeks and months thereafter

Celenia Chevare, principal of NEST M, for sharing space with the PS 89 community

Ron Chaluisan and Sonnet Takahisa, leaders of the Museum School, and Rob Menken and Sheila Breslaw, leaders of the Upper Lab School, for welcoming IS 89 into their school community at the O. Henry complex

Lee McCaskill, principal of Brooklyn Technical High School, for welcoming the Stuyvesant High School community

JoAnna Frank, principal of Norman Thomas High School for welcoming the Economics and Finance High School community

Charles Bonnie of Fashion Industries High School for welcoming the High School for Leadership into their community

Rebecca Bravo of the Ed Horan School for welcoming Carol Silverstein's 721M at Stuyvesant into their school community

Mental Health providers including, NYU Child Study Center, St. Vincent's Hospital Medical Center, Jewish Board of Family and Children's Services, Staten Island Mental Health, and the many local mental health providers of New York City

Dr. Catherine Hickey of the Archdiocese of New York for allowing PS 234 to recreate their school at St. Bernard's

Superintendents Helen Santiago, Tony Sawyer, Shelley Harwayne, and Susan Erber for their tireless efforts on behalf of their students and staff

Kevin Gill, Richard Scarpa, and the staff of the Office of Pupil Transportation, School Food, and Nutrition Services and the Division of Instructional Technology

Bernie Orlan, Director of Environmental Health and Safety

Eric Weinbaum, Bronx/Manhattan Area Manager, Division of School Facilities

Francine Goldstein and the Staff of the Division of Student Support Services

Dr. Terri Marks, Chief Physician, New York City Public Schools

Joseph Nappi and the staff of the Division of School Facilities

Chief Raymond Diaz and the staff of the New York City Police Department, Division of School Safety

Randi Weingarten, President, United Federation of Teachers

Jill Levy, President, Council of Supervisors and Administrators

And finally, a deep and heartfelt thank you to all of our friends at Heinemann. Educators have long looked to your fine publications for inspiration and information. Now we can add support, guidance and broad shoulders to lean on in an emergency. Thank you for your generous donations, your devotion to the plight of our city, and your passionate commitment to turning this dream of a book into a reality. Thank you especially to Lesa Scott (Vice-President/General Manager) for her total commitment to this project, Leigh Peake (Editorial Director) for her determination and expertise, Lois Bridges (Literacy Publisher) for tirelessly rallying educators throughout the land, and to the numerous Heinemann staff who dedicated their time and expertise to the project, including Lisa Fowler, Renee LeVerrier, Deborah Burns, Steve Bernier, Maura Sullivan, Chad Vanderbeck, Eric Chalek, and Kären Clausen. A final special note of thanks to Louise Richardson who made this one-of-a-kind book almost manageable.

From the Publisher
The additions to the ledger would be incomplete if we didn't recognize the extraordinary work of Plainspoke. The exquisite sample of book design you hold in your hands emerged from their unique combination of superior talent and heartfelt dedication to the project itself. Quite simply, without Nicole Comtois, Amy Becker-Jones, and Connie DiSanto, this book would not have happened. Matt and Diane Ralph's leadership and willingness to contribute the work of their studio and staff are emblematic of their commitment to both quality and kindness.

From design to final book is a long road, and that road was made shorter and gentler through the expert advice and hard work of the staff at Jay's Publishing Services; Lindenmeyr Book Publishing Papers (in particular, Stephen Wright and Ernie Etling); Jaguar Advanced Graphics (special thanks to Ellie Mariano and Kelly Ortiz); RR Donnelly (particularly John Carollo and Dave Hudson).

TOP TEN LISTS FOR
BEAUTIFUL SHADE GARDENS

Seeing Your Way
Out of the Dark

52 Garden-Transforming Lists, Money-Saving Shortcuts,
Design Tips & Smart Plant Picks for Zones 3 through 7

Kerry Ann Mendez

LONE OAK PRESS

14 Dec. 02
B+T
21.95 (1866)

Top Ten Lists for Beautiful Shade Gardens: Seeing Your Way Out of the Dark
52 Garden-Transforming Lists, Money-Saving Shortcuts,
Design Tips & Smart Plant Picks for Zones 3 through 7

Copyright © 2011 Kerry Ann Mendez.

ISBN: 978-1-935534-94-5

Plant Characters: Created by artist, book writer, and teacher, Daniele Ippoliti owner of Character of Nature. www.CharacterofNature.net. (518) 878-4837

Photo Credits: Bailey Nurseries (www.baileynurseries.com)
                 Bluestone Perennials (www.bluestoneperennials.com);
                 John Scheepers (www.johnscheepers.com)
                 Gardener's Supply Company (www.gardeners.com);
                 Leonard Perry (www.perrysperennials.com);
                 Perennial Resource (www.PerennialResource.com);
                 Perennially Yours (www.pyours.com);
                 Plant Delights Nursery (www.Plantdelights.com)
                 Proven Winners (www.provenwinners.com);
                 Sunny Border Nurseries (www.sunnyborder.com);
                 and Terra Nova Nurseries (www.terranova.com).

Cover Photos: Perennially Yours gardens

Book Design: Melissa Mykal Batalin

Printed by: The Troy Book Makers
                 Troy, New York
                 www.thetroybookmakers.com

Publisher: Lone Oak Press
                 Ballston Spa, New York

Editing: Margaret Morrone, Rita Fassett, Sergio Mendez and Evan Mendez

Book orders: Perennially Yours,
                 P.O. Box 144, Ballston Spa, NY 12020
                 Phone: (518) 885-3471
                 Email: pyours@nycap.rr.com

To order additional copies of this title, visit www.pyours.com,
contact your favorite local bookstore, or visit www.tbmbooks.com

*This book is dedicated to
the dearest men in my life who
continually support and encourage me.
To my wise, uncompromising father;
my loving, patient husband;
and my son, Evan,
who keeps me laughing
and riding roller coasters.*

Acknowledgements

My sincerest thanks to family, friends and hundreds of dear patrons that encouraged me to write this book on shade gardening. I am richly blessed with a great cheerleading squad. I also salute Wynne Trowbridge, owner of Shades of Green Nursery, for her inspirational display beds and collection of shade plants, many of which are in my gardens. And where would I be without the outstanding photographs, kindly provided by Bailey Nurseries; Bluestone Perennials; John Scheepers; Gardener's Supply Company; Dr. Leonard Perry; PerennialResource.com; Plant Delights Nursery; Proven Winners; Sunny Border Nurseries; and Terra Nova Nurseries? Once again, Daniele Ippoliti's delightful nature characters dance their way across the pages, as they did in my first book, *The Ultimate Flower Gardener's Top Ten Lists*. Daniele's web site, www.characterofnature.net, is a treasure chest of the artist's products and services. Special thanks to Barry Glick, owner of Sunshine Farm and Gardens, and Heather Poire, horticultural expert for Proven Winners, for their help composing the top ten lists for Hellebores and annual shade combinations for containers, respectively. My kudos to Rita Fassett and Margaret Morrone for once again applying their masterful editing skills to my second book. And above all, praise to the Lord who provides a lamp unto my feet and a light unto my path.

Contents

Chapter 8: Garden Care _____ 147

Chapter 9: Creature Comforts _____ 171

This book is written for all of you who are frustrated by your dark side. I'm talking about those dimly lit areas on your property that have succeeded in making you think they are untouchable. Before you grab a chainsaw and attack those lovely canopy trees, allow me to shed light on the situation. The truth is you have a gold mine in disguise; a treasure waiting to be uncovered.

Unfortunately it is a myth that sunny beds are prettier and easier than their shadier cousins. How did this fairy tale get started? I believe it's because most people are more familiar with sun-loving plants and therefore conclude shade gardening offers few plant choices; translating to *boring*. But just because you haven't been introduced to the magical and exquisite world of shade plants, doesn't mean they don't exist. In reality, there are many super perennials for shade that have unparalleled beauty and provide color spring, summer and fall. And I am not referring to just Hosta. I'm talking Foamflowers, Bishop's Hat, Siberian Bugloss, Bugbane, Toad Lily, Masterwort, Ligularia, Hepatica and many other exotic beauties.

I much prefer shade gardening. Shade beds have a special mystique. They're more intriguing and provocative than sun gardens plus they require much less maintenance. That caught your attention! There are four reasons why shade gardens provide more time in the lounge chair. Typically they demand less water, have fewer weeds and require less deadheading, a task I detest. Many shade perennials will not rebloom after deadheading. You can whack them off or leave the dried flowers for interest. The fourth

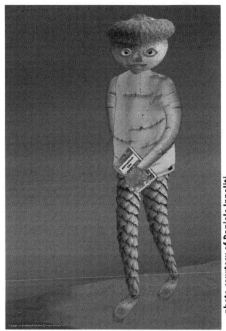

factor contributing to less work in shade beds has to do with sunlight. Because there is less light, plants tend to grow more slowly which means less frequent dividing. Yes, dividing is good in that you get more plants and it stimulates new roots and better flowering, but it also takes *your* time and energy - not good.

So let's start down this shady path together and rejoice in the journey. I bet after reading this book you may just head out to a garden center to buy a shade tree. And another lounge chair.

I know you're anxious to jump right to the pretty plant descriptions and pictures but let's first do a little primer on assessing your garden site. I promise I'll make this fun and easy. And this checklist is practical for both shade or sun gardens.

photo courtesy of Daniele Ippoliti

CHAPTER ONE

Lights, Camera.....STOP!

Reality 101

It is time to stop the madness. You know what I'm talking about. Each year when March 20th arrives, the first day of spring, we race off like wild banshees to garden centers. Actually, if we are really honest with ourselves, we start cruising the neighborhoods weeks earlier, watching for the first sign of inventory being rolled out at greenhouses. And in all fairness, who can blame us? We are color-starved gardeners that have just made it through another long, cold winter. Our motivation is high, dreams are big, and the adrenaline is pumping. We jump into our cars, rev the engines, and race off to buy a bunch of plants covered with flowers. Rarely do we have enough self-discipline to purchase plants that bloom later in the season; instant gratification is all consuming. We throw common sense to the wind, along with the site conditions of our garden. The scene quickly changes only months later as we walk away from our gardens, hunched over in exhaustion, frustration and disappointment, tossing the garden spade in the compost pile as we go. I don't know about you, but I got tired of this annual emotional and physical roller coaster ride that cost me a lot of money in the process. It reminded me too much of my attempts at dieting. Each time I ended up in worse shape than when I started. This book will bring your sanity back and help you better understand your shade gardens.

The first step to having million dollar shade gardens is to be honest with yourself and your landscape. Gardeners have a tendency to blur the lines between reality and fantasy when it comes to their gardens. Sometimes the most recent garden you coveted in *Better Homes and Gardens* magazine has a hallucinogenic effect on what you think you can grow in your own yard. You want that same sun-bathed, Texan garden in your shady, New England property. I don't think so. I'm here to gently knock some sense back into your head, as others have done for me. My gardens and I have thrived as a result, and I trust the same will be for you. You can talk yourself into buying pants that are two sizes too small, but I won't let you fudge the facts about your garden. And the good news is that the truth need not hurt. There are terrific plants for every garden challenge, including dry shade. So

photo courtesy of Daniele Ippoliti

let's start with a bear knuckle assessment of your garden's site and let truth reign…as well as gorgeous, low maintenance shade gardens. If you follow my tried and proven recommendations, someday you'll be looking at your own Better Homes and Gardens masterpiece while saying "Pinch me, I think I'm dreaming"…and you won't be.

The other reality check needed before we go any farther is the 'T' factor. Time. We fight it all the time (there is that word again), from battling age lines on our faces, racing to pick up kids up from after school activities, filing our tax forms at the twelfth hour, and mailing that belated birthday card to Uncle Ed. We always have less time than we think. My husband shakes his head at my attempt to cram ten tasks into a time frame that realistically can accommodate two (if I'm lucky). Part of my disillusioned thinking comes from the fact that I have a type A personality. This has its pluses and minuses, but a whirling Tasmanian devil can be dangerous and trying to all who fall into its path, including gardens. So let's take a deep breath, admit that many of us are time-deficient gardeners, and design shade gardens that boldly meet this challenge.

So it's time to remove your rose tinted glasses as we begin down the path of honestly assessing your shady site. Come on now, I'm waiting. It is time to face your fears…and overcome them. By candidly and honestly evaluating each of the following areas, you'll be well on your way to a 'bravissima' garden. We will take each assessment one step at a time, in easy-to-chew, manageable bites. Here comes the appetizer…

Can You Please Shed Some Light?

Unfortunately there is much confusion over shade definitions. Part Shade, Light Shade, Dappled Shade, Half Shade, Shade and Deep Shade. And then of course there are those half shaded circles. Do they mean Part Sun or Part Shade? Perspiration builds on the forehead. I am going to take the liberty to simplify all of this muckety-muck.

Most of you reading this book probably fall into one of two categories: Part Shade and Shade.

Part Shade: This is two hours or less sun between 10:00 a.m. and 4:00 p.m. OR it can be dappled light throughout the day.

Shade: Early morning sun (before 10:00 a.m.) or late day sun (after 5:00 p.m.)

I'm commonly asked what time of year is best to assess a garden's light. Earth Science 101: the sun is lower in the sky in fall than it is in the spring, increasing the amount of shade cast by an object. This means sections of our garden may be shaded in September but be in full sun in June. This seasonal fluctuation is unchangeable. We should follow suit and stop changing our minds about our garden's light category. When we waffle in our assessment, we resemble a squirrel darting back and forth across the road. Pick one light category and stay the course. I recommend folks track sunlight between May and July. If trees are a factor in creating shade, no fair evaluating hours until they are fully leafed out. Naughty, naughty.

Most plants, especially perennials, are surprisingly flexible regarding their daily sunlight dose. Many will bloom in less light than their label dictates, although stems may grow longer than usual as they stretch for light. Flowers may also lean towards the light. You have several choices when this happens. Embrace this graceful, loose habit; stake stems so they remain upright; or look the other way.

Few folks try to garden in deep shade, although I applaud the tenacity of those that do. Deep shade is where there is very little light and air flow. Examples would be under a raised deck, in a narrow alley between tall buildings, or beneath low-hanging tree branches such as Norway Maples or Canadian Hemlocks. My first response when asked about what will grow in these conditions is "Why?" Why not apply a layer of shredded mulch as an attractive blanket under the tree? It's not as if there are a lot of weeds to suppress in those hellish conditions. Or you could limb up some of the tree branches and create a more hospitable site. And wouldn't it be easier to nail lattice to the deck and grow colorful flowering vines up the structure? Vines with fragrant flowers would be especially delightful. Try blocking the view of an alley with a colorful gate or a panel decorated with a striking piece of art such as a copper sun. Think outside the flower box!

Bottom line, we need to 'lighten up' when it comes to shade gardening. It really isn't as difficult as we make it out to be. The majority of plants in this book can cross the imaginary 'big divide' between part shade and shade, agreed, some better than others. Here is one way to boil it down to the simplest assessment technique. Learn the signs of a sunburned shade plant. The leaves look bleached out, may have brown, crispy edges and are limp from lack of moisture. Apply 'suntan lotion' by moving it to a shadier spot. And what are the signs of a shade plant in too much shade? That's pretty easy. Little or no flowering, diminished vigor and stunted growth. Move it into a little more sun. Of course these could also be signs of poor soil but this book will cover how to have healthy soil so that will *not* be a factor.

Don't Zone Out

Another party killer for glorious shade gardens is purchasing perennials, bulbs, shrubs and trees that are outside our hardiness zones. If you are not sure of your zone, please refer to the USDA Hardiness Zone Map at www.usna.usda.gov/Hardzone/ushz-map.html. The majority of the plants in this book are for Zones 3 to 8.

If a plant is not rated for your area, why invest a lot of time and money just so it can kick the bucket come winter? This book is all about making smart choices for beautiful gardens that are not time and money hogs. Sure, there is room in our low maintenance gardens for some annuals and tropicals but these are placed with realistic expectations. We need to be very choosy about which prima donnas are escorted into our beds. Tough, hardy perennials and flowering shrubs that can survive winters without any blankies (winter mulch) are a must. Heartless as it sounds, I refuse to give any of my perennials winter protection. They must meet me on the other side of Old Man Winter's best blows, if not, I'll find a plant that will.

Hardiness zones represent a range of average annual minimum temperatures in a region. There are eleven zones in the USDA Plant Hardiness Zone Map. Zone 1 is the coldest; zone 11 is the warmest. Zones are divided into ten degree sections. If you really want to get technical, these sections are further divided into two subsections, A and B (A being the colder half). Personally, I don't get bogged down with the A's and B's (except when it comes to my son's report card). Most plant descriptions don't go into this detail anyway. If a plant is rated to a certain hardiness zone, let's say zone 5, it should survive winters in that zone as well as warmer, higher numbered zones. Notice I said should. If you can't stand the thought of seeing a few dead plants in spring then go with plastic or silk flowers. There are simply no guarantees in life, other than my teenage son not putting his dirty laundry in the hamper.

Many folks like to push the envelope when it comes to deciding their hardiness zone. Let's be honest. It's all about shopping. The warmer the zone you decide, the more plants there are to choose from. I'm here to help you fight the temporary insanity that overtakes us as we drool over knockout plants requiring more temperate climates. Stop dreaming. But don't dismay, there are many fabulous plants for our zones so let's stay the course and zone in accurately. If after staring at the zone map you are still confused, contact your regional cooperative extension, local garden club, garden center, or neighborhood Master Gardener for advice.

So What's The Dirt?

Unfortunately for many gardeners, soil falls into the same taboo category as religion or politics. Whenever I start teaching a class on soil assessment, I notice averted eyes, people pretending to quietly clear their throats, or a sudden need to use the restrooms. And it only gets worse if part of the homework assignment was to bring in a soil sample for analysis. Gee, you'd think I asked for a urine sample. People arrive with baggies carefully tucked in their purses, canvas totes, or in crumbled brown bags, all held closely to their bodies. This shouldn't be. We need to tackle our soil issues unashamed, head-on, and learn how to become chest-puffing owners of 'Black Gold'.

Most people put blinders on when it comes to their soil. Truth be told; dealing with soil is not very exciting. Actually, it can be a drag. It's a lot more fun to race out to garden centers, buy pretty perennials, come home and stuff them into the ground. We gently remove them from containers filled with rich potting soil and then use a shovel to dig a hole in our 'sandbox' or a pick ax to break through heavy clay. We pop the plants in the ground and walk away with the absurd expectation that they will flourish year after year. If we want magnificent gardens that don't need a lot of handholding, we need to think differently about our soil. Great soil leads to great roots, that leads to great flowers, that leads to oohs and ahhs from envious admirers.

As promised, I am not going to overcomplicate this soil thing. I've found that most people who garden as a hobby, can go through life just fine without knowing the percent of Boron in their soil. If you understand your soil type (sandy, clay or loam), its pH and drainage, then you and your plants can usually get along just fine. I'm not saying you shouldn't have a complete soil test done if you have a nagging curiosity to know the exact percentage of clay, sand, silt, macro and micronutrients, and organic matter in the gardens, as well as its pH. But in more than twenty-five years of gardening, I have never had a complete soil analysis done. I must say, if my gardens were showing signs of stress and I couldn't figure out why, then I would be the first in line. So far, so good. A slacker I be.

What's Your Soil's Complexion?

Let's start with your soil type. Soil particles are defined by their size. Sand is the largest particle; next in size is silt, and the smallest is clay. Your soil is made up of all three, along with air, water, organic matter and living organisms. The percentage of each particle will determine the soil type. Borrowing from a popular fairy tale: sandy soils are "too big" (composed of mostly larger particles that drain too quickly and lose nutrients); clay soils are "too little" (composed of smaller particles that pack together tightly resulting in poor drainage and little air space); and loam is 'just right'. Most experts consider great garden loam to consist of at least 5% organic matter and be approximately 40% sand, 40% silt, and 20% clay *or* an equal mix of all three.

Okay, that was a really simple soil 101. To know which soil type you have, do one of the simple soil tests provided or take a sample to your county cooperative extension office and they will test it for you.

KISS *(Keep It Simple, Silly)* SOIL TESTS

Watch what happens after a steady rain. If your soil drains really fast and hardly looks like it was even watered, hello sand. If water puddles quickly on the surface or runs off, bring in the potter's wheel (clay). If it drains nicely but the soil remains slightly moist to the touch after it has been watered, hallelujah loam.

The ball test. Take a small amount of soil in the palm of your hand and moisten it. Squeeze your hand into a fist and then open it up. If the sample never holds a shape, you have sandy soil. If it forms a mound that gently falls apart, loam. And if it remains in a tight little ball, clay.

The Mayonnaise jar test. Put a cup of soil in a clear quart jar, fill with water from the sink, and shake, shake, shake (put the top on first). Let the jar sit for at least 24 hours. The soil will settle into layers. Sand will be at the bottom, topped by silt, then clay. You can now estimate the percentage of each in your soil by measuring the depth in inches of each layer. If you get ¼ inch sand, ¼ inch silt, and ½ inch clay then you have clay soil. Actually if you have more than ¼ inch (25%) clay, you *still* fall into the clay category. If there is 50% or more sand, you have sandy soil.

You are a winner if the 'soil wheel of fortune' landed on loam. But, what if you fall into the sand or clay category? Join the gang. Most of us are not blessed with rich, crumbly loam from the get-go. We will need to apply some oomph to transform our good-for-nothing 'dirt' into loam. How? The magic ingredient is organic matter. Humus is just another name for this finished, decomposed plant material that is usually dark brown or black and smells 'earthy'. 'Earthy' is a hard term to describe, but what it is not is a rotten, sour, reeking, or ammonia-like aroma. Instead is like the fresh smell you inhale when walking in the woods after it rains.

Whatever amendment you add to your soil, it should accomplish two things. One, it should increase the fertility of the soil, providing nourishment for your plants, with the addition of nitrogen, phosphorus, potassium and other nutrients. Just like people, the better nourished your plants, the healthier and better they will perform. Secondly, it should improve the soil's structure, the way the soil particles fit together. The goal is for sandy soils to retain water and nutrients better, while clay soils should drain faster and have more air space between particles. The adjacent chart includes some recommended organic soil amendments. Some may be more readily available and less expensive than others depending on where you live. And brace yourself. You should add organic matter every year since it continually breaks down (much appreciated by our plants). The good news is this is easily done by applying it as a seasonal mulch around your plants.

ORGANIC SOIL AMENDMENTS

Compost (decayed leaves, grass, other yard wastes)
Composted animal manure
Mushroom compost
Peat moss
Biosolids (treated sewage)
Leaf mold (decomposed leaves)
Grass clippings (untreated and composted)

Allow me to digress for a moment on animal manures, a topic that at times has raised quite the ruckus among my students. Who would have ever guessed that some people would become bragging, chest-puffing 'parents' over their manures? Kids, I can perhaps understand. But *!#*@? I've heard bragging rights over horse, cow, pig, sheep, chicken, turkey, rabbit, alpaca, llama, guinea pigs, and worm doo. But two folk's bravado topped all others. One petite, sophisticated-looking lady raved about her bat barn that was solely dedicated to harvesting guano. Every few weeks she dons her gas mask and shovels black bat droppings into garbage cans that are then rolled out to her garden beds. Interesting. But the winner has to be the woman who smugly said we were all thinking too small. Imagine the class's reaction when she burst out with elephant dung. She follows county fairs around in summer and scouts out the elephant tent. Much to the surprised delight of the animal keeper, she happily shovels big piles into hefty bags and carts her treasure away.

Two cautions about organic soil amendments. Many people mistakenly believe peat moss is *the* preferred amendment. Actually, peat moss only contributes one of the two qualities we want from amendments. It is a soil conditioner but it contains almost zero nutrients. Peat moss is the 'iceberg lettuce' of amendments – crunch but few nutrients. Its claim to glory is its ability to hold water, like a huge sponge. This is an extremely desirable as-

photo courtesy of Daniele Ippoliti

set for sandy soils, but a detriment to their clay counterparts. Plus peat moss is extremely acidic, which can negatively affect your soil's pH (we will talk about this later). Those of you with sandier soils should absolutely add peat moss to your soil, but always along with another amendment such as manure or compost. And please stop putting peat moss in planting holes for shrubs and trees. This used to be the recommended protocol but has now been refuted as it may actually wick moisture away from trees roots. My second caution is short and sweet. You cannot use cat or dog droppings in your gardens. These may contain bacteria and organisms that can cause disease.

I used to think pH was only something that Master Gardeners, professional landscapers, or chemists had to be concerned with. Boy, was I wrong. It makes a huge difference in how your plants grow. To explain, I will use the KISS approach (Keep It Simple, Silly). PH affects a plant's ability to take up nutrients in the soil. If your soil's pH is not in the optimum range, then your plants can become anemic, weakened, prone to disease, and stunted in growth. Allow me to use my son's love of macaroni and cheese as an illustration. I could put a huge bowl of that awful, fluorescent orange, boxed macaroni and cheese (his favorite) in front of him and then tie his hands behind his back so he couldn't (theoretically) get it into his mouth. All of that 'good stuff' is right there next to him but he is unable to eat it. Same thing with nutrients and your plants' roots. You could put a lot of sweat equity into working organic amendments into your soil and if the pH is off, you are not seeing the results you worked so hard to get. The askew pH acts like an invisible wall between the root hairs and the nutrients in the soil. And if you try to make up for the garden's lackluster appearance with fertilizer, you would just be wasting your money as the fertilizer also bypasses the roots.

Soil pH is measured on a scale from 1-14. Seven is considered neutral. Anything above 7 is considered alkaline (also referred to as basic or sweet). Anything lower than 7 is acidic (also referred to as sour). Most perennials, annuals, bulbs, shrubs and trees prefer to be in the 6.0 – 7.0 range. Of course there are always exceptions to the rule. Acid loving shrubs like Rhododendrons, Azaleas, Mountain Laurels, blue Hydrangeas, blueberry bushes, and Japanese Andromedas prefer a pH range of 5.0 - 5.5. Many woodland perennials like a pH between 6.0 to 6.5.

Having said all of this, given my no-fuss approach to gardening, I refuse to micromanage pH. I find most plants to be quite flexible. As long as my lawn and gardens fall somewhere in the low 6's to 7.0 pH range, I sleep just fine at night. The only exception I make for micro-managing pH is for my acid loving shrubs, as noted above. More on this shortly.

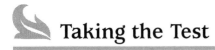

Taking the Test

Thankfully no studying is needed for a pH test. It's simple. Most garden centers sell pH test kits or pH meters. RapiTest is a top-rated, easy to use, inexpensive test kit. Meters are also easy to use. You just stick the probe into the soil and read the meter. Steer clear of cheaper probes (under $15); they tend to lose their preciseness after a few uses. If you are not a do-it-yourselfer or simply prefer a master's hand, take your samples to the local cooperative extension office and they will do this for a nominal fee. Many garden centers also do pH tests for a small fee, or sometimes for free, as they sell products to correct pH. Some areas in your yard are particularly prone to pH extremes. Refer to the chart for potential trouble spots.

POTENTIAL pH PROBLEM AREAS

Likely to be Alkaline	Likely to be Acidic
Where limestone is a predominant rock	under oak and pine trees
Where there is a lot of stonework, retaining walls	where peat moss has been used
Along the foundation of older homes	woodlands, especially evergreens
Near lawns that have been annually limed	where pine needles are used as mulch

When collecting samples, each area should be tested separately. Brush away any surface mulch or debris; dig down about 5" to 6" into the soil; slice a ½ cup sample from the sides and bottom of the hole with a stainless steel trowel or large spoon; and place in a baggie. Label each baggie so you know where the sample came from. Also note what is, or will be, planted there (i.e., perennial gardens, Rhododendrons and other evergreens, lawn, vegetable garden). Recommended soil pH will vary based on the plantings. If the area to be tested is large, collect five to eight samples from different spots, mix them together in a clean plastic bucket or mixing bowl, and scoop ½ cup into a baggie as the representative sample. When preparing a new garden bed, take the sample *after* all the soil amendments have been incorporated.

A word of caution. Many pH test kits require the sample to be dry (RapiTest does not). If there is a lot of moisture in it, results can be skewed. I usually put my samples on plastic plates on our kitchen counter and let them air dry a few days before testing. One harried student of mine had a different approach. He was running late from work and had forgotten to collect a soil sample for my class that night. Unfortunately it had rained all day and the ground was soaked. He called on his cell phone and asked if he could microwave it. I chuckled and said no, this would affect the reading. He was quiet for a moment and then asked if he could blow dry it on low. Now that's creative!

Editing the Red Marks After the Test

If a pH adjustment is needed, apply lime to raise pH, sulfur to lower pH. Alternative amendments are provided in the chart. Follow package directions for the amount needed based on the desired change. If your soil was tested by a service, the summary will include what amendment is recommended and its specific amount. Simply work the recommended number of pounds per one hundred square feet into the top few inches of soil with a cultivator or hoe and then water it in well. This all may sound more complicated than it really is. As you've gathered by now, I'm into simplicity. Being a visual learner, the first time I needed to make a correction, I took four garden stakes and a tape measure out to my gardens. I then measured out one hundred square feet (length times width) and put stakes at the corners. Next I grabbed a bag of elemental sulfur (in my case I needed to lower pH), an empty coffee can, and my bathroom scale. I put the can on the scale and poured sulfur into the can until I hit the necessary poundage per one hundred square feet. I then donned pharmaceutical gloves and cast the sulfur by hand as evenly as I could inside the staked area. Once I saw how the particles covered the required area I replicated this on other beds. Not terribly scientific, but it worked. This approach works with many dry fertilizers as well. I am always cautious to err on the side of under-applying, versus over-applying. Please do the same.

ALTERNATIVES TO LIME AND SULFUR

To raise pH	To lower pH
Woodash	Peat moss
Sweet peet	Coffee grinds or used tea bags
Chopped maple leaves	Chopped oak leaves
	Pine needles

Lime and sulfur (*especially sulfur*) are slow moving agents in the soil. Translation: you cannot race out the following week to retest your pH. Patience is a virtue. You need to wait a full three to six months. I personally wait a full six months before a 'redo' so I don't overcorrect and cause myself more problems.

A commonly asked question is how to deal with acid-loving shrubs when they are planted among less acid-loving neighbors (which they usually are). No problem. Both lime and sulfur tend to move vertically in the soil, versus horizontally. You can scratch in sulfur around the base of the shrubs and the nearby plants won't 'feel a thing'. And to all of you Miracid fans, this pendulum-swinging fertilizing practice is not good for your plants, plus it is a poor substitute for a pH correction made directly to the soil.

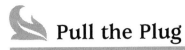

Pull the Plug

Proper drainage is another consideration. Sandy soils can be exasperating with their bad habit of quickly drying out but wet, poorly draining soils can be deadly. As explained earlier, clay or heavily compacted soils are composed of tightly packed particles. After soaking rains, water quickly fills the narrow channels between particles, displacing air needed for crucial gas exchange by the roots, resulting in plant stress or death by suffocation. Unlike worms that can come to the surface for air after the soil is flooded, your plants' roots are trapped below. Crown rot is another casualty of wet soils. The crown (the area where the stems meet the roots at the soil's surface) is so waterlogged that it gives up the ghost. And if crown rot didn't get some plants, winterkill may. Many people blame cold winters for plant loss but in reality, more plants are lost to extended periods of excessive moisture rather than to cold temperatures.

Signs of poor drainage include puddling water, soggy soil, difficulty in rewetting the soil after it has dried, and cracks running through the soil's surface after extended dry spells. A simple test for potential roto-rooter problems is to dig a hole one foot wide and about 8 to 12 inches deep. Fill the hole with water and allow to drain. Fill again with water. If it takes more than an hour to drain the second time, get the plunger.

You have several options for loosening tight soil and increasing percolation. You can build raised beds. An additional 8 inches or more of loamy topsoil will greatly enhance drainage. And for even better results, first loosen the top 4 to 6 inches of your hard packed soil before adding the topsoil. Other remedies include working with plants that don't mind wet feet (see the Top Ten lists for these), incorporating plenty of organic matter, and, if all else fails, installing drainage tiles (an expensive solution).

This book is patterned after my first book, *The Ultimate Flower Gardener's Top Ten Lists*. Similar to that book, my mission is to cut to the chase and give you only necessary, scale-turning gardening tips and plants for low-maintenance, breathtakingly beautiful shade gardens. Superfluous verbiage is for the compost pile.

I'm a list maker. Not because I love 'em. But because a concise, easy to follow format doesn't overwhelm me. If I see a lot of text or side tangents on a topic, my head starts swimming and I lock up. It's the same way when I shop for clothes. The lists in this book are practical, time-tested and to the point. Rejoice, turn the page and embrace the shade!

photo courtesy of Daniele Ippoliti

CHAPTER TWO

Top Ten Perennial Lists for Shade

Top Ten Spring Blooming Perennials

❧⊹Lenten Rose (Helleborus) 12" - 24". This 2005 Perennial Plant of the Year has nodding flowers in white, yellow, pink, red, burgundy as well as multicolor. Deep green leathery leaves are semi-evergreen in zones 5 and colder, a questionable benefit when they are buried under a foot of snow. Plants are ignored by deer, rabbits and other munchers thanks to their poisonous nature. 'Ivory Prince' is one of a number that break the traditional nodding flower posture. It has upward facing blooms. This allows you to better appreciate the delicate stamens without lying on your back. Lenten Rose is drought tolerant once established. See the Top Ten Hellebores list for more great cultivars. Zones 4 - 9

⊹Siberian Bugloss (Brunnera) 10" - 15" Bright blue, forget-me-not like flowers billow above mounded, heart-shaped leaves. Leaves can be solid green or have silver, creamy yellow or white markings. I prefer the variegated cultivars for their ability to reflect light in shadier spots. Plus the green leaved plant, macrophylla, seeds a bit too enthusiastically for me. 'Jack Frost' has silvery leaves with green veins; 'Looking Glass' has solid silver leaves; and 'Variegata' and 'Hadspen Cream' have green leaves with bold white margins. I 'deadleaf' Siberian Bugloss periodically in summer to remove foliage with brown edges. This also stimulates new leaves to unfurl. Zones 3 - 8

❧⊹Barrenwort, Bishop's Hat, Fairy Wings (Epimedium) 4" - 20" This is my favorite groundcover for dry shade. It sneers at thirsty maple tree roots. Although it is frequently labeled a groundcover, I find it moves at a polite pace. Flowers can be white, pink, sulfur yellow, orange and bicolor. All flowers dangle from wiry stems that rise above elongated, heart-shaped foliage. Barrenwort's leaves take on a pleasing burgundy cast in spring and sometimes again in fall. It partners beautifully with Hellebores. Zones 4 - 8

⊹Bleeding Heart (Dicentra spectabilis) 2' - 3' I can't imagine a garden without old fashioned Bleeding Heart. Gracefully arched stems with dangling white or pink flowers are a spring hallmark. 'Gold Heart' displays all of the same graceful characteristics of its siblings but it has screaming yellow foliage that glows in shade. Some might call it gaudy with its bright pink flowers and yellow leaves; I say encore! After long cold winters 'Gold Heart' is a refreshing sight. Most spectabilis varieties start to die back and go dormant in mid-summer. The more sun they get, the faster the 'adios'. Surprisingly, 'Gold Heart' usually remains unfazed by warmer weather. I give it a quick trim after flowering and it becomes a pretty backdrop to summer bloomers. The best time to divide all spectabilis varieties is when they start to go dormant. Speed up their retreat by whacking back the foliage to within 6" of the ground, dig up the clump and cut it into sections with a sharp knife. Reset the divisions, water in well and smile. Zones 3 - 9

❧drought tolerant ⊹deer resistant

Foamflower (Tiarella) 8" - 13" Foamflowers are charming native wildflowers. They have delicate white or pink flowers on wiry stems carried above colorful foliage. There are many different leaf shapes, most displaying rich black markings. Some of my favorite cultivars are 'Black Snowflake' (white flowers), 'Pink Bouquet' (pink flowers), and 'Mint Chocolate' (creamy white). Most Foamflowers are clump formers but 'Cascade Creeper' and 'Running Tapestry' will root along their stems to create pretty, drought-tolerant groundcovers. Check out the Top Ten 'Ellas' list for more no fuss Foamflowers. Zones 4 - 9

Lungwort (Pulmonaria) 10" - 15" These shade stalwarts always make me smile. Most varieties have flowers that start out pink and then turn blue as the flower matures. 'Sissinghurst White' is a white flowering cultivar and 'Bertram Anderson' is a lovely gentian blue. Leaves can be solid green, spotted, silvery or green with white margins. 'Redstart' is the earliest to bloom. Lungwort does have a bad habit of getting yucky looking leaves from powdery mildew after flowering. Fix the unsightly problem by cutting back all foliage to within 2" of the ground. The emerging new growth will look great. Are you wondering how Pulmonaria got the catchy common name of Lungwort? When the Bubonic Plague ('Black Death') swept across Europe in the 1300's, Pulmonaria was used along

PerennialResource.com

with another herb, wormwood, as a possible cure. Pulmonaria was also sometimes referred to as "Herb of Mary" and used to supposedly prove if a person was a witch or not. I bet it was a hot seller at Halloween. Zones 3 - 9

Dwarf Crested Iris (Iris cristata) 4" - 6". This charming little spring native never fails to entertain visitors. Small, sword-shaped leaves spring from petite rhizomes. Flowers are blue, violet or white. Like its larger cousin, German Bearded Iris, Dwarf Crested Iris does not like to have its rhizomes buried under soil or mulch. Leave the top half enjoying fresh air. Dwarf Crested Iris needs very little soil to sink its roots into and is quite drought tolerant. I like planting it around trees, especially near tough to plant spots next to a trunk's flare line. One word of caution. If you have children or pets that are 'ground feeders', think twice about Crested Iris. Its rhizomes are poisonous. Zones 3 - 8

Shooting Star (Dodecatheon) 8" - 20" Shooting Star's dart-shaped flowers dangling from long green stems are a joy to behold. Flowers are white or pink. The leaves are crinkly, medium green and hug the ground. By midsummer, Shooting Stars go dormant. They are in the ephemeral plant category. After blooming in spring and as the temperatures rise, they 'sink'. But don't despair. They'll cheerfully return next spring. Shooting Stars look especially nice next to fuller bodied plants like Hosta. Zones 3 - 9

✤**Paeonia japonica (Woodland Peony)** 15" - 24" Hold the phone! Here is an enchanting Peony for part shade. It has papery white petals and bright yellow stamens. It is probably the most asked about plant in my spring gardens. And the show doesn't stop after it blooms. The seed pods open in August to reveal bright pink shells and blue seeds. The leaves of Woodland Peonies look quite different from traditional peonies. They are grayish-green with three lobes. These exotic beauties are slow to get going, but once happy and settled in, they develop into a nice clump. A word of caution about dividing these. I assumed they would be easy like other Peonies so I whacked mine in late summer. Sadly, only one of five potted divisions survived, along with my 'mother plant' in the garden. Woodland Peonies can be hard to find at garden centers. You can find these at Plant Delights Nursery (www.plantdelights.com) and Seneca Hill Perennials (www.senecahillperennials.com), both great mail-order sources. Zones 4 - 8

🍂✤**Dead Nettle (Lamium)** 4" - 8" These are workhorses for dry shade. There are many varieties, although most gardeners are only familiar with silver leaved ones. 'Beedham's White' has chartreuse leaves with a white strip down the center; 'Anne Greenaway' is green, gold, and white; 'Aureum' has solid gold leaves and 'Friday' has green and yellow leaves. All march across the soil and set roots from their stems, creating more self-sufficient plants. Zones 3 - 8

⚘Astilbe (Astilbe) 8" - 4' Astilbes can handle sun or part shade. They really don't bloom well in full shade. I prefer the chinensis cultivars that are more drought tolerant than others. How can you tell if an Astilbe is in the 'camel-like' chinensis group? You will either see that word chinensis or c. before the single quote marks. For example, Astilbe c. 'Visions'. To enjoy these colorful white, pink, red, lavender, or purple blooms throughout the summer, make sure to buy Early (mid-June through early July), Mid (July) and Late blooming (mid-July through mid-August) varieties. Astilbes are heavy feeders. To encourage impressive plumes, work in some slow-release fertilizer such as Plant-Tone (organic) or Osmocote (14-14-14) into the soil once a year in early May. Zones 3 - 9

⚘Ligularia (Ligularia) 20" - 4' What a funky group of plants. They all have intriguing leaves, both in shape and color. The flowers are 'crunchy' too. The most common, 'The Rocket', has tall yellow spikes in July reaching 4' - 5'. 'Little Rocket' takes it down a notch at 3' tall. 'Othello' and 'Desdemona' have chocolate scalloped leaves. 'Britt-Marie Crawford' goes the extra mile with dark chocolate-purple foliage and purple undersides. 'Othello', 'Desdemona' and 'Britt-Marie Crawford' all have orangey-yellow, daisy-like flowers in August. Ligularias want a moisture-rich site. Along a water's edge is super. If you don't have a wet area, create a mini-bog by digging a hole, lining it with some pond liner or heavy plastic, backfill with soil amended with organic matter (compost or aged manure along with some peat moss) and plant. Zones 4 - 9

⚘Cardinal Flower (Lobelia) 24" - 5' Cardinal Flowers hit their peak in late July and August. Cardinalis is very popular with its electric red flower stalks that can reach 4'. It can be finicky and short-lived for some. 'Monet Moment' with rosy pink flowers and 'Red Beauty' tend to be more reliable. L. siphilitica has stunning blue flowers in August and September. Although it can seed around, blue is such a rare color in late blooming perennials, I'll take it. 'Queen Victoria', with its captivating burgundy foliage and red flowers, has never overwintered in my gardens, despite its claim to be hardy to Zone 5. Liar. Zones 3 - 9

Hosta (Hosta) 3" - 4' Call me snobby, but I primarily buy Hosta for their foliage. I usually whack off the flowers. There are a few excep-

PerennialResource.com

tions. I love white flowering Hosta for reflecting light in shady spots. Hosta with white flowers include sieboldiana 'Elegans' (blue leaves), 'Frances Williams' (blue and chartreuse leaves), 'Love Pat' (blue leaves) and 'Spilt Milk' (white streaks on blue leaves). Fragrant flowers are another plus. Check out the Top Ten list for fragrant Hosta. In general, the thicker the leaves (substance), the more resistant a Hosta is to deer, slug and snail damage. Most Hosta with blue leaves have a heavy substance. Zones 3 - 9

Corydalis (Corydalis) 9" - 16" These are 'Ever-Ready Bunnies' in shade or part sun. They bloom May through September with no deadheading. They can be short-lived and seed about if happy, but a perennial that bangs away flowers that long can have a spot in my bed. C. lutea has cheerful yellow flowers with ferny-green leaves. Less common but as impressive is the white corydalis, ochroleuca. Be wary of C. sempervirens, a pink and yellow flowering lady that gets very leggy and is a biennial, not a perennial. The blue flowering Corydalis ('Blue Panda' and 'China Blue') go dormant in warmer temperatures and can be short-lived. 'Berry Exciting' is a newcomer with screaming yellow foliage and purple flowers. This one is on my wish list. Zones 4 - 9

✛Fringed Leaved, Fern-Leaved Bleeding Heart (Dicentra) 8" - 15" These pick up the baton where larger, earlier blooming Bleeding Hearts quit. Ferny, blue green foliage complements pink, white or reddish-pink flowers. They dislike dry shade and may go dormant in these conditions. The Heart series is exceptional with frosty blue leaves and a heavy flowering habit. Look for 'King of Hearts' (deep pink); 'Ivory Hearts' (white), 'Candy Hearts' (medium pink) and 'Burning Hearts' (rosy-red with white edges). Fern-Leaved Bleeding Hearts can be challenging to divide. They don't always respond well (read between the lines). If you are going to divide them, attack in spring. Zones 3 - 8

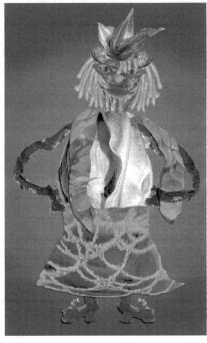

photo courtesy of Daniele Ippoliti

🌿Coral Bell (Heuchera) 6" - 20" Many Coral Bells thrive in shade, especially those with yellow, peach or purple leaves. Mounds can be only 4" tall or as large as 12". Most flowers are a non-descript creamy-white or pale pink but 'Hollywood', 'Hercules', 'Veil of Passion' and 'Cherries Jubilee' are bright red; 'Rave On' and 'Dolce Mocha Mint' are rich pink. One of my favorites is 'Caramel' with large, showy marmalade leaves. It is one of the few I've found that handles sun or shade with equal flare. Zones 4 - 9

🌿drought tolerant ✛deer resistant

⁜Pink Turtlehead (Chelone) 2' - 4' Pink or white flowers decorate dark green, glossy leaves starting in August. Turtlehead can handle sun or shade as well as drier conditions, despite its fame as being a moisture lover. I had a sweep of these under a silver maple tree and they thrived. That is until the maple was struck by lightning and everything came a'tumblin' down. 'Hot Lips' has deep pink flowers and stays more compact at 2' to 3' than C. lyonii that can reach 4'. I am not impressed with white Turtlehead. It looks ho-hum. All Turtleheads have stiff stems that can be pinched in early June for more compact, heavier blooming plants. Zones 3 - 7

⁜Athyrium niponicum (Japanese Painted Fern) 8" - 22" Ferns are a natural for shade. 'Pictum' is the most widely available Japanese Painted Fern with silver, red and dark green fronds. Nice, but if you want to turn up the color meter, plant 'Silver Falls', 'Ursula's Red', 'Regal Red' or 'Burgundy Lace'. 'Ghost' is almost all silver and very upright and vase-like in appearance. Japanese Painted Ferns contrast nicely with Hosta and plumy Astilbes, especially the darker red Astilbes that provide a color echo to the fern's burgundy veins. Zones 4 - 9

Bellflower (Campanula) 4" - 3' Campanulas do fine in part shade, especially the gold-leaved ones that tend to fry in full sun. I love using 'Dickson's Gold' along shady paths. It has gold, mounded foliage and lavender-blue flowers. The glowing mounds act like runway lights spring through fall. By positioning these at various intervals on each side of a path, the viewer's eye is gently directed forward. Peach-Leaf Bellfowers (persicifolia) also do well in part shade. Flowers can be white, blue or purple. 'Blue-Eyed Blond' has blue flowers and bright yellow foliage. 'Alba' has white flowers and green leaves. Deadheading always helps extend the bloom period of Bellflowers but all those little flowers drive me bananas. So I wait until most flowers are spent and then I shear them all off, knowing that some fresh buds were sacrificed in the process. So be it. Zones 3 - 8

Top Ten Fall Blooming Perennials

Yellow Waxbells (Kirengeshoma palmata) 3' Yellow Waxbells have delicate, buttery-yellow flowers that dangle from 3' arching stems. The foliage is soft green and looks similar to a maple tree's leaf. Yellow Waxbells form a neat 3' X 3' clump. It rarely needs dividing. It makes a handsome pairing with Astilbes, Toad Lilies and Hosta. Zones 4 - 8

Toad Lily (Tricyrtis) 18" - 36" These unique looking flowers are in the orchid family. Blooms can be solid white, yellow, white with pink or purple markings. Leaves are solid green, green and white, or green and creamy-yellow. All Toad Lilies have arching stems with flowers formed along their stem length. The flowers are petite in size so it's best to plant a number of Toad Lilies together to create a nice show. Plant them near the front of a bed where these beauties can be appreciated. Zones 4 - 8

Gentian (Gentiana) 8" - 30" These uncommon plants make a fetching display in bloom. Most need at least part sun but a few can handle part shade. 'True Blue' has bright blue, upward facing, bell-shaped flowers that open in mid-summer and continue into early fall. It gets 24" - 30" tall. Closed Gentian (andrewsii) has deeper blue, 'closed' tubular flowers and stays shorter at 12" - 18". There is also a pure white variety. Crested Gentian (Gentian septemfida) has brilliant blue, open-faced flowers with white throats. It stays low at 8". Cady's Falls Nursery (www.cadysfallsnursery.com) in northern Vermont carries a large selection of these delightful plants. Zones 4 - 7

PerennialResource.com

⊹Bugbane, Snakeroot (Cimicifuga) 4' - 6' There are green and chocolate leaved varieties of Bugbane. Chocolate foliaged cultivars have incredibly fragrant flowers. I find the aroma of green leaved ones unpleasant. Most Bugbanes send up long, bottlebrush flowers in August and continue into fall. My favorite chocolates include 'Brunette' and 'Hillside Black Beauty'. I have tried 'Black Negligee' several times with no success, in the garden or bedroom. 'Pink Spire' is promoted as having pink flowers, but the blooms were so pale, it required imagination to 'see' pink. Two of the green leaved varieties that I love for masses of floating 'candlesticks' are Simplex, (blooms in September and October) and racemosa (blooms July and August. Zones 3 - 8

⁂Leadwort, Plumbago (Ceratostigma plumbaginoides) 8" - 12" Leadwort is a lovely blue flowering perennial that opens in August and continues through September. It can handle full sun to part shade. The more sun it gets, the more burgundy the leaves turn in cooler weather. When happy, it can be a slow spreading groundcover that effectively smothers weeds. Some catalogs list it as a Zone 5, others Zone 6. In colder climates it does best in a sheltered area, on the east side of the house or near stonework. I have lost it to Old Man Winter a number of times but it is so gorgeous, I keep buying it. Call me foolish, I'm lovesick. Zone 5/6 - 9

⁑⁂Fall Blooming Joe Pye Weed (Eupatorium 'Chocolate') 3' - 5' 'Chocolate' grows in dry shade and features billowy clouds of white flowers September through October. It also does well in full sun. Despite its height, I have never had to stake it. It is also a lovely cut flower for late season bouquets. Zones 3 - 7

⁂Monkshood (Aconitum) 12" - 5' These resemble Delphinium but are longer-lived and can handle shade. Plus nothing eats Monkshood as it's poisonous. Some Monkshood like nappellis (blue, 4' - 5'), 'Bi-color' (white with blue edges, 4' - 5') and 'Blue Lagoon' (blue, 12") bloom in July and August. Others postpone the show until fall. 'Arendsii' (violet, 4'), 'Barker's Variety' (violet-blue, 5') and carmichaelii or fischeri (wedgewood blue, 4') start in September and bloom for weeks. Many Monkshood have deep green, shiny leaves. Zones 3 - 6

Top Ten Fragrant Perennials

Fragrance is the most powerful of all our senses for triggering memories. Scents can quickly transport us back in time. As I child I delighted in pressing my nose next to my Grandma's tea roses. Mm-mmm, heavenly. So were her gingersnap cookies. There is nothing like a sublime fragrance to renew our souls.

To get the most bang for your buck when designing with nature's 'Air-Wicks', consider the following:

PerennialResource.com

- Site them in a sheltered location so the perfume lingers. Usually the warmer the space, the more concentrated the aroma. Many fragrances are often stronger in the evening. This is to attract pollinating night moths. Place 'sense-sational' plants near your evening retreats.
- Take note of the direction of the prevailing breezes. Locate your garden down-wind.
- Remember that low spots in your landscape also capture fragrance.
- Place fragrant plants near doors, entertainment areas, patios, open windows, screened porches, gazebos and pathways.

Here are a few tips for purchasing fragrant perennials:

- Older flower varieties tend to be more fragrant. Hybridization for bigger and better blooms has not always benefited fragrance.
- Pick a mix of spring, summer and fall blooming fragrant plants for constant perfume.
- In general, the lighter the flower color, the stronger the scent. White flowers tend to be the most fragrant. Others include off-white, pink, mauve, yellow and lavender.
- When researching plants, look for those labeled 'strongly or powerfully scented' verses 'lightly scented' to be sure you'll be able to easily smell them without being right on top of them.
- Don't place too many fragrant perennials close together. Stronger scents can overwhelm more delicate ones, plus when strong scents mingle the effect can be overpowering. Think of being in car full of teenage boys 'cologned up with Axe' before a dance. I've been there. Nasty.

Note: There is a separate Top Ten List for fragrant Hosta.

Oriental, Trumpet and Orienpet Lilies (assorted Liliums) 16" - 6' Sun - Part Shade. Summer bloomer. White, pink, red, yellow, orange, reddish-purple or bicolor flowers. I know. You thing I have 'sniffed' too many flowers and have lost my 'senses'. Nope. You can actually grow many Liliums in part shade. The only adjustment you need to make is an allowance for stretching as the stem seeks more sun. So if the plant tag states the lilium will reach 28", I'll guesstimate that in a shadier spot it will be more like 34" to 40". I can't give you a 'resizing' formula. Experience will be your guide. Thankfully, if you guessed wrong and the bulb is not the right height when it blooms, you can dig it up and move it to a better spot afterwards. Plant Lilium bulbs as you would spring blooming bulbs, at a depth of three times the height of the bulb. To protect them from bulb munching critters put chicken grit (crushed oyster shells) or Harvest Crab Shells in the planting holes. Gravel also works. Trumpet and Orienpets are usually taller than Orientals. All have yellow pollen that stains clothes or skin so don't get too close to sniff. You shouldn't need to. As far as blooming, Trumpets are usually first out of the blooming gate in late June, followed by Orienpets, and Orientals bring up the rear in August. By planting all three you will have fragrance in the garden for months. Most Liliums are hardy to Zones 4 - 8

❧ Daylily (Hemerocallis) 18" - 30 + " Sun - Part Shade. Summer bloomer. All flower colors except blue. White and yellow daylilies are most fragrant. Daylilies will behave like Liliums in part shade. Their stems (scapes) will usually stretch for the sun. Respond by planting them a little farther back in the bed. You may also need to stake the elongated stems to support the weighted flower tips. Some Daylilies are labeled as fragrant but your really have to use your imagination to smell anything. The following have some real oomph to them: 'Sunday Gloves' (white, 27" tall), 'Hyperion' (yellow, 40"), 'Buttered Popcorn' (yellow, 32"), 'Barbara Mitchell' (soft pink, 20") and 'Amazing Grace' (yellow, 24"). Zones 3 - 9

❧ Bugbane, Snakeroot (Cimicifuga) 2' - 6' Part Sun - Part Shade. Late summer, fall bloomer. White or soft pink flowers. If I had to pick one perennial that was the most fragrant, it would be the chocolate-leaved Bugbanes. Their elegant, long 'candle-stick' flowers transmit sweet aroma all over the property. The dark, ferny foliage is an elegant 'vase'. 'Brunette', 'Hillside Black Beauty' and 'Atropurpurea' get 4' to 5' tall. 'Chocoholic' is the shortest at 2' to 3'. All have creamy white flowers. 'Pink Spires' has very soft pink blooms. If like me, you are itching for more of these beauties to plant around the property or to give to special friends, the best time to divide them is in spring. Zones 3 - 8

Tree Peony (Paeonia suffruticosa) 2' - 5' Sun - Part Shade. Spring bloomer. White, pink or red flowers. Most people are familiar with the traditional herbaceous Peony in the lactiflora group. Time to step on the wild side and grow Tree Peonies. These exotic Peonies have massive flowers in colors unavailable in common Peonies: dreamy apricot, purple, near black and wisteria blue. Of course red, whites and pinks abound too. Tree Peonies never require pruning and can handle full sun or dappled shade. Their flowers last longer in less sun. These long-lived plants are quite drought tolerant once established. But be patient with them; they are slow growing but worth the journey. When planting, make sure to place the grafted union a good 4" - 6" below the soil surface. This is where the stem meets the large root mass. Eventually the grafted section will develop its own roots and be very hardy. Don't be surprised if the first year or two you don't have many flowers. As the root system settles in and expands, you will be rewarded with more and more buds. Do not trim Peonies in the fall. Leave them be! The woody stems carry buds for next year's show. Not all Tree Peonies are fragrant. Some perfumed cultivars include 'Alice Harding' (semi-double petals, yellow), 'Ruffled Sunset' (single petals, creamy rose), 'Wauceda Princess' (semi-double petals, pink) and 'Boreas' (semi-double petals, dark red). Zone 3 - 8

Sweet Autumn Clematis (Clematis paniculata) 15'- 20' Sun - Part Shade. Late summer bloomer. White flowers. This heavily flowering Clematis has small white blooms that bury the leaves, resembling a 'blanket of snow'. It can be whacked down to within 8" of the ground each spring and it still scrambles to great heights and blooms in August. It looks divine sweeping over fences, stonewalls, arbors and shrubs. Zones 3 - 8

Lily of the Valley (Convallaria) 6" - 8" Sun - Shade. Spring bloomer. White or pink flowers. Lily of the Valley is a well-known, fragrant groundcover for its ability to handle extreme conditions. Let me emphasize the word groundcover. It will follow you into the house if you're not watching. The point is, think before you plant it. Be realistic and happy. You can try to control its enthusiasm by sinking it in a deep-sided pot but sometimes the long spaghetti-like roots can magically escape the 'box'. Most cultivars have single petals but there are double forms available. There is also a variegated variety, C. Albostriata, with sassy white striped leaves. C. Rosea has pink flowers. Sometimes the foliage will get scrappy and start to die back later in the season, especially in hot, dry summers. It is going dormant. You can try giving it more water, or simply wave good-bye, look the other way, and it will resurface next spring. All parts of this plant are poisonous. Zones 3 - 8

Sweet Woodruff (Galium odoratum) 6" Part Sun - Shade. Spring bloomer. White flowers. Sweet Woodruff's foliage and flowers are both lightly scented. The delicate looking leaves are a nice shade of soft green. This is a sweet groundcover. Zones 3 - 7

⚜Woods Phlox (Phlox divaricata) 6" - 14" Sun - Shade. Spring bloomer. White, pink, shades of blue, or lavender flowers. Woods Phlox boasts masses of flowers for a good five weeks. All are extremely fragrant! Woods Phlox are equally happy in sun or dappled shade. After flowering, shear them to within two inches of the ground for a pleasing green mat. New cultivars include those with variegated foliage. 'Lemon Slice' from Plant Delight's Nursery has gold bands in the center of each leaf. And there is even a tri-color variety, Montrose Tri-color, available from my friend, Dawn Foglia's delightful nursery, WildThings Rescued in Valley Falls, NY. Closely related is Phlox glaberrima (Smooth Phlox) and g. 'Triple Play' hits it out of the park with its green and white leaves, dark red stems and pinkish-lavender flowers. Finally, Woods Phlox is my pick over the more common Creeping Phlox (sometimes called Moss Phlox). Woods phlox is fragrant, weed-smothering, longer blooming, and deer resistant; not so Creeping Phlox. Zones 3 - 8

⚜Summersweet (Clethra) 3' - 8' Sun - Part Shade. Summer bloomer. Pink or white flowers. Summersweet is such a perfect name for this flowering shrub. It's flowers perfume the summer air with fragrance. Summersweet is one of the few shrubs that can handle wet soil as well as average soil. They stress out in dry soil. Flower buds are set on new wood so prune in late winter or early spring. 'Sixteen Candles' (28", white flowers), 'Ruby Spice' (3 - 6', pink flowers), 'Hummingbird' (30", white flowers) and 'Vanilla Spice' (3 - 6', white flowers) are all butterfly magnets with showy golden foliage in fall. Zones 3 - 9

⚜Carolina Allspice, Sweetshrub (Calycanthus) 5' - 10' Sun - Part Shade. Late spring, early summer bloomer. Maroon, yellow or chocolate flowers. This old fashioned shrub has to be smelled to be appreciated. And I mean that literally. Different cultivars have different scents. Some are quite pleasant, others will have you plugging your nose. But then again, fragrance is highly subjective in the 'nose' of the beholder. Carolina Allspice's leaves are also fragrant with a clove-like aroma. Carolina Allspice benefits from pruning each season after flowering to keep it compact. In shadier spots it will be more open branched and 'relaxed' looking. 'Athens' has lovely yellow flowers and gets 6' tall. 'Michael Lindsey' has reddish-brown flowers and grows between 6' - 10'. 'Venus' has sweet magnolia-like, white flowers that are supposed to smell like strawberries, melons, and spices. Grab your eating utensils! Zones 5 - 8

Top Ten 'Blue'-tiful Perennials

Blue is such a cheerful, fetching color, especially in shade. Blue calms the soul. The lighter the blue (tint), the easier it is to see from a distance versus darker shades that fade away from the viewer. In either case, you can help blue flowers pop by placing them near yellow or chartreuse foliage. Magnificent.

⫶Virginia Bluebells (Mertensia) 12" - 24" Part Sun - Shade. Spring bloomer. Delicate, nodding flowers adorn soft green leaves on arching stems in April and May. After the mesmerizing plant awes bystanders, it goes dormant in early summer. But do not fear, it will come back next spring. Because Virginia Bluebells is an ephemeral, place it where its absence will go unnoticed. I plant it between large Hosta. When the Bluebells disappear, large unfurling Hosta leaves cover their exit. Zones 3 - 9

⫶Siberian Bugloss (Brunnera) 10" - 15" Part Shade - Shade. Spring bloomer. Siberian Bugloss is also commonly known as False Forget-Me-Not because of its dazzling blue flowers that look just like Forget-Me-Nots on elongated stems. Mounded leaves can be solid green or display silver, creamy yellow or white markings. 'Jack Frost' has silvery leaves with green veins; 'Looking Glass' has solid silver leaves; and B. 'Variegata' and 'Hadspen Cream' have green leaves with bold white margins. 'Spring Yellow' has yellow leaves in spring that become light green as the season progresses. Zones 3 - 7

⫶Bellflower (Campanula) 4" - 3' Sun - Part Shade. Summer bloomer. Most bellflowers prefer sun but there are two groups that do fine in part shade. Bellflowers have charming, cup-shaped blooms. Peach-Leaf Bellflower (in the persicifolia group) has long stems that shoot up from narrow-leaved foliage mounds. 'Telham Beauty', 'Takion Blue' and 'Blue' are nice green-leaved picks. 'Blue-Eyed Blond' has seductive blue eyes atop flashy yellow foliage. In the carpatica group (mounded Bellflowers), 'Dickson's Gold' has notched, golden leaves with blue flowers. Zones 3 - 8

⫶Gentian (Gentiana) 8" - 30" Sun - Part Shade. Summer, early fall. These uncommon plants make a fetching presentation. Most Gentians need at least part sun but a few can handle part shade. 'True Blue' has bright blue, upward facing, bell-shaped flowers in mid-summer. It gets 24" - 30" tall. Closed Gentian (andrewsii) has deeper blue, 'closed' tubular flowers and stays shorter at 12" - 18". Crested Gentian (Gentian septemfida) has brilliant blue, open-faced flowers with white throats. It stays low at 8". Zones 4 - 7

Liverleaf, Liverwort (Hepatica) 4" - 6" Part Shade - Shade. Spring bloomer. These dainty woodland perennials have three-lobed leaves that resemble a liver. There are two groups of Hepaticas: pointy-lobed and round-lobed. Both groups are evergreen. The early spring leaves are actually last year's, providing the backdrop for lovely flowers that bloom atop hairy, silver stems. Once flowering is finished the foliage dies back and a fresh new round of leaves takes its place. Hepatica nobilis 'Lithowanian Blues' has striking blue flowers as does nobilis 'Czeck'. These will be harder to find at garden centers. Mail-order is probably your best bet. Zones 3 - 9

⁘Lungwort (Pulmonaria) 8" - 12" Part Shade - Shade. Spring bloomer. Many Lungworts have pink buds that open to bluish-violet flowers but there are a few cultivars that have brilliant blue flowers. 'Bertram Anderson' has very narrow, spotted leaves, 'Blue Ensign' sports dark green, spotless leaves, and 'Samourai' has glistening silver leaves. All Lungworts can get powdery mildew after flowering. Don't tolerate this. Whack the leaves back to within a few inches of the ground when they look ratty and they will respond with a nice new set. Zones 3 - 7

⁘Monkshood (Aconitum) 12" - 5' Part Sun - Shade. Summer, fall blooms. These resemble Delphinium but are longer-lived and handle shade. Plus nothing eats them because they're poisonous. Some Monkshood like nappellis (blue, 4' - 5') and 'Blue Lagoon' (blue, 12") bloom in July and August. Others postpone the show until fall. 'Arendsii' (violet, 4'), 'Barker's Variety' (violet-blue, 5') and carmichaelii or fischeri (wedgewood blue, 4') start in September and bloom for weeks. Most Monkshood have deep green, shiny leaves. Zones 3 - 6

Corydalis (Corydalis) 8" - 12" Sun - Shade. Late spring, early summer bloomer. 'Blue Panda' and 'China Blue' have gentian blue flowers over ferny green foliage. These beauties are only for those gardeners who love challenges and are risk takers. The blue flowering Corydalis will usually go dormant in mid-summer. This delicate plant is also not long-lived. But the seductive blue flowers will lure many to try them, including me. I struck out but my twin sister in Kennebunk, Maine has had good luck. The yellow flowering C. lutea and C. ochroleuca with white flowers are much easier to grow, don't go dormant in summer, and bloom into fall. But they are not blue. Choices, choices. Zones 4 - 8

🌿✥Dwarf Crested Iris (Iris cristata) 4" - 6". Sun - Part Shade. Spring bloomer. This charming little spring perennial is a winner. Small, sword-shaped leaves spring from petite rhizomes. 'Powder Blue Giant' lives up to its name with large, soft blue flowers. Like its larger cousin, German Bearded Iris, Dwarf Crested Iris does not like to have its rhizomes buried under soil or mulch. Leave the top half enjoying fresh air. I like planting Dwarf Crested Iris around trees, especially near tough to plant spots by a trunk's flare line. It needs very little soil to sink its roots into and is quite drought tolerant. One word of caution. If you have children or pets that are 'ground feeders', think twice about Crested Iris. Its rhizomes are poisonous. Zones 3 - 8

✥Primrose (Primula) 4" - 24" Part Sun - Shade. Spring bloomer. Primroses come in many colors but shimmering blue cultivars are 'Revere', 'Eugenie' and 'Striped Victorians', all in the Barnhaven polyanthus series. P. vulgaris 'Blue' is commonly found in grocery stores around the spring holidays and is reliable grower with brilliant yellow centers. Most Primroses are easy to grow as long as they have enough moisture. Primroses can be divided after blooming. Just pull apart the foliage rosettes with your hands and replant. Zones 5 - 8

What are these? Peek-a-boo perennials that emerge in spring, bloom, set seed, and then disappear (go dormant) as the warmer temperatures arrive in summer. Ephemerals get their business done before deciduous trees leaf out and shade the ground floor. Their entire above-ground playtime is only six to eight weeks. Despite their elusive nature, these woodland beauties are magical and contribute an unequaled beauty to shade gardens. But ephemerals also require more thought on your part, given they leave vacant spaces for months. I like to plant them between large Hosta. The ephemeral blooms as the awakening Hosta is just pushing through the ground. Then the Hosta's unfurling leaves provide a discretionary screen as the ephemeral changes into its dormant clothes. Astilbes, Ferns, and Toad Lilies are also nice partners because their leaves unfurl later than other perennials in spring. Another way to fill the void is to plant shade-loving annuals over the sleeping beauties. The roots of annuals are not a long-term competition for ephemerals. If an ephemeral takes too long to depart and its ratty leaves bother you, speed up their departure by cutting back foliage to within an inch of the ground.

Many botanical gardens have woodland gardens as one of their educational displays. These gardens provide an outstanding arena for viewing ephemerals and companion plantings. And needless to say, spring is the time to visit. One of my favorite spots is Garden in the Woods, managed by the New England Wildflower Society in Framingham, MA. They also have a fabulous nursery where you can buy many of these woodland gems. Just make sure when you get home not to delay getting them in the ground or they may go dormant on you in the pot.

⚜Shooting Star (Dodecatheon) 6" - 20" Part Shade - Shade. White, pink or red flowers.
The dangling, dart-shaped flowers of Shooting Stars are a joy to behold. The leaves are a crinkly, medium green and lay close to the ground. Some different varieties to check out include 'Sooke' (red-purple, 6" - 8"), 'Album' (white, 14"), and 'Queen Victoria' (rose-purple, 10" - 14"). Shooting Stars look especially nice next to fuller bodied plants like Hosta. Zones 4 - 8

Liverleaf, Liverwort (Hepatica) 4" - 6" Part Shade - Shade. Pink, purple, blue or white
flowers. These dainty woodland perennials have three-lobed leaves that resemble a liver. There are two groups of Hepaticas: pointy-lobed and round-lobed. Both groups are evergreen. The early spring leaves are actually last year's crop, providing the backdrop for lovely flowers that bloom atop hairy, silver stems. Once flowering has finished, the older leaves die back and a fresh new round of leaves take their place. Pretty cool. Zones 3 - 9

⚜Fairy Bells (Disporum) 1' - 3' Part Shade - Shade. White or yellow flowers. D. sessile
'Variegatum' has green and white striped leaves and dangling white flowers that echo

the white leaf markings. D. flavum, with green leaves, showcases soft yellow, nodding flowers on 2' stems. The leaves are solid green leaves. Both have black berries and will slowly naturalize over time. Zones 4 - 9

Lady's Slipper (Cypripedium) 10" - 2' Part Shade - Shade. Yellow, white, pink or bicolor flowers. Lady's Slippers are not a flower for beginners. They can be very temperamental and finicky and at $60 or more per plant, mistakes can be costly. Lady Slippers like organically rich soil with good drainage. A protected wildflower, it is illegal to harvest these from the wild. That is why legally propagated ones grown from seed are so expensive. It can take a minimum of seven years to grow one to flowering size. Plant Delights Nursery (www.plantdelights.com) and Roots & Rhizomes (www.rootsrhizomes.com) both carry these beauties. Zones 3 - 8

Wakerobin (Trillium) 8" - 12" Part Shade - Shade. Pink, white, maroon, red or yellow flowers. Trilliums are quite easy to grow and will slowly spread to form a showy display. I mixed white, pink and red ones in a shady spot for an attractive display. The word arresting brings to mind that these are also protected wildflowers and you should buy them from reputable growers. One of my favorites is Trillium lutea. It has soft yellow flowers with dark green and silver mottled leaves. There are also double petaled forms of the white Trillium that are highly prized (and priced). Zones 3 - 9

⁑Jack in the Pulpit (Arisaema) 15" - 36" Part Shade - Shade. White, pink, yellow or mixed striped flowers. This Dr. Zeus plant has always fascinated me. It just makes you want to squat and look under the 'hood' to see Jack. Then after flowering the brilliant red seed heads carry on the show. Please stand and applaud. Mine have seeded happily but it takes several years for seedlings to get 'Jacked'. Zones 4 - 8

Bloodroot (Sanguinaria canadensis) 6" - 14" Part Shade - Shade. White flowers. This delicate woodland plant gets its common name from the red juice that is released from crushed roots. Native Americans used the juice as a dye for baskets, clothing, war paint and insect repellent. S. canandensis has a single petaled, white flower that appears above a large, single lobed, gray-green leaf. 'Multiplex' has double petaled, white flowers. Heads up, the roots are poisonous. Zones 3 - 9

⚜Virginia Bluebells (Mertensia virginica) 12" - 24" Part Sun - Shade. Purplish-pink buds open to brilliant blue flowers. Soft green, smooth leaves adorn arching stems that drip gorgeous blue flowers from their tips. These dainty flowers will colonize where happy. Virginia Bluebells make a bewitching combination with yellow Daffodils. Their only pet peeve is wet soil. Zones 3 - 9

Himalayan Blue Poppy (Meconopsis) 25" - 30" Part Shade. Blue flowers. Heavenly, true blue, poppy flowers are like the 'Holy Grail' to gardeners. The plant is not long-lived and usually waits to bloom until its second or third year. Himalayan Blue Poppy has the well earned reputation of being very challenging to grow (not to kill) and has been my personal challenge for years. I refuse to give up in my quest for this elusive blue gem in the garden. Bragging rights are seductive. They demand cool, nutrient rich (lots of compost or manure), well drained soil. Zones 5 - 8

Largeflower Bellwort (Uvularia) 12" - 16" Part Sun - Shade. Yellow flowers. Pale green, nodding stems dangle pretty, buttery-yellow flowers. Not as showy as some other ephemerals but sweet. They look similar to Fairy Bells. Zones 2 - 9

Top Ten 'Ellas' (Tiarella and Heucherella)

Tiarellas and Heucherellas are super heroes for dry shade. They win our hearts and praise. At least mine.

Tiarellas, commonly known as Foamflowers, flower in spring, with many reblooming in summer. Flowers can be pink or white. They got the nickname Foamflower because blooms appear to foam forth and hover just above attractive leaves. Most Foam-flowers are clump forming perennials but some like 'Eco Running Tapestry', 'Running Tiger' and cordifolia that are stoloniferous. What? They have stems that scramble across the soil and set root as they press forward. These make tremendous flowering ground-covers for dry shade.

Tiarella is one of Heucherella's parents. Some brilliant plantsman crossed Tiarella with Heuchera (Coral Bell) and presto, Heucherella was born. Heu-cherella, commonly called Foamy Bells, captures some of the best characteristics of both parents. Heuchera contributes additional foliage colors and an evergreen nature. Tiarella adds cool shaped, dissected leaves with central leaf colorations plus its woodland heritage.

Both Tiarella and Heucherella make colorful companions for Hostas, Astilbes, ever-blooming Bleeding Hearts, and ornamental grasses. They are easy to mix and match and can be used to create a breathtaking shade tapestry. Heucherellas are more drought toler-ant while Tiareallas are more deer resistant.

The height noted for all of these 'Ellas' is the foliage mound's height, not that of the 'see through' flowers.

Top Five Tiarellas

'Heronswood Mist' 6" Part Shade - Shade. Spring bloomer. Pink flowers. This Tiarella makes you want to pet it, just like Lambsear. 'Heronswood Mist' has creamy-white, green and pink leaves with fuzzy leaf 'hairs'. It has pink flowers that repeat through the summer. Zones 4 - 9

'Neon Lights' 8" Part Shade - Shade. Spring bloomer. Pink and white flowers. This bold-leaved Tiarella has bright green, large leaves with burgundy-chocolate centers. It occasionally reblooms in summer. Zones 4 - 9

'Eco Running Tapestry' and 'Running Tiger' 6" - 8" Part Shade - Shade. Spring bloomer. Pinkish-white flowers. Both of these have maple-shaped, fuzzy leaves with light purple-maroon markings. They happily spread across open ground, smothering weeds in their path. Zones 4 - 9

'Sugar and Spice' 8" Part Shade - Shade. Spring bloomer. Pink and white flowers. Dan Heims is a brilliant, internationally recognized plantsman and he states this is the best Foamflower yet. It has glossy, dark green, dissected leaves with purple centers. Prolific blooms are icing on the cake. Some say it is an improved 'Spring Symphony'. Zones 4 - 9

'Mint Chocolate' 8" Part Shade - Shade. Spring bloomer. White flowers. I have hungered for 'Mint Chocolate' for several years but have yet to put my hands on it. It has slightly more elongated, dissected green leaves with chocolate markings than others in the 'box'. Zones 4 - 9

Top Five Heucherellas

'Stoplight' 6" Sun - Shade. Spring bloomer. White flowers. 'Stoplight' is an improvement on Heucherella 'Sunspot'. It has bolder colored leaves with red markings. I have also found that 'Stoplight' is much hardier and vigorous. I placed a sweep of these under a burgundy, thread-leaf Japanese Maple and the combination was electric. Zones 4 - 9

'Golden Zebra' 10" Sun - Shade. Spring bloomer. White flowers. This is a super-sized Heucherella 'Alabama Sunrise', which in turn is a super-sized 'Stoplight'. One upsies. 'Golden Zebra' has very large, yellow leaves with the boldest red markings of all the Heucherellas. 'Golden Zebra' rivals some of the showiest annual Coleus, but it comes back every year. Bingo! Zones 4 - 9

'Sweet Tea' 20" Sun - Shade. Spring bloomer. White flowers . This knockout has apricot, orange and burgundy spring leaves that shift to a cinnamon, orangey-yellow display in summer and fall. It has a Heuchera villosa heritage so it sneers at heat and drought. Zones 4 - 9

'Berry Fizz' 10" Sun - Shade. Spring bloomer. Pink flowers. 'Berry Fizz' is the first variegated Heucherella. 'Burnished Bronze' Heucherella may have been planted too close to Heuchera 'Midnight Splash' and some shananigans occurred. 'Berry Splash' has rich purple, dissected foliage with a bronzy shine plus pink splashes through the leaves. Zones 4 - 9

'Sonic Smash' 12" Sun - Shade. Spring bloomer. White flowers. 'Sonic Smash' has vavoom leaves that are almost 4" - 5" across. The foliage is not as flamboyant as others in this genus, but this is a nice change of pace. The leaves feature rich purple veining, back-dropped by silver, and rimmed by green margins. It looks sort of like a larger Heuchera 'Green Spice'. Heuchere villosa is in its 'veins' so it is quite heat and drought tolerant. Zones 4 - 9

Top Ten Hellebores

To write this Top Ten Hellebores list, I had to go to the King of Hellebores, Barry Glick. Barry is the owner of Sunshine Farm & Gardens in West Virginia, a 60-acre botanical garden, arboretum and nursery that grows over 10,000 different plants. The nursery is dedicated to uncommonly rare and exceptional plants for the discriminating gardener and collector. Barry is a popular national speaker, writer and breeder.

In addition to running a thriving mail-order nursery, Barry also breeds Hellebores. He has introduced many outstanding specimens, including the 'Sunshine Selections'. These plants are specially propagated by hand pollination to insure the most brilliant colors and hybrid vigor. He ships plants all over the world to thousands of happy gardeners. To do this, he maintains more than 50,000 flowering stock plants for seed propagation - and I thought I was busy!

Barry Glick

Why are Hellebores such outstanding perennials for part shade and shade gardens? There are many reasons but let me start with their extensive bloom time of usually six weeks or more; the mesmerizing beauty of their blooms; their dislike by deer; and they make great cut flowers. Barry has put together the list below with much effort, the effort being from trying to narrow these remarkable plants down to only ten. Despite his plea to expand the list to at least thirty, I held my ground, given the theme of the book. You'll have to go to his web site for all of the others!

Hellebores are easy to grow. They enjoy shade in moisture-retentive soil. Like Astilbes, they are heavy feeders and enjoy a time-released fertilizer such as Plant-Tone or Osmocote (14-14-14) in spring. Barry encourages folks to have fun and hybridize their own Hellebores by cross pollinating selected plants to see what the 'boucin' baby' looks like. You can also divide Hellebores in spring but it may be a year or so before the 'c-sectioned' plant pops out flowers due to 'surgery'. The three most popular groups of Hellebores are Lenten Roses (Helleborus X hybridus), Christmas Rose (Helleborus niger) and Stinking Hellebore (Helleborus foetidus). It's the lacy leaves of Stinking Hellebores that are supposed to be nose-turning. I have them and disagree. They are striking plants.

Barry's web site, www.sunfarm.com, is a wealth of information as well as a source for fascinating plants at great prices. Enjoy his following picks and write-ups as well as those on his web site.

Helleborus x hybridus 'Sunshine Selections' These plants are the results of the ongoing breeding processes at Sunshine Farm & Gardens that started almost 30 years ago. They encompass breeding stock from Hellebore enthusiasts from every corner of the world and include pollen from Hellebore species such as *H. torquatus, H. purpurascens, H. viridis, H. multifidus, H. orientalis* and many other species, each of which brings a different range of color and leaf form. These long lived plants prefer light to medium shade but can tolerate sun in northern climes. They are long lived and flower in late winter through mid spring. Hellebores hold up for a long period as a cut flower also. Zones 4 - 10

Helleborus x hybridus 'Sunshine Spectaculars' The "anemone centered" and "double" selections from the above *Helleborus x hybridus* 'Sunshine Selections' . Actually the term "Double" is a misnomer as they should really be referred to as "Semi Doubles" since they still have their sexual parts intact and viable. In these selections, the nectaries (aborted petals in Helleborus x hybridus) have become petaloid and are quite colorful and showy. In the "Anemone Centered", they are semi petaloid. Zones 4 - 10

Helleborus foetidus I wholeheartedly agree with Kerry when she says that this plant has a bad rap being called the "Stinking Hellebore"! If you crush the foliage, it has a strong chlorophyll scent, nothing objectionable though. Anyway, who would want to harm the delicate, lacy foliage of this graceful plant. Helleborus foetidus appreciates a bit of sun and needs good drainage. Although it is not nearly as long lived as Helleborus x hybridus, it will happily seed itself around your garden. Zones 3 - 10

Helleborus foetidus 'Frenchy' A friend who was hiking the French Alps stumbled across a colony of *Helleborus foetidus* that had red coloration, not only on the stems, but on the tips of the newly emerging foliage. As with all plants produced from seed strains and not vegetatively propagated, there is quite a bit of variability. Zones 3 - 10

Helleborus foetidus 'Miss Jekyll' This English selection of Helleborus foetidus has been around for quite some time. Named in honor of landscape pioneer Gertrude Jekyll, it has very glossy foliage and an almost tree like "Standard" habit. Zones 3 - 10

Helleborus niger Ahhhhh, the "Christmas Rose", often blooming around Christmas or shortly thereafter depending on your location, this species of Helleborus produces copious stems of large. pure white flowers that age slowly and gracefully to a pink color. Growing conditions are similar to *Helleborus x hybridus*. The foliage on this species tends to be less erect, thereby creating a bit of a shorter plant. Zones 4 - 10

Helleborus argutifolius Part sun and excellent drainage is a requirement for the "Corsican Hellebore". The specific epithet (second part of the scientific name) is quite apropos as "argute" means rough in Latin and the leaf margins are so very dentate that they even look like little saw blades. Large green flowers hang somewhat pendulously in early Spring from a very erect tree like plant. Zones 4 - 10

Helleborus lividus Although not hardy in most of the U.S., the exquisitely silvery marbled foliage is quite a treat. Worthy of a little extra work to grow as a container plant to be moved inside for the winter in all but zone 9 or 10 gardens. The flowers are not very showy, but are attractive none the less. Zones 9 - 10

Helleborus x sternii First successfully performed by Dr. Frederick Stern in 1939, this hybrid, is an interspecific cross *Helleborus lividus* and Helleborus argutifolius. The influence of the H. argutifolius parent brings a hardiness to the plant of about zone 6, possibly 5. A small amount of the silvery marbling of the H. lividus comes through. Zones 5 - 10

Helleborus x ericsmithii 'Sunmarble' What a pedigree this plant has, first you cross *Helleborus lividus* with Helleborus argutifolius to make Helleborus x sternii as I explained above and then cross Helleborus x sternii with Helleborus niger. This complex yet super easy to grow and super hardy hybrid plant has magnificent silvery marbling and huge white flowers. It was named in honor of Eric Smith, a very famous and beloved gardener and nurseryman in England in the 50's and 60's. Zones 4 - 10

Shade and ferns go frond in frond. Heck, there are even ferns that do fine in full sun. Ferns are incredibly resilient and contribute luxurious texture to a garden. Some are clump growers while others slowly march along (naturalize). There are ferns for wet spots and others thrive in dry soil. All are quite resistant to disease, insect and wildlife damage. Please don't snub your nose at them just because they don't have flowers.

Ferns are especially good companions for heavier framed perennials like Hosta. The positive tension generated from this combination adds interest. Just think of the comedian duo of Laurel and Hardy. See? Ferns also partner well with spring blooming bulbs and ephemerals. Their unfurling fronds cover up the sloppy exit of these rascals as they go dormant until the following year. And big boys, such as Ostrich and Cinnamon Ferns, placed near homes are great at masquerading as shrubs. Their 5' tall frames block the view of the foundation during the growing season but they don't require protection from crashing snow or blasting snowblowers in winter. By November they have disappeared underground. Finally, many Ferns make graceful, low-maintenance groundcovers.

⁜Japanese Painted Fern (Athyrium niponicum) 8" - 24" Part Shade - Shade. All Japanese Painted Ferns are lovely accents. Their silver and green fronds, injected with burgundy veins, are fetching. 'Pictum' is the most commonly available. If you want more brilliance and contrast, than reach for 'Burgundy Lace', 'Ursula's Red' or 'Silver Falls'. All Japanese Painted Ferns do best in a moisture-retentive soil and can be divided in spring and early summer. Zones 4 - 9

⁜Maidenhair Fern (Adiantum pedatum) 18" - 24" Part Shade - Shade. Soft green, whirled fronds dance atop skinny black stems. This is one of the most delicate looking ferns. It contrasts nicely with ribbed or puckered Hosta. I am always mesmerized each spring by how elegantly the black stems unfurl from the warming earth. Enchanting. Zones 3 - 8

⁜Tatting Fern (Athyrium filix-femina) 12" - 18" Part Shade - Shade. 'Friselliae' is an unusual looking fern with small, crinkled, very narrow fronds. The look is commonly described as beads on a necklace. Frizzy. Light green. Skinny and petite. These are words that come to my mind. Zones 3 - 8

⁜'Ghost' Lady Fern (Athyrium filix-femina X niponicum) 2' - 3' Part Shade - Shade. There was some hanky-panky going on between filix-femina and niponicum. 'Ghost' was the resulting bouncy baby frond. 'Ghost' grows taller than others with Japanese Painted Ferns in their parentage. It is

PerennialResource.com

very upright and vase-shaped, with apple-green and silvery-white fronds. It really glows in shade. Zones 3 – 8

⁘Dre's Dagger' Lady Fern (Athyrium filix-femina) 12" - 18" Part Shade - Shade. This fern looks like it put a frond in an electrical outlet. It has narrow, medium green fronds with little pinnae that cross each other. Hard to describe but I love the fern and have several in my display beds. In addition to funky looking fronds, it has a nice overall arching form. Zones 4 - 8

⁘Crested Hart's Tongue Fern (Phyllitis s. 'Cristatum') 14" - 20" Part Shade - Shade. Flat, wide, slightly shiny and undivided fronds with wavy edges make this a very strange looking fern. Perfect conversation piece. This one needs good drainage. I lost it one winter but put the replacement in a spot with gravely soil and it has been happy for years. Zones 5 - 8

⁘Christmas Fern (Polystichum acrostichoides) 9" - 18" Part Shade - Shade. Really dark green, shiny, leather-like, evergreen fronds that remain evergreen make this a popular fern. I find it pretty drought tolerant even though the descriptions don't state this. It gets its common name from the fact that people use the rich green fronds for Christmas greenery. Zones 3 - 8

⁘Ostrich Fern (Matteuccia struthiopteris) 3' - 5' Part Shade - Shade. This is my favorite mega fern. The huge upright fronds are vase-shaped. 'The King' is a cultivar that gets taller than its native parent (M. struthiopteris), reaching 4' - 7'. This fern will spread quickly where happy. Zones 3 - 8

⁘Autumn Fern (Dryopteris erythrosora) 18" - 24" Part Shade - Shade. This fern is distinguished by its bright, coppery-pink fronds in spring. 'Brilliance' is a showier form that holds its color longer into summer. Zones 5 - 8

⁘Hayscented Fern (Dennstaedtia punctiloba) 12" - 18" Sun - Shade. This is one of the ferns that handles full sun. It has soft green fronds and can spread quickly. Hayscented Fern's other notable attribute is its gorgeous golden fall color. The common name describes its smell when the fronds are dried. Zones 3 - 8

photo courtesy of Daniele Ippoliti

Astilbes are one of my most popular perennial picks for sun or shade. You read right. Most folks assume Astilbes are only shade plants. They are, but they can also handle full sun as long as they are in moisture-retentive soil. And they are snubbed by deer and rabbit. Can I hear an Amen?!

Early: 'Fanal' (red, 24"), 'Peach Blossom' (light pink, 20"), 'Washington' (white, 24")
Mid: 'Montgomery' (red, 20"), 'Bressingham Beauty' (rich pink, 36"), 'Darwin's Snow Sprite' (white, 12"), 'Veronica Klose' (rosy-purple, 16")
Late: 'Finale' (pink, 15"), 'Pumila' (lilac-rose, 10"), 'Hennie Graafland' (soft pink, 16")

Astilbe plumes can be light and airy or dense and clumpy. Flower colors are pink, red, burgundy, purple, white or lavender. There are early, mid and late blooming Astilbes. To have the showiest garden, use a combination of all three. Generally speaking, early blooming Astilbes flower from mid-June to early July; mid-season bloomers go from early July to late July; and late season cultivars finish the race from late July through mid-August. Below are a few of favorites sorted by bloom time.

Astilbes are piggy eaters. They tend to quickly gobble up many of the nutrients surrounding their roots. By giving them a slow release, organic fertilizer like Plant-Tone in early May, food is I.V.'d into their systems over three to four months, resulting in showier blooms and heftier clumps.

Astilbes can develop woody roots that require the old heave-hoe when dividing. This is not a time to be timid. I like using a sharp butcher knife, spade, machete or hand saw. Astilbe should be divided in spring, before they go into bloom. Dig out a clump, lay it on its side, and then eyeball where the 'great divide' will occur. As long as you have a stem and a piece of root, you've got a division. The size of the division is a personal choice. The larger the division, the more quickly it will go back into bloom the next season. Replant the divisions, toss some Plant-Tone (5-3-3) or Rock Phosphate (0-3-0) into the hole, pour in water, and then backfill with soil and tamp down. Smile with satisfaction.

Most Astilbe prefer soil with more moisture. It need not be heavy and wet, but on the other hand, sandy soil can be a killer. To increase the water holding capacity of soil, work in some compost or manure. If you want Astilbes flowering around the base of a tree where root competition is an issue, then select Astilbes in the chinensis group. These are more drought tolerant and more accommodating of drier soil. Chinensis cultivars should also be the pick for those who water inconsistently or not at all. A sign of a thirsty Astilbe is brown, crispy leaf edges. And one last note about watering Astilbes. Be sure they get a big drink of water in fall before the ground freezes. Well hydrated roots in fall are more likely to produce fabulous plumes the next season.

Astilbe leaves can be deep green, shiny and petite or large, lighter green and coarse.

Most of the chinensis varieties fall into the coarser group. 'Colorflash' has green leaves that turn red, yellow and orange in fall. 'Color Flash Lime' has lime-colored leaves during summer that have orange-red tinges in fall. Both have pink flowers. 'Key West' has rich burgundy-tinged leaves with deep magenta flowers as icing.

Many gardeners wait to cut Astilbes back in spring. The dried plumes make great winter ornaments, especially if they are spray painted (not a typo). Once the flowers have dried, grab a can of your favorite color and spray away. I've had some real head turning results with fluorescent lime-green. Glittery silver and gold make a more refined statement. But don't stop at Astilbes. Spray paint can also dress up dried Hydrangea, Goat's Beard, Masterwort, and Allium blooms.

All of the following are hardy for Zones 3 - 8.

꙳'**Milk and Honey**' 30" Creamy-white, frothy plumes turn soft pink as they age. A very long bloomer! Mid season. Medium green leaves. Chinensis variety.

꙳'**Fanal**' 20" Blood-red plumes. Early. Dark green foliage has a burgundy cast in spring.

꙳'**Finale**' 15" - 18" Medium pink blooms that slightly arch. Late. Medium green leaves. Chinensis variety.

꙳'**Montgomery**' 20" - 24" Rich red plumes, Flower stems are dark red with rich green leaves. Mid season. Some other terrific picks similar to 'Montgomery' are 'August Light' (28") and 'Red Sentinel' (20" - 24").

꙳'**Maggie Daley**' 28" Brilliant pinky-purple plumes over dark green, shiny foliage. Mid season. Chinensis variety.

꙳'**Bridal Veil**' 18" Glistening white blooms, slightly nodding at the tip. Deep green, glossy foliage. Early.

꙳'**Peach Blossom**' 24" Peachy flowers with a sweet fragrance. Early. Shiny green foliage. Another early blooming, fragrant Astilbe is 'Deutchland' with white flowers, reaching 24".

꙳'**Visions**' 14" - 16" Raspberry-red, thick dense plumes. Mid season. Dark green, coarse foliage. Chinensis variety. 'Visions in Pink' and 'Visions in White' are other top sellers.

꙳'**Cattleya**' 36" Rose-pink, narrow plumes. Mid season. Medium green foliage.

꙳'**Purple Candles**' 42" Violet-red, narrow plumes. Mid season. Dark green, coarse foliage. Chinensis variety.

You've hit 'The Easy Button' with Coral Bells. They are no-brainers. Perfect for my approach to gardening. I incorporate them into my garden the same way I do Hosta. I focus on foliage; color, leaf size and the overall plant form. The flowers are icing on the cake. Gorgeous, low-maintenance gardens can be created by simply quilting a tapestry of colorful leaf mounds. Who cares when they bloom? Flowering time is one less factor to take into consideration when arranging Coral Bells. Similar to Hosta, Coral Bells come in petite, medium and large 'servings'. Two top ten lists, one for large Coral Bells, with foliage domes reaching 12" or higher, and another list for petite to medium sized plants that are under 12". Before we jump into the lists, let's first go over some helpful tips for growing these 'Easy Buttons'.

- Coral Bells are quite flexible regarding light conditions. In general, the solid green varieties prefer sun to part sun. As the shade deepens, so do their frowns. On the other hand, most other Coral Bells enjoy part sun to shade. When I say shade, I am not referring to heavy shade. Some dappled light, reflected light, or breaks of sun during the day are appreciated. How can you tell if your Coral Bell is unhappy? If it is getting too much sun, the leaves bleach and the outer rims turn crispy. If it is starving for light, it will lose its vibrant leaf color and decline in vigor. It is gasping for light. Please move it.

- Coral Bells have a bad habit of popping out of the ground in late winter and early spring as a result of soil temperature fluctuations. Correct the 'uprising' by pressing them back down into the soil with your hand, or have fun gently stepping on them as I do. You do not want the roots to be exposed to air. Not good. Like a fish out of water.

- In the spring and once in summer, deadleaf Coral Bells for their best appearance. The lower, outer leaves can get ratty looking. Grab a hand pruner and snip these off. This simply 'surgery' gives plants a fabulous facelift.

- Coral Bells should be divided when they get large and 'woody'. Usually this is after three or four years of growth. Dig the clump out of the ground and use a sharp knife to cut it into sections. The plant may look a bit awkward to divide as the soil falls off the gnarly roots. Make sure as you're eyeing the specimen, that each potential division has a root and one or more stems. Once I decide where to make the slice, I just 'do it' as the Nike ad says. Fast and with commitment. A slow, drawn out cut is agonizing both for you and the Coral Bell. If the Coral Bell has flowers on it, shear these off. When replanting the divisions, set them 1" to 2" deeper then they were originally. Before backfilling with soil, toss a tablespoon of Rock Phosphate (0-3-0) or organic Plant-Tone fertilizer (5-3-3) into the hole, add water, fill with soil, and tamp down gently.

- If you feel bored and would like to deadhead the flowers, be my guest. Sure, in most cases this will prolong the bloom time. But there are few cultivars that move me to put forth this effort. 'Hollywood', 'Hercules', 'Dolce Mocha Mint' and

'Rave On' are a few I'll aim my pinchers at. They have bold red or pink flowers that complement the showy leaves. Flowers that are wishy-washy white or pale pink are whacked off so not to distract from the gorgeous foliage. Am I heartless?

- If you live in a region with high heat and humidity, select cultivars from the *villosa* line. Many of these were introduced by Thierry Delabroye of France. These Coral Bells sneer at sizzling temperatures that cause others to weep, plus *villosas* are very robust in their growth habit. 'Caramel' is one of the best examples of their sturdy natures. Some popular choices in this group include 'Christa' (orange-caramel); 'Pinot Noir' (dark leaves with silver overcast); and 'Beaujolais' (burgundy leaves with silver overcast). Others are included in the Top Ten list.

- A few cultivars that I have been disappointed in based on my own growing experience are 'Amber Waves', 'Crème Brulee' and 'Ginger Ale'. I found these to fizzle out over time. Even 'Marmalade' went a little sour on me. These lacked the vigor of other Coral Bells. But then again, I am not one to baby my plants. You shouldn't either.

- Very dark purple or black Coral Bells can be difficult to see, especially if surrounded by dark mulch. Help the mounds pop to attention by placing bright yellow-leaved plants nearby. This striking contrast does the trick. Some possible 'illuminators' with yellow leaves are Yellow Creeping Jenny (this can be invasive in some areas); Lamium 'Beedham's White' (white flowers); Campanula 'Dickson's Gold' (blue-purple flowers), Hosta 'Gold Drop', 'Lakeside Down Sized' or 'Bitsy Gold'; Sedum 'Angelina'; or Veronica 'Trehane' or 'Aztec Gold' (blue flowers).

- Some Coral Bells can be chameleons. For example, cooler weather brings on a dramatic wardrobe change for 'Miracle' and 'Tiramisu'. 'Miracle' has electric chartreuse foliage in spring that changes to rich, brick-red in summer with a chartreuse margin. It has pink flowers. 'Tiramisu' has leaves that start out yellow with red splashes and matures to a chartreuse and silvery leaf with creamy-white flowers.

- When quilting a tapestry of Coral Bells, it is best not to place too many different variegated varieties next to each other. The result is similar to combining stripes and plaids. A tad distracting. Break up the busyness with some solid-colored varieties.

- Deer and rabbits typically, let me repeat, typically leave Coral Bells alone. If Bambi and Thumper are radicals in your neighborhood, then spray Coral Bells with a taste and smell repellant such as Liquid Fence, Plantskydd or Hinder. I've also found my teenage son's dirty soccer socks to be effective.

Now on to the lists! All of the following Coral Bells are hardy to at least Zone 4 and are drought tolerant.

I define large as those with foliage mounds that typically get around 12" or taller. The flower stalks are not included in the height.

'Caramel' 12" Villosa parentage. This has to be one of my favorites. A robust habit is an understatement. Flashy orange-yellow leaves with a fuzzy surface create large, compact mounds adorned by creamy-white flowers. Zones 4 - 9

'Earth Angel' 15" A subtle beauty with purple leaves in spring that transform to coppery-green in warmer weather. The flowers are petite and red. Zones 4 - 9

'Sparkling Burgundy' 18" Villosa parentage. Mama Mia! These large, rosy-burgundy leaves develop a silvery-white sheen in summer and then change to a rich burgundy in fall. The flowers are creamy-white on purple-red stalks. This beauty won first place at the Royal Bulb Flower Association show in 2008. Zones 4 - 9

'Berry Smoothie' 18" Villosa parentage. The pinkish-purple leaves are magnificent! The large leaves pop in shade. White flowers in summer. Zones 4 - 9

'Frosted Violet' 14 + " Rich plum-purple leaves have burgundy veins. The soft, silvery hairs that emerge from the leaves give them a 'frosted' look. Sweet pink flowers in summer. Zones 4 - 9

'June Bride' 12" This fashionable 'bride' is one of the few white flowering Coral Bells with truly eye-catching blooms. The flowers are larger than most and the mounds are covered in …June. The large leaves are solid colored and light green. Zones 3 - 8

'Georgia Peach' 14" Villosa parentage. Yummy! Soft, peachy leaves are brushed with a silver cast. Pink flowers are a nice accessory. Zones 4 - 9

'Brownies' 24" Villosa parentage. This massive 'Brownie' will have you falling backwards in awe. It is the largest Coral Bell I have grown in my garden. Just one will make you full! It has large chocolate leaves that gradually turn olive-brown in summer. Zones 5 - 9

'Stormy Seas' 16" Large ruffled leaves start out purple and develop silver markings throughout the leaf. Striking purple undersides are delightfully visible due to 'crinkly' edges . Creamy-white flowers. Zones 4 - 9

'Southern Comfort' 14" Villosa parentage. Bodacious cinnamon-peach leaves slowly turn coppery then amber in cooler weather. The leaves go down smoothly with their creamy-white flowers in summer. Zones 4 - 9

Top Ten Medium to Petite Coral Bells

This group of lovelies has foliage mounds 10" or smaller. The flower stalks are not included in the height.

'Obsidian' 10" Villosa parentage. Jet black, sultry leaves have a magical shine to them. Add to this mystique, purple undersides and you have a head-turner. Dark stems and buds open to creamy-white flowers. 'Blackout' and 'Black Bird' are two additional black-leaved cultivars. Zones 4 - 9

'Citronelle' 10" Villosa parentage. This is my top pick for yellow-leaved coral bells. The large leaves have a silvery underside and a fussy surface that reflects light in shady spots. And it usually holds is bright color even in full shade. Creamy-white flowers are an afterthought. Zones 4 - 9

'Electra' 8" Villosa parentage. Get my sunglasses! This striking coral bell has yellow leaves with red veins. It has its best color in spring and fall. White flowers emerge in summer and stay low to the mound. Zones 4 - 9

'Green Spice' 9" The tricolor leaves and dense mounding habit make this Coral Bell ir-resistible. Dark green leaves, splashed with silver and mottled with burgundy-red veins, are magnificent. Creamy-white flowers bloom a good 12" or more above the foliage. Zones 4 - 9

'Peach Flambé' 7" Yummy peachy leaves grow even more delicious as the cooler weather approach-es. Maroon-red color flushes the leaves in fall. A striking Coral Bell! 'Peach Crisp' looks similar but has ruffled leaves. 'Peach Melba' and 'Marmalade' both have less of an orange hue to them. Zones 4 - 9

Terra Nova Nurseries

'Hercules' 10" This Coral Bell has brilliant foliage and flow-ers. Dense mounds of green and creamy-white variegated leaves support bright red flowers in summer. And the variegated leaves are very stable, not being 'bad boys' and reverting to a solid green leaf as many variegated plants are prone to doing. 'Snow Angel' has a similar leaf but bright pink flowers. Zones 4 - 9

'Ruby Bells' 8" This solid green leaved Coral Bell is ablaze for weeks with shocking red flowers. Even though, like most Coral Bells, the flowers are petite, the plant makes a brilliant display thanks to masses of red-topped stems. 'Firefly' is another top pick for sizzling red flowers. Zones 3 - 9

'Plum Pudding' 8" This is one of the richest, purple-leaved Coral Bells I have ever worked with. The leaves are plum colored with purple veins and deep purple under-sides. It is equally good in full sun and shade. Soft cream flowers spring up from the mounds. 'Plum Royal' is a new selection that is supposed to have even richer purple foliage. Zones 4 - 9

'Vesuvias' 8" This was the first burgundy-purple leaved, red flowering Coral Bell I ever planted and it still holds a premier place in my garden. Rich red flowers keep pushing forth from attractive, dark mounds through summer. A good rebloomer. Other dark-leaved, red flowering Coral Bells are 'Hollywood' and 'Cherries Jubilee'. Zones 4 - 9

'Midnight Rose' 10" Villosa parentage. This one is psychedelic! A sport of black-leaved 'Obsidian', it looks like someone splashed hot pink paint over the leaves. And this striking coloration is unfazed by warmer summer temperatures. The white flowers are definitely a distraction. Zones 4 - 9

'Petite Pearl Fairy' 6" A sweet little thing with masses of bright pink flowers in late spring and early summer. Because of its diminutive size, three or more make the best presentation. Other dark-leaved coral bells with rich pink flowers include 'Rave On' and 'Milan'. Zones 4 - 9

Top Ten Monster Hosta

Behemoth Hosta are the 'Big Dogs' in shade gardens. They cover a lot of ground so less plants are needed per square foot; their massive leaves shade the ground to reduce weeds; they act like shrubs but don't need protection from crashing snow when sited near the house; and they provide shade for lower growing shade lovers. To give you an idea of the size I'm taking about, 'Frances Williams' is smaller than these. Uh-huh. The only downside of these 'Monster Trucks' could be if you needed to relocate or divide one. A backhoe might be in order. Or you could just move. All of the below are drought tolerant, grow in part shade to shade, and are hardy to Zone 3.

'Sum and Substance' Huge yellow, ribbed leaves up to 2' across. Lavender flowers. The leaves are 'thicker' than other yellow Hosta, making them more slug resistant.

'Sum of All' A sport (offspring) of 'Sum and Substance'. It has huge green, ribbed leaves with a yellow margin. Lavender flowers. Also more slug resistant.

'Blue Angel' Frosty blue, ribbed leaves with some puckering. The leaves can get 12" wide and 16" long. White flowers. Slug resistant.

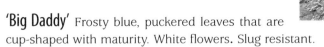

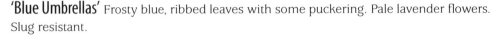

'Earth Angel' A sport of 'Blue Angel'. Blue-green, ribbed leaves with wide, yellow margins that turn white in summer. Lavender flowers. Slug resistant.

'Big Daddy' Frosty blue, puckered leaves that are cup-shaped with maturity. White flowers. Slug resistant.

'Blue Umbrellas' Frosty blue, ribbed leaves with some puckering. Pale lavender flowers. Slug resistant.

'Empress Wu' Stand back. This is known as the largest Hosta in commerce. Mounds can reach 3' - 4'. Giant green, ribbed leaves. Soft violet flowers.

'Krossa Regal' Frosty gray-green, ribbed leaves that extend upward in a vase shape. Lavender flowers. Slug resistant.

'Regal Splendor' A sport of 'Krossa Regal'. Frosty blue leaves have a wavy edge and gold margins. Lavender flowers. Slug resistant.

'Komodo Dragon' Dark green, ribbed leaves with wavy edges. Pale lavender flowers. Slug resistant.

Kerry Ann Mendez   drought tolerant ⊕deer resistant

Top Ten Medium to Large Hosta

Let me start by saying it impossible to pick only ten in this popular size range. The Hosta on this list range in height from 11" - 28" tall, the height being that of the foliage mound. For this book's purpose, I made myself pick ten varieties out of my 'Hosta wheelbarrow of greats'.

'June' Ribbed leaves with bright gold centers and wide, frosty-blue margins. Pale lavender flowers. Slug resistant. 15"

'Remember Me' A sport of 'June'. Bright yellow centers with narrow, blue-green margins. Lavender flowers. Slug resistant. 15" A portion of each plant sold goes to breast cancer research.

'Striptease' Green ribbed leaves with narrow gold centers and skinny white stripes running between the green and gold. Pale violet flowers. 20"

'Patriot' Heart-shaped, ribbed leaves with wide, white margins and medium green centers. Lavender flowers. Very sun tolerant. 22'

'Sagae' Wide, heart-shaped, frosty gray-green, ribbed leaves with yellow margins. Lavender flowers. 28"

'Sun Power' Bright yellow, ribbed leaves with a slight twist to each leaf. Upright and vase-shaped. Soft lavender flowers. 24"

'Great Expectations' Very thick, puckered, frosty blue, heart-shaped leaves with chartreuse center. White flowers. Slow grower but worth the wait. 20"

montana 'Aureomarginata' Huge, elongated, frosty green, ribbed leaves with wide gold margins. Pale lavender flowers. 27"

'Love Pat' Rich blue, cup-shaped, puckered leaves. White flowers. Slug resistant. 14"

'Frances Williams' Huge frosty blue, puckered leaves with wide gold margins. White flowers. 22"

Top Ten Mini to Small Hosta

These are sweet little darlings. They range in size from 3" to 10". Give them their own space to play in so they don't get bumped around by the big Hosta. Small Hosta are perfect for rock or alpine gardens as well as containers. Remember, the more petite the plant, the more needed to make an impact. One mini Hosta all by itself would look lonely.

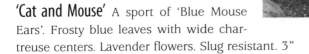

'Pandora's Box' Blue-green leaves with white centers. Purple flowers. 4"

'Alakazaam' Very long, narrow, wavy green leaves with yellow margins. Lavender flowers. 5"

'Blue Mouse Ears' Frosty blue, mouse ear-shaped leaves. Pale lavender flowers. Slug resistant. 8"

'Cat and Mouse' A sport of 'Blue Mouse Ears'. Frosty blue leaves with wide chartreuse centers. Lavender flowers. Slug resistant. 3"

'Maui Buttercups' Bright gold, cupped and puckered leaves. White flowers. Slug resistant. 10"

'Cameo' Frosty, gray-green centers with white margins. Purple flowers. 4"

'Cherry Tomato' Narrow, long green leaves with creamy yellow centers. Purple flowers on red scapes (stems). 4"

'Little Treasure' Pointy, frosty blue-green leaves with white centers. Lavender flowers on creamy-white scapes (stems). 6"

'Teeny Weeny Bikini' Pale yellow leaves with narrow, medium green margins. Purple flower. 4"

'Uzo No Mai' Very shiny, green leaves than lie almost flat against the ground. A very unusual Hosta. Lavender flowers. 1"

Top Ten Fragrant Flowering Hosta

Fragrant flowering Hosta are the Oriental Lilies of the shade world. These scented ladies can be white or light lavender and start blooming in early, mid or late summer. Unlike fragrant roses, Hosta blooms aren't bothered by Japanese beetles. And there are no red lily beetles attacking them as they do Oriental Lilies like 'Casa Blanca'. And even though slugs and snails can be a drag, rarely do these slimers hike it all the way to the top 'flower floor'. So sprinkle these heavenly scented Hosta around patios, sitting areas, decks, and other places where noses can enjoy them.

'Royal Standard' Shiny, rich green, ribbed leaves. White flowers. Late summer bloomer. 26"

'Honeybells' Medium green, slightly shiny leaves. Lavender flowers. Late summer bloomer. 26"

'Aphrodite' Shiny green, ribbed leaves. Double white flowers. Late summer bloomer. 24"

'Fragrant Blue' Smooth frosty blue, heart shaped, lightly ribbed leaves. Light lavender flowers. Early to mid-summer bloomer. 18"

'Fragrant Bouquet' Very light green, ribbed leaves with soft yellow margins. White flowers. Mid-summer bloomer. 20"

'Fragrant Queen' Similar to 'Fragrant Bouquet' but deeper green leaves and much wider, creamy to white margins. White to light lavender flowers. Late summer bloomer. 16"

'Guacamole' A sport of 'Fragrant Bouquet'. Large, chartreuse to light green, ribbed leaves with dark green margins. White flowers. Late summer bloomer. 22"

'Fried Bananas' A sport of 'Guacamole'. Large, green-gold, shiny leaves. Pale lavender to white flowers. Mid-summer bloomer. 23"

'Stained Glass' A sport of 'Guacamole'. Long, striking gold leaves with wide, dark green margins. Pale lavender flowers. Late summer bloomer. 15"

'So Sweet' Green leaves with white margins. Lavender flowers. Late summer bloomer. 22"

Top Ten Perennial Thugs

As low maintenance, want-to-be gardeners, we wouldn't *knowingly* plant perennials that have aggressive, unrelenting roots. We need to be very choosey about what we allow into our beds. Perennials that can't keep their roots to themselves are bad boys. But usually these thugs sneak under our surveillance cameras because they were delivered by friends, or marked for only $1 at a garage sale, or we mistakenly believed the word 'vigorous' on the plant's tag refers to the plant's ability to perform well. Mistake, mistake, mistake.

Before you jump to the list below, please know I am not condemning these plants. I have most of them in my garden but I am a drill sergeant about keeping them in line with one of the following restraining methods:

- ❧ Plant the thug in a garden pot in the ground. Recycle your plastic pots (2 gallon or larger) by cutting the bottom off, leaving a good 6" of side attached. Dig a hole in the garden, insert pot (leave about 1" above ground), place the thug in the pot, back fill with soil and tell it to 'Stay!' It will. You can also use large plastic tubs or old plastic swimming pools. Or imprison the thug with heavy-duty landscape edging. One of my clients created a huge heart with landscape edging and filled it with red Bee Balm.
- ❧ Don't give it a second thought when you need to ruthlessly plunge a spade into the thug to remove a section where it overstepped its bounds. Share the piece with a 'friend'.
- ❧ Plant it where you want it to be a flowering groundcover.
- ❧ Understand that when a plant's description states it is a groundcover, it is. Use it as a groundcover and you will not get frustrated. Be realistic.
- ❧ If there is a variegated cultivar of the thug, consider using this. Variegated plants do not have as much chlorophyll in their leaves, so there is less 'food' is manufactured to fuel their 'takeover'.
- ❧ Whatever you do, don't fertilize the thug. You are just throwing gasoline on the fire.
- ❧ Site the thug more adverse growing conditions. For instance, if a plant likes (thrives) in moisture-retentive soil, plant it in sandy soil.

I did not include mint on this list since most of us already know about its enthusiastic nature.

⊹ White Gooseneck (Lysimachia clethriodes) 24" - 36" Sun - Part Shade. Summer bloomer. White flowers. White Gooseneck has white arching flowers that resemble a goose's neck. It is enchanting in flower arrangements. It is a tough bird, handling all types of soil conditions with ease. That's the problem. But when massed as a groundcover it is breathtaking. Zones 3 - 9

⁜Circle Flower (Lysimachia punctata) 36" - 48" Sun - Part Shade. Early summer bloomer. Yellow flowers. Circle Flower has yellow flowers circling each stem at intervals. 'Firecracker' has small, light yellow flowers and chocolate foliage in spring that slowly turns greenish-bronze in summer. 'Golden Alexander' is a slower paced variegated cultivar with light green leaves and creamy-yellow margins. 'Alexander' has pink, light green and creamy-white foliage that changes to mostly green and white in summer. Zones 3 - 8

PerennialResource.com

⁜Chameleon Plant (Houttuynia) 6" - 9" Sun - Shade. Summer bloomer. White flowers (very insignificant). This plant is all about its heart-shaped red, gold, pink and green leaves that race, very quickly, across the ground. It gets its best color in moisture retentive soil and full sun. It wakes up late in the spring so don't get excited too quickly if you think you've finally gotten rid of it in unwanted areas. Take a second look. Don't get me wrong. This is an outstanding groundcover in areas where you want it to be a groundcover. Be decisive before planting. And if you decide to divide it, or when yanking at it, hold your nose. It has an awful smell. Zones 3 - 8

Bishop's Weed, Snow-on-the-Mountain (Aegopodium) 6" - 10" Sun - Shade. Summer bloomer. White flowers. It takes everything in me just to type this entry. Bishop's Weed has been a pain in my.....neck for years as I strive to weed it out of my perennial bed. It came in with another plant...that my friend gave me. Plants can have solid green or variegated green and white leaves. On the plus side, the flowers are pretty. They look like Queen Anne's Lace. But we don't need a whole acre of them. Some use 'Variegatum' as a groundcover around trees. This looks nice until the leaves get infected by a rust later in summer. Enjoy fixing the problem by weed-whacking the plants to the ground. New clean foliage will spring up and look nice again. Zones 3 - 8

Bugleweed (Ajuga) 2" - 6" Sun - Shade. Spring bloomer. Pink, blue or white flowers. Many gardeners curse Bugleweed for its 'gift' as a groundcover but it does have its place if used properly. It is extremely shallow rooted and can cling to areas with little soil coverage. I like 'quilting' different Bugleweeds together to create a colorful and functional tapestry. 'Black Scallop' has shiny black leaves, 'Party Colors' has creamy white, pink and dark green leaves (it's an improved sport of 'Burgundy Glow'), 'Toffee Chip' is the most petite variety only getting 2" tall with creamy-yellow and grey-green leaves, 'Chocolate Chip' gets a tad taller at 3" with green and purplish leaves, and 'Caitlin's Giant' has large, bronzy-green leaves. Most Bugleweeds have blue flower spikes in spring but 'Purple Torch' has pink spikes and 'Alba' has white ones. Zones 3 - 10

❦✠Comfrey (Symphytum) 12" - 24" Sun - Shade. Spring bloomer. Blue, pink, yellow or white flowers. Comfrey has dangling, bell-shaped flowers, blue being the most commonly available. It is happy in dry or wet soil. Most cultivars have solid fuzzy green leaves but 'Axminster Gold' has striking green leaves with brilliant yellow margins. Because of its variegation, it is less enthusiastic than others in this family. I saw it once in a client's garden and it was love at first sight. Unfortunately it is difficult to find. Zones 4 - 8

✠Giant Japanese Butterbur (Petasites) 36" - 42" Sun - Part Shade. Spring bloomer. Green or white flowers. This monster looks like it could eat you but I have never gotten close enough to find out. Massive leaves look a bit like Rhubarb on steroids. Butterbur needs lots of water to keep its leaves happy, and not wilting. Best used in wet areas or along the water's edge. There is a variegated variety, j. 'Variegatus', with creamy-yellow splotches on the leaves and white flowers. True, it will not spread as fast as the solid leafed version but don't let your guard down. Zones 4 - 9

❦✠Lily of the Valley (Convallaria) 6" - 8" Sun - Shade. Spring bloomer. White or pink flowers. Lily of the Valley is a well known groundcover for its ability to handle extreme conditions. Its heavenly fragrance is a harbinger of spring and a popular scent for air fresheners, laundry sheets and perfumes. There is a less aggressive variegated variety, C. Albostriata, with sassy white striped leaves. Sometimes the foliage will start to look scrappy and die back later in the season, especially in hot, dry summers. It is going dormant. You can try giving it more water, or simply wave good-bye, look the other way, and it will resurface next spring. All parts of this plant are poisonous. Zones 3 - 9

Spiderwort (Tradescantia) 12" - 24" Part Sun - Shade. Summer bloomer. Pink, purple, blue, white or violet flowers. Spiderwort is a pretty flower that opens in the cool of the morning and then melts away (closes) in afternoon heat. It has grassy foliage that can be green, blue-green or yellow. It spreads by roots as well as by seeds. Unrelenting! Most Spiderworts get floppy by mid-July. Whack them back by two-thirds and they'll usually reward you with a second flush of flowers in late summer. If they don't, so what. At least the plant looks neater. 'Sweet Kate' is one of the few Spiderworts that is a behaved clumper. Some confuse its brilliant gold blades to be an ornamental grass. The only bad habit I've noticed is an occasional effort to revert to solid green leaves. When you see rebellious green blades emerge, pinch these off at their base or divide them out. Zones 3 - 9

✠Labrador Violet (Viola labradorica) 3" - 6" Sun - Part Shade. Spring bloomer. Violet-blue flowers. It was the purplish-green, petite, heart-shaped leaves that first lured me to buy one Labrador Violet. Maybe it was my imagination, but I thought I heard the word "Sucker" whispered from the 4" pot. No question that it is lovely but it can seed around with abandon. I just apply the same approach when I thin it from the garden. Zones 3 - 7

CHAPTER THREE

Perennials for Challenging Sites or Specific Uses

Top Ten Perennials for Dry Shade

Dry shade can be a tough nugget but with the below tips and plant lists, you just might find yourself shopping for shade trees. Two Top Ten Lists are provided: one for spring and early summer bloomers and another for mid-summer and fall winners. I did not include Hosta. They have their own Top Ten lists.

⚜Bugleweed (Ajuga) 2" - 6" The majority of Bugleweeds have flamboyant blue or blue-violet flowers that holler for your attention. That's okay, they're nice eye-candy. Other flower colors are pink and white. After flowering, shear off spent blooms so the attention goes to its weed-smothering foliage. Foliage can be green; burgundy and green; bronzy green; black; green, pink and white; and soft gray-green and light yellow. I like 'quilting' different Bugleweeds together to create a colorful and functional tapestry. 'Black Scallop' has shiny black leaves, 'Party Colors' has creamy-white, pink and dark green leaves (it's an improved sport of 'Burgundy Glow'), 'Toffee Chip' is the most petite variety only getting 2" tall with creamy yellow and grey-green leaves, 'Metallica Crispa Rubra' has crinkled, reddish foliage at 3" - 4", 'Chocolate Chip' has 3" tall green and purple leaves and 'Caitlin's Giant' has large, bronzy-green leaves. 'Caitlin's Giant' makes one of the best, weed suppressing mats due to its larger leaves. Zones 3 - 10

⚜Barrenwort, Bishop's Hat, Fairy Wings (Epimedium) (4" - 20" The roots of this plant were thought to cause barrenness in women, hence its name. Although Barrenwort is frequently labeled a groundcover, there are some cultivars that move more at a snail's pace. Flowers can be white, pink, sulfur yellow, orange and bicolor. Barrenwort's leaves have a pleasing burgundy cast in spring and sometimes again in fall. These make great underplantings for spring and summer flowering shrubs. A few favorites are rubrum (pink flowers), 'Niveum' (white), 'Sulfureum' (light yellow), 'Bandit' (white), 'Frohnleiten' (soft yellow), 'Amber Queen' (bright yellow), 'Fire Dragon' (pink and yellow), and 'Orange Queen' (orange-yellow). Zones 4 - 9

Solomon's Seal (Polygonatum) 4" - 6' All varieties of Solomon's Seal have graceful, arching branches. Heights vary greatly. Sweet 4" tall humile makes a delightful groundcover while Giant Solomon's Seal (biflorum var. commutatum) towers 5' to 6' in the air. Dangling, white tubular flowers appear in spring and then morph to shiny black berries. Most Solomon's Seals have green leaves but 'Variegatum' has white margins and 'Striatum' has white streaking throughout the leaf. Another cool aspect of Solomon's Seal is how it emerges out of the ground in spring, it's very alien looking. Zones 3 - 9

⚜Lenten Rose (Helleborus orientalis) 12" - 24" Lenten Rose's nodding flowers can be white, yellow, pink, red, burgundy or multicolor. Deep green leathery leaves are semi-evergreen in zones 5 and colder. Plants are ignored by deer, rabbits and other munchers. Newer cultivars like 'Ivory Prince', have upward facing flowers so you can better appreciate the delicate stamens. There are also enchanting double-petaled plants like 'Phoebe' (soft pink) and 'Mrs. Betty Ranicar' (double white). Heronswood Nursery (www.heronswood.com) and Sunshine Farm and Gardens (www.sunfarm.com) offer a large inventory of unique choices. 'Foetidus', also known as Stinking Hellebore, is an odd duck. It has an upright growth habit with long narrow leaves and greenish bell-shaped flowers. At first I thought it would make a good conversation piece in the garden but then the awful smelling leaves (not flowers) got to me. Bye-bye. Helleborus niger (Christmas Rose) can be more challenging to grow. I recently had one winter over and I was dancing like a kid at Christmas when I saw it bloom. It blooms weeks earlier than Lenten Rose. All Hellebores are quite drought tolerant once established. See the Top Ten Hellebores list for more winners. Zones 4 - 8

⊹Siberian Bugloss (Brunnera) 10" - 15" Bright blue, Forget-Me-Not flowers billow over heart-shaped leaves. Siberian Bugloss's leaves come in a number of styles. 'Jack Frost' has silver leaves with green veins; 'Looking Glass' has solid silver leaves; and B. 'Variegata' and 'Hadspen Cream' have leaves with green leaves with bold white margins. 'Langtrees' has silvery markings on the outer leaf edge. 'King's Ransom' has creamy-yellow margins while 'Spring Yellow' has totally yellow leaves that slowly change to soft green in summer. My vote is still out on 'Spring Yellow'. I think the plant looks on the sickly side. Zones 3 - 7

⊹Big Root Geranium (Geranium macrorrhizum) 8" - 15" Big Root Geranium makes a spectacular groundcover or individual specimen for dry shade. Spring blooming flowers are either white or pink. It's the only perennial Geranium with fragrant leaves, plus the foliage turns a burgundy-red tinge in fall. I've grown 'Bevan's Variety' (deep pink, 10") and 'Ingwerson's Variety' (soft pink, 10") for over 15 years with great satisfaction. A client of mine used Big Root Geraniums as the sole groundcover under limbed up pine trees in the woods behind his house. Pine needle paths weaved through the drifts of these geraniums. It was magical looking and no work. Big Roots are best divided after they bloom. When transplanting, lay the scrappy looking roots almost horizontally in the soil, just 3" beneath the surface. Zones 3 - 7

Foamy Bells (Heucherella) 6" - 18" Foamy Bells are a cross between Coral Bells (Heuchera) and Foamflowers (Tiarella). The resulting offspring retain some of the best characteristics of both parents: showy leaves, drought tolerant, and airy sprays of soft pink or white blooms on long stems. Frankly, I think the leaves steal the show. 'Stoplight', an improved 'Sunspot', has bright yellow leaves with red blotches in the center. 'Alabama Sunrise' looks similar to 'Stoplight' but the leaves are more delicate looking. 'Golden Zebra' pushes it one farther. It has even bolder red markings and the leaves are large and dissected. 'Sweet Tea' had me ordering more the minute after I planted one. It has apricot, orange and burgundy spring leaves that shift to a cinnamon, orange-yellow in summer and fall. 'Burnished Bronze' dazzles with shimmering bronze leaves and pink flowers while 'Silver Streak's has silver and purple leaves with white flowers. 'Quick-

❦drought tolerant ⊹deer resistant

silver' was one of the first to come to market with its soft pink flowers and burgundy-purple leaves splashed with a silver overlay. Zones 4 - 9

✥Pig Squeak (Bergenia) 8" - 18"

I just had to include this one for its fun common name, Pig Squeak. Most varieties handle full sun or shade. Pig Squeaks have architecturally interesting leathery, cabbage-like leaves that turn bronzy-red in fall. The more sun they get, the richer the coloring. Stalks of pink or white flowers pop up from succulent leaves in spring. This is a plant that you will either love or hate because of its unique look. I choose love. Why is it called Pig Squeak? If you take a wet leaf between your fingers and rub it, you hear what sounds like a squealing pig (imagination required). Zones 3 - 8

✥Dead Nettle (Lamium) 4" - 8"

These are work-horses for dry shade. There are many leaf variations to choose from. 'Beedham's White' has chartreuse leaves with a white strip down the center; 'Anne Greenaway' has green, gold, and white leaves; 'Aureum' has solid gold leaves and 'Friday' has green and yellow leaves. All march across the soil and set roots from their stems, creating more self-sufficient plants. Almost all varieties of Lamium are terrific plants but there are a few I steer clear of. 'Beacon Silver' tends to get rust on its leaves and 'White Nancy' is prone to wimping out over time. Zones 3 - 9

Golden Star (Chrysogonum virginianum) 3" - 6"

This is a uncommon plant that always draws attention from onlookers in my garden. Cheerful, bright yellow flowers sit just above medium green leaves that form a weed-smothering mat. It blooms for at least four weeks with no deadheading. Zones 5 - 10

Top Ten Mid-Summer and Fall Bloomers for Dry Shade

⊹Chinese Astilbe (Astilbe Chinensis) 6" - 4' All of the chinensis Astilbes are more tolerant of dry soil than others in this family. Would they prefer more moisture-retentive, organically rich soil? Sure. Tough. Chinese Astilbes can be ground-huggers like 'Pumila' with its 6" lavender-pink spikes in August or towering like 'Purple Candles' with rosy-lavender plumes in July that reach 4'. Other great chinensis groupies include 'Visions' (raspberry-red, 15", July), 'Finale' (light pink, 18", August), 'Superba' (lilac, 4', July), 'Diamonds and Pearls' (white, 24", July), 'Veronica Klose' (reddish-purple, 16", July) and 'Maggie Daley' (rosy-purple, 28", July). All Astilbes will generously reward you with richer plumes if you work organic Plant-Tone or Osmocote fertilizer around their base in early May. After they finish blooming, you can spray paint the plumes bright colors for late season color. Is nothing sacred? The best time to divide astilbe in colder zones is in spring, not fall. Their roots can get woody and require a handsaw to split. A 'fall saw' can be a little too much stress for them to handle before Old Man Winter barrels in. Zones 3 - 8

⊹Wood Fern and Christmas Fern (Dryopteris and Polystichum) 12" - 4' There are many sensual ferns for shade beds but some are more tolerant of dry soil than others. Wood Fern and Christmas Fern are two forgiving choices. The Wood Fern group encompasses many fine specimens including the Crested Male Fern and the Log Fern. The Christmas Fern has dark green, leathery fronds that remain evergreen. All ferns make great companions to Hosta, Astilbe and Lamium. Zones 3 - 8

⊹Fall Blooming Joe Pye Weed (Eupatorium rugosum) 3' - 5' 'Chocolate' grows in dry shade and features billowy, small white flowers September through October. The foliage is chocolate-green and the stems are deep purple. 'Chocolate' also handles full sun. Despite its height, I have never had to stake it. If you want shorter, more compact plants, pinch the stems by half their height in mid-June Zones 3 - 7

⊹Leadwort, Plumbago (Ceratostigma plumbaginoides) 8" - 12" Leadwort is a lovely blue flowering perennial that opens in August and continues through September. It enjoys sun to part shade. The more sun it gets, the more burgundy the leaves turn in cooler weather. Where happy, it can be a slow spreading groundcover that effectively smothers weeds. Some catalogs list it as a Zone 5, others Zone 6. It works great on slopes and it a butterfly magnet. Zone 5 - 9

Shredded Umbrella Plant (Syneilesis) 18"- 24" This is one fun plant. When it emerges in spring, it looks like fuzzy white, 'closed umbrellas'. It then opens up to deeply divided, flat green leaves. Most catalogs suggest the flowers are secondary. I find them as fascinating as the leaves. It took my plants three years to finally produce flowers. Small pinkish-white blooms emerged on thin stems above the foliage. And prior to this I thought it couldn't get any stranger looking! Zones 5 - 8 (probably Zone 4)

⁙Martagon Lily (Lilium Martagon) 3' - 6' These fascinating beauties are rarely seen in gardens, one reason why you want people oohhing at them in yours. Plus they are rarely browsed by deer, which is rare for lilium bulbs. Martagons bloom in June and July with small, downward facing flowers that have reflexed petals. Blooms can be white, pink, magenta or rose. They are slow growers but once established, they're breathtaking. To help them 'bulk up' apply a time-released fertilizer like organic Plant-Tone in spring. I have 'Alba' (white) near a light green, Japanese thread-leaf maple and the combination is bewitching. One that is on my wish list is 'Mrs. P.O. Backhouse' from Plant Delights Nursery. It is golden-orange with purple speckles. Martagons are hard to find at garden centers. It is easier to purchase them online at www.vanscheepers.com, www.plantdelights.com or www.oldhousegardens.com. But be forewarned. These beauties come at a price: $10 or more per bulb. Zones 3 - 6

Toad Lily (Tricyrtis) 18" - 36" These unique looking flowers are in the orchid family. August, September and October blooms can be solid white, yellow or white with pink or purple markings. Leaves are solid green, green and white, green and creamy-yellow, and tricolor pink, white and green. All Toad Lilies have slightly arching stems with flowers formed along their stem. The flowers are petite so it's best to plant a number of Toad Lilies together to make a nice show. Some of my favorites are 'White Towers' (pure white), 'Miyazaki' (white with maroon spots), 'Jim's Tall Towers' (white with purple spots), 'Tojen' (lavender-pink with white center) and 'Gilt Edge' (green leaves with creamy yellow margins plus white flowers with purple spots). Zones 4 - 8

Coral Bells (Heuchera) 6" - 24" Coral Bells come in all sizes and colors. They are all drought tolerant. Almost all Coral Bells, other than green-leaved cultivars, do fine in part shade to shade. For more on Coral Bells, see the Top Ten Coral Bells lists.

⁙Lily Turf (Liriope) 10" - 18" Spiky white, purple, lavender or violet flowers that look like Grape Hyacinths decorate shiny, arching, strappy leaves in late summer. This is a common groundcover or lawn substitute in warmer climates. Leaves can be solid green or green and white striped. An extremely non-demanding plant that remains evergreen for winter interest (if it isn't buried under snow). 'Monroe White' has white flowers, 'Variegata' has variegated leaves with lavender flowers, and 'Big Blue' has violet flowers. Zones 5 - 10

⁙Nodding Allium, Nodding Onion (Allium cernuum) 6" - 3' This group of Alliums dances in the shade. Nodding flowers can be pink or lavender-purple and burst into bloom later in summer. Some complain that it reseeds too enthusiastically. I have not found this to be an issue. Allium moly has soft yellow flowers that nod over bluish-green foliage and only gets between 6" - 12". Zones 3 - 9

Top Ten Perennials for Moist Shade

Most perennials really resent (okay, die) if they are left sitting in wet, soggy soil for an extended period. But the ones on this list are pigs in mud. They love it.

If you don't have a naturally wet area in your shade garden, then you can try placing thirstier plants:

- at the base of a rain downspout or where water funnels off the roof
- at the base of an incline where water flows
- in your own man-made bog. Dig an area, line it with pond liner or heavier plastic and backfill with moisture-retentive soil (topsoil mixed with compost and a little peat moss or coconut fiber). Old plastic children's swimming pools also work well.
- in the vicinity of your (or your neighbor's) sump pump
- where you have added water-retentive polymers like Sta-Moist, Soil Moist, Water-Gel Crystals and Watersave to the planting holes. These little crystals can hold water up to 400 times their density in water, slowly releasing it to thirsty roots. It works best to hydrate the crystals first in a bucket and then place them around the plant's roots. Otherwise when the crystals take on water, the swelling might heave plants right out of the soil. These environmentally-friendly, non-hazardous crystals will last up to five years in soil.

⁜Pink Turtlehead (Chelone) 2' - 42" Sun - Part Shade. Late summer, early fall bloomer. Pink or white flowers. Chelone glabra, a pale pink 4' native, is commonly known as Swamp Turtlehead. 'Hot Lips' gets 2' to 3' and has deeper pink flowers with shiny, dark green leaves. 'Hot Lip's' side kick, 'Pink Temptation' has rich pink flowers too but stays more compact at 15" - 18". 'Alba' has white flowers and gets the tallest at 42". Unfortunately I have never been impressed with 'Alba'. It looks very ho-hum in bloom. All Turtleheads have stiff stems that can be pinched in early June for shorter, heavier blooming plants. Zones 3 - 7

⁜Astilbe (Astilbe) 8" - 4' Sun - Part Shade. Summer blooming. White, pink, red, lavender or purple blooms. When purchasing these plumy wonders, make sure to buy Early (mid-June through early July), Mid (July) and Late blooming (mid-July through mid-August) varieties for six to eight weeks of color. Astilbes in the Arendsii, Japonica, Simplicifolia and Thunbergii groups do super in moist soil. To encourage impressive plumes, work some slow-release fertilizer such as organic Plant-Tone into the soil once a year in early May. Zones 3 - 9

⁜Ligularia (Ligularia) 20" - 4' Part Sun to Part Shade. Summer bloomer. Yellow or orange flowers. Ligularias are an interesting group of plants. They all have intriguing leaves, both in shape and color plus funky flowers. 'The Rocket' has tall yellow spikes to 4' in July. 'Little Rocket' takes it down a notch at 3'. 'Othello' and 'Desdemona' have

🍂drought tolerant ⁜deer resistant

chocolate-green scalloped leaves. 'Britt-Marie Crawford' has even darker foliage with purple undersides. 'Japonica' has huge, deeply lobed, green leaves. All four of these have orange flowers. Finally, 'Osiris Fantaisie' and 'Osiris Café Noir' have large, leathery, serrated leaves with colors that vary from dark chocolate to bronzy green. Both have yellow flowers. In mid-summer the older leaves of all Ligularias can get ratty looking so I prune these off at the plant's base. Zones 4 - 9

⁜ Cardinal Flower (Lobelia)

24" - 5' Sun - Part Shade. Summer, early fall bloomer. Red, white, blue, pink or purple flowers. Cardinal Flowers hit their peak in July and August. Cardinalis is a native and the most common with electric red flower stalks that reach 4'. It can be finicky and short-lived but reseeds easily. 'Monet Moment' with rosy-pink flowers and 'Red Beauty' with rosy-red blooms can be longer lived. L. siphilitica has stunning blue flowers in August and September. 'Gladys Lindley' has white stalks and 'Vedrariensis' boasts deep purple flowers. All of these usually grow around 3' tall. Spicata with pale blue to white flowers and 'Grape Knee-High' with rich purple blooms are more compact, staying between 1' - 2' tall. I have never had luck over wintering the chocolate foliaged Cardinal Flowers like 'Fan Scarlet' and 'Queen Victoria'. How I wish otherwise, they are beauties. Zones 3 - 8

⁜ Rodger's Flower (Rodgersia)

30" - 4' Part Sun - Shade. Early summer bloomer. Creamy white or soft pink flowers. These are cool, tropical-looking plants. They have large, heavily textured, 'five-fingered' palmate leaves that are green or bronze. The flowers look like giant Astilbe plumes. R. aesculifolia has greenish-bronzy leaves and ivory flowers with a soft pink blush. The leaves of 'Chocolate Wings' start out chocolate and change to bronze. 'Elegans' and 'Die Shone' have pink flowers. 'Dark Leaf' has burgundy-red leaves in spring, turning to green in summer. Zones 4 - 7

⁜ Primrose (Primula)

4" - 24" Part Sun - Shade. Spring bloomer. Red, white, purple, yellow, blue and pink flowers. Most primroses are easy to grow as long as they have enough moisture. The earliest to pop open in my garden are the drumstick varieties (denticulata). These are followed by polyantha and vulgaris types with Japanese Primroses (japonica) being the last to swoon the crowds. Primrose will seed where happy, especially japonicas. One that looks just darling is in the kisoana group. These petite beauties have soft green, fuzzy leaves with pink or white flowers. Two Primrose series that have eye-popping varieties are Barnhaven and Bullsiana. Primroses are easy to divide after blooming. Just pull apart the foliage rosettes with your hands and replant. Zones 3 - 8

⊹Astilboides (Astilboides tabularis) 3' Part Shade - Shade. Summer bloomer. White flowers. Astilboides looks like it is from another planet. It has monstrous, bright green leaves that can measure over 2' across. Give this big boy plenty of room, it can get 3' – 5' wide. White, astilbe-like flowers decorate it in July. As with all gigunda-leaved plants, water is a must! Zones 5 -7

❦Nodding Ladies Tresses (Spiranthes cernua odorata) 12" - 24" Part Shade - Shade. Fall bloomer. White flowers. I have yet to plant this hardy native orchid in my garden but I expect this to change shortly. 'Chadds Ford' has fragrant, white flower spikes that arise from clumpy foliage rosettes. Zones 4 - 8

⊹Bugbane, Snakeroot (Cimicifuga) 2' - 6' Part Sun - Part Shade. Late summer, fall bloomer. White or soft pink flowers. Chocolate-leaved Bugbanes have deliciously fragrant flowers in August and September. The dark, ferny foliage is an elegant 'vase' for dancing, candle-stick like flowers. 'Brunette', 'Hillside Black Beauty' and 'Atropurpurea' all get 4' to 5' tall. 'Chocoholic' is the shortest at 2' to 3'. All have creamy white flowers. Bugbanes can get crispy edges in dry soil. Zones 3 - 8

⊹Sedge (Carex) 9" - 3' Sun - Part Shade. Foliage. Technically, Sedges are not true grasses but they look like them so what the hey. A few of my favorites are Carex glauca and g. 'Blue Zinger' with steel blue blades. These will slowly spread as 9" - 20" groundcovers. 'Evergold', a clumper, has striking foliage with yellow centers and green margins. 'Ice Dance' will spread where happy. It has green 1'- 2' blades with crisp white edges. 'Bowles Golden' features skinny, brilliant gold blades with a slightly arching habit. It can get between 2' - 3'. Zones 4 - 8

Groundcovers are great problem solvers. They are marvelous at:

- Thriving in tough areas under trees where grass won't grow
- Creating a weed-suppressing blanket around perennials, shrubs or trees
- Substituting for high maintenance lawns
- Controlling erosion on slopes
- Filling crevices in walls, between pavers and stepping stones
- Substituting for grass or mulch in areas that are difficult to mow
- Covering large expanses with low-maintenance plants

Probably the two most commonly used groundcovers for shade are Pachysandra and Vinca (myrtle). No doubt about it, these are good groundcovers, but let's be more creative, shall we?

To help groundcovers spread faster (which is the whole point) fertilize them each spring with Plant-Tone, a slow-release, organic fertilizer. Apply this right before it rains or water it in immediately afterwards to wash off any fertilizer that landed on leaves. You can also use a nutrient-rich, light-weight mulch (aged compost or horse manure). I apply this by shaking a shovel full of mulch over the groundcover so the material sifts down between the plants.

Another way to cheer on many groundcovers is to mow or weed-whack them back in spring. This stimulates fresh new growth and also thickens up existing plants.

Prepping the area to be covered also helps a groundcover's success. This does not have to be a labor-intensive process. Simply loosening the soil to three or four inches deep will help, especially if the area is compacted. Tossing in some compost, aged manure, leaf mold or other organic amendments will also reap tremendous benefits.

When using groundcovers around trees that have a lot of surface-feeding roots, such as maple trees, pick drought tolerant plants that can compete in this challenging environment.

Many Hostas are stoloniferous, making them great low-maintenance picks. There are separate Top Ten Lists for Hosta but a few prized for ground-covering speed are 'Ginko Craig' (narrow green leaves with white margins, purple flower, 10"), 'Stiletto' (very narrow green leaves with white margins, purple flowers, 8") and lancifolia (green leaves, lilac-blue flowers, 18").

Plant Delights Nursery

Barrenwort, Bishop's Hat, Fairy Wings (Epimedium) 4" - 16" Part Sun - Shade. Spring bloomer. White, pink, yellow, orange or multicolor flowers. This is one tough perennial. Spring flowers top dark, wiry stems. The leaves have a lovely burgundy cast in spring and occasionally in fall. To maximize spring leaf color, shear back the plants to within an inch of the ground in late winter. I like planting yellow Trout Lily bulbs (Erythronium) among white or pink Barrenworts for a fetching spring display. One of the most vigorous (remember that word?) of all Barrenworts is 'Sulfurem' with soft yellow flowers. Zones 4 - 9

Big Root Geranium (Geranium macrorrhizum) 8" - 15" Sun - Shade. Spring bloomer. Pink or white flowers. Big Root Geranium makes a spectacular groundcover. It has large leaves that are pleasantly fragrant. The more sun the plant gets, the richer burgundy-red the leaves turn in fall. 'Bevan's Variety' (deep pink, 10") 'Czakor' (rosey magenta, 15"), 'Spessart' (soft pinkish-white, 15") and 'Ingwerson's Variety' (soft pink, 10") are great picks. Zones 3 - 7

Deadnettle (Lamium) 3" - 8" Part Sun - Shade. Spring, summer bloomer. White, pink or purple flowers. Lamiums move pretty quickly across the soil, thanks to their stoloniferous stems. They also seed around. Foliage can be silver; green and white; green, yellow and white; or yellow and white. There are many fine cultivars to choose from. 'Pink Chablis', at 6", is promoted as one of the longest, consistently blooming Lamiums. 'Cosmopolitan' is the baby of the group, only getting between 3" - 6" tall. I allowed silver-leaved 'Pink Pewter' Lamium to sweep around my blue, mophead Hydrangeas and the combo is delightful! Lamiums do not like wet soil or areas where winter snow piles are slow to melt in spring. Zones 3 - 9

Chinese Astilbe 'Pumila' (Astilbe chinensis) 6" - 10" Sun - Shade. Summer bloomer. Lavender-pink flowers. This creeping astilbe has matt-forming, ferny leaves covered with spiky flowers in late July and August. You will get more flowers if you treat it to some time-released fertilizer in spring. It has very tight, ground-hugging leaves making it an extremely effective weed suppresser. Smile for the camera! Zones 3 - 8

Sweet Woodruff (Galium odoratum) 6" Part Sun - Shade. Spring bloomer. White flowers. Sweet Woodruff's foliage and flowers are both lightly scented. Some claim it smells like vanilla. The delicate, finely-cut leaves are a nice shade of soft green. To jazz up the display, tuck in spring and fall blooming bulbs. Possible choices include spring blooming Crocus, Trout Lily, dwarf Daffodils and Checkered Lilies. Late summer and early fall bloomers are Colchicums and fall blooming Crocus. Zones 3 - 8

Bugleweed (Ajuga) 2" - 6" Sun - Shade. Spring bloomer. Blue, blue-violet, pink or white flowers. Most Bugleweeds have stunning blue or blue-violet flowers that holler for attention in spring. After flowering, shear off spent blooms so the crisp, ground- hugging leaves become the focus. Foliage can be green; burgundy and green; bronzy green; black; green, pink and white; and soft gray-green and light yellow. Two of my favorites are 'Toffee Chip' that only gets 2" tall with creamy yellow and grey-green leaves and 'Black Scallop' with shiny black leaves reaching 4" - 6". Zones 3 - 8

⚜Wild Ginger (Asarum canadensis) 4" - 8" Part Shade - Shade. Spring bloomer. Purply-brown flowers. Wild Ginger, also called Canadian Ginger, has soft green, heart-shaped leaves. The Dr. Seus-like flowers lie on the ground under the leaves waiting for pollinating beetles. The leaves overlap nicely to suppress weeds. This is the hardiest of all Gingers, growing in Zones 2 - 8. European Ginger (Asarum europaeum) has very dark green, shiny, round leaves and stays shorter at 4" - 6". This spreads slower than canadensis and is hardy from Zones 4 - 9. One I have coveted is Chinese Wild Ginger (Asarum splendens). It has heart-shaped, dark green leaves mottled with silver and grows in Zones 6 - 9 (many catalogs list Zone 5).

⚜Archangel, False Lamium (Lamiastrum) 8" - 18" Part Shade - Shade. Spring bloomer. Yellow flowers. There are two commonly sold Lamiastrums. One is a much faster runner than the other. The gold medal goes to L. galeobdolan 'Variegatum'. It's almost vine-like as it scrambles over the ground, and it sets roots where the stems hit the ground. 'Variegatum' has silver 'V' markings on green leaves. Much more refined is Lamiumstrum g. 'Herman's Pride'. It only gets 8" tall and has striking white flecks in the leaves. 'Herman's Pride' is more of a clumper, although it will widen its girth over time. Zones 3 - 7

❧Dwarf Japanese Solomon's Seal (Polygonatum humile) 6" - 8" Part Shade - Shade. Spring Bloomer. White flowers. Little arching stems pop from the earth and have petite white flowers dripping from the tips. The leaves are light green. They are very drought tolerant and can travel in tight spots where other groundcovers would have trouble. Zones 3 - 9

❧⚜Foamflower (Tiarella) 10" - 12" Part Shade - Shade. Spring bloomer. White and pinkish-white flowers. There are many Foamflowers on the market but only a few are impressive groundcovers that enthusiastically set roots from stems running along the ground. The pacesetter in the line-up is cordifolia, a native plant with white flowers and solid green, maple-shaped leaves. More striking are its progeny, Tiarella cordifolia 'Eco Running Tapestry', with shapely, dissected leaves marked by dark veining and cordifolia 'Eco Running Tiger' that shines with lighter green leaves decorated by purple-maroon veining. Both have pinkish-white flowers. Zones 4 - 9

Top Ten Perennials for Full Shade

There are not many perennials that thrive in low light. This list features the 'bottom feeders' that are up to the challenge. But let's be realistic. There must be some light, even if it is only reflected, for a plant to conduct photosynthesis and live.

When I refer to full shade, I am not talking about what I refer to as a dungeon, also known as heavy or deep shade. Examples would be spots under decks, stairs or low hanging evergreen branches. When I say full shade, this is where leaves see 'the light of day' at some point. This may be on the north side of the house where early morning sun slips in or underneath a stand of trees. It could also be sunlight reflected from a lighter colored surface.

Below are a few tips to make the most of full shade gardens:

- If you plan to create a woodland garden, deciduous trees are easier to garden beneath than evergreens. At least there is spring sunlight reaching plants before the canopy fills in.
- Closely related to the above, when selecting which trees to plant under, aim for those that have deep roots with fewer surface feeders. Perennials will face less competition for needed water and nutrients. Oaks and Tulip trees (Loriodendron) have deep diving roots. On the other hand, many Maple trees, especially Norway or Silver Maples, can be a nightmare with their thick, netted surface roots.
- If planting a shade garden near a structure, consider painting the backdrop white or a light color to reflect sunlight to plants. If a wooded area is a garden's backdrop, consider adding a fence or living wall (hedge) as a backdrop otherwise the garden gets lost in the dark void behind it.
- Tuck bright colored objects in the garden to add interest. Accessories could be a decorative armillary, container, statue, urn, funky garden art, stonework…use your imagination! I have spray painted old birdbaths cobalt blue or electric yellow for striking accents. A huge fern in a large antique urn painted bone white presented a more subtle statement.
- Place containers bursting with brilliant shade annuals among full shade plantings. If the annuals start to decline after a few weeks due to low light, replace the container with a fresh one. Place the ailing one in more sun and fertilize with a liquid fertilizer, such as Neptune's Harvest, to rejuvenate. It should be ready to return to the 'front line' in several weeks.

🌿**Hosta (Hosta)** 3" - 36" + Summer bloomer. White, lavender or purple flowers. The best Hostas for full shade are blue leaved cultivars. The blue color is actually caused by a waxy coating

Neptune's Harvest

🌿drought tolerant ⊹deer resistant

on the leaves. This 'melts away' in sun, revealing green leaves beneath. To prevent blue Hosta from turning green, give them as much shade as possible. Some great blue cultivars are 'Blue Angel' (36" foliage mound, lavender flowers); 'Big Daddy' (24", white flowers), 'Abiqua Drinking Gourd' (18", white flowers); 'Blue Mouse Ears' (8", lavender flowers); 'Love Pat' (14", white flowers); sieboldiana 'Elegans' (20", white flowers); 'Hadspen Blue' (14", lavender flowers); 'Halcyon' (18", blue-violet flowers); and 'Fragrant Blue' (18", light lavender, fragrant flowers). Zones 3 - 9

Cinnamon Fern and Christmas Fern (Osmunda cinnamomea and Polystichum acrostichoides) 1' - 5' Foliage. Cinnamon Fern grows between 2' and 5' tall and gets the name from what looks like a big cinnamon stick rising from the center of the large fronds. It prefers moist areas but can tolerate drier soils. Christmas Fern grows between 1' to 3' tall and has very dark green, leathery fronds. Zones 3 - 8

❦ Solomon's Seal (Polygonatum) 4" - 6' Spring bloomer. White flowers. All varieties of Solomon's Seal have graceful, arching branches. Heights vary greatly. 4" tall humile makes a petite groundcover while Giant Solomon's Seal (biflorum var. commutatum) towers 5' to 6' in the air. Dangling, white tubular flowers appear in spring and then morph to shiny black berries. Most Solomon's Seals have green leaves but 'Variegatum' has white margins and 'Striatum' has white streaking throughout the leaf. The variegated cultivars are more noticeable in lower light. All have glowing golden foliage in fall. Zones 3 - 9

❦ Partridge Berry (Mitchella repens) 2" Summer bloomer. White flowers. This is actually a dwarf woody shrub that creeps along the ground and pops forth small, white flowers in summer that become bright red, edible berries later that season. There are actually two white flowers that bloom right next to each other and after fertilization occurs, the flowers fuse and produce one large red berry. Great team work! Zones 4 - 9

Toad Lily (Tricyrtis) 18" - 36" Fall bloomer. White, yellow or white with pinkish or purple spotted flowers. These unique looking flowers are in the orchid family. Leaves are solid green, green and white, green and creamy-yellow, and tricolor pink, white and green. All Toad Lilies have slightly arching stems with flowers formed along their length. 'White Towers' and 'Shirohotogisu' show best with white flowers. Zones 4 - 8

Meehan's Mint (Meehania cordata) 6" - 10" Late spring bloomer. Blue flowers. Now don't skip over this one just because you see the word mint. It is actually very striking and a stalwart native for shady sites. Think of it as a good companion for Ajuga, Lamium or Herman's Pride Lamiastrium. Meehan's Mint is a recent discovery for me and I'm delighted with my new treasure. Zones 5 - 8

Bunchberry (Cornus canadensis) 4" - 6" Spring bloomers. White flowers. This cute little ground-cover smothers itself with white flowers in spring, followed by cheerful red berries in summer. Picture a beautiful Dogwood tree in the movie, 'Honey, I Shrunk the Kids' and shazam, you have a miniaturized Dogwood. I've read that Bunchberry enjoys a moisture-retentive soil that is periodically amended with decaying wood. I must admit I lost the first Bunchberry I planted before discovering this tip. I'm up for another try! Zone 2 - 7

photo courtesy of Daniele Ippoliti

Wild Ginger (Asarum canadensis) 4" - 8" Spring bloomer. Purple-brown flowers. Wild Ginger has soft green, heart-shaped leaves. The Dr. Seus-like flowers lie on the ground under the leaves waiting for pollinating beetles. The leaves overlap nicely to suppress weeds. This is the hardiest of all the Gingers, growing in Zones 2 - 8. European Ginger (Asarum europaeum) has dark green, shiny, round leaves and stays a tad shorter at 4" - 6". This spreads slower than canadensis. Zones 2 - 9

Jack in the Pulpit (Arisaema) 15" - 36" White, pink, yellow or mixed striped flowers. Peek a boo. How can you not delight in squatting to look under Jack's hood to see him? Bright red, berry 'popsicles' appear in late summer and provide as much splash as any flower. Zones 4 - 8

Mukdenia 12" Spring bloomer. White flowers. This is a very unusual perennial that I bought for the leaves. They look sort of like a maple leaf but are more fringed at the edges. The outer margins are supposed to turn bronzy-red in late summer but I find this not to be true in full shade. This coloring comes with part shade. The white flowers (which I have yet to see on mine but I have faith) emerge in spring on leafless stems. Zones 4 - 8

Top Ten Climbing Vines for Shade

Reach for the sky! Many folks overlook vertical gardening. Please don't. It adds such a dynamic element. Drawing the eye upward provides another landscaping dimension, especially important for smaller properties. The sky, or graceful tree branches and leaf canopy, becomes a 'borrowed view', making the garden appear bigger than it really is.

Climbers can fulfill a number of other roles as well by:
- Contributing colorful flowers or foliage
- Camouflaging ugly walls, fences and other eye-sores
- Creating an interesting backdrop for gardens
- Acting as a groundcover when allowed to scramble along the ground
- Decorating shrubs and trees by twining up and over them
- Attracting hummingbirds and other desired wildlife
- Providing privacy

When choosing climbers, it is important to know how they ascend. This will dictate what kind of structure they need to achieve their goal. There are three ways for climbers to get where they want to go – up:

Twiners: The plant twists all, or a part of itself, around trellises, poles, string, chain-link fences and other structures. Some plants such, as Wisteria, wrap their whole 'body' around a structure. Other plants use slender tendrils or leaf stalks (petioles) to twirl around supports such as chicken wire, netting, string, fishing wire or trellises. Clematis and Morning Glories are in this group. Most climbers fall in the twiners category.

Clingers: These vines attach themselves to solid surfaces by aerial roots or adhesive discs. Potential supports include large trees, masonry surfaces, wood fences and other rough surfaces. Climbing Hydrangea and False Climbing Hydrangea fall into this group.

Scramblers or Ramblers: These plants don't actually climb on their own, they need a helping hand. You need to tie their stems to supporting structures with twisty ties, rope twine, old nylons or clasps. Climbing roses fall into this category.

Also consider the following when selecting and placing vines:
- The mature height and weight of the vine.
- The location's light, soil type and ease to get to for maintenance.
- Don't put vines with sucker-like discs on wooden surfaces, brick or stone walls that could be damaged by their aggressive grip.
- If you are using a climber to create privacy, think about an evergreen vine, like

English Ivy, for year-round functionality.

- Dress-up ugly chain-link fences with dense climbers like Climbing Hydrangea or Dutchman's Pipe.
- Use heavier vines to support secondary, lighter vines. For example, Clematis or annual flowering vines can be trained up Climbing Hydrangea.
- If you need to get to a wall behind a trellis for maintenance, consider using a hinged trellis that can be pulled down without damaging the vine.
- Chicken wire or black netting work well as supports when wrapped around posts, fences, trees and along walls because they are hard to see.
- Tomato cages can be used for smaller growing vines in perennial gardens.

A few specific comments about Clematis:

- There are many varieties, colors, bloom times and heights to choose.
- Most Clematis like full to part sun but a few are more shade tolerant like the ones on the list below.
- Clematis use leaf stalks (petioles) to twirl around slender supports like chicken wire, string and narrow trellis slats.
- Clematis can be allowed to scramble over perennials and ornamental shrubs in the garden for an interesting look.
- Make sure to prepare the planting hole well. Dig a hole 1' X 1' and work in plenty of organic matter such as compost or aged manure.
- Pruning varies depending on the type of Clematis. Clematis can be in Group I, II or III depending on when they set their flower buds. The easiest Clematis to grow are in group III. These only bloom on new wood. Translation: you can cut the vine to within 6" to 8" of the ground each fall when cleaning up perennial beds. They can also be cut back in late winter or early spring. Group III should be pruned as recommended or they develop tangled, unsightly bare lower stems with new growth towards the top. Group I plants bloom early in spring on old wood. Many of these have smaller, nodding flowers. Prune these right after they bloom. Group II Clematis bloom on old and new wood. This makes them a tad tricky. They flower in early summer on old wood (buds set on the prior year's wood, like Lilacs) and then set buds on new wood that grows from older stems. A light pruning can be done right after the initial bloom and then again after the second flowering.
- To train Clematis to climb through branches of small trees and shrubs, plant roots on the shady side of the trunk and the vine will work its way to the side with more light. The vine will need a support, such as a bamboo stake, to reach the lower branches.
- When setting Clematis in a planting hole, place the crown (where the stem meets the roots) 1" to 2" below the soil surface. Also angle the plant slightly in the direction you want it to go.
- Clematis wilt is a nasty fungal disease that causes entire stems to rapidly die back

to the soil. The fungus typically attacks the vascular system at the stem's base. Infected stems should be cut off and trashed, but not in the compost pile. The disease does not affect the roots so the vine will grow back. Unfortunately many times new stems will also be affected. You can treat this fungal disease with a sulfur product but I have had mixed results doing this. The best solution I found was to dig out the infected plant and 'junk' it. Then I dug the soil out where it was planted (a 2' X 2' area and 18" deep). I filled the hole with 'clean' soil amended with compost or aged manure and planted a new Clematis. This has worked every time. Another way to avoid the angst of Clematis wilt is to only work with Group I varieties that are rarely bothered by it.

❧ Patio Clematis are great choices for smaller areas or containers. They only reach 2' to 4'. After flowering you can cut all the stems back to 6" from the ground and this usually stimulates another flush of flowers.

Clematis 6' - 10' Sun - Part Shade. Summer, early fall bloomer. There are oodles of Clematis on the market but only a few will tolerate part shade. Most desire full to part sun. 'Comtesse de Bouchaud' has charming lavender-pink flowers for at least 6 weeks and is a Group III lady. Another Group III pick is 'Hagley Hybrid' with soft shell pink flowers. 'Silver Moon' glows in shade with silvery-lilac flowers. 'Nelly Moser' will also dance in part shade with pink petals marked with burgundy-red stripes. Both 'Nelly Moser' and 'Silver Moon' are Group II groupies. 'Roguchi' is a new Japanese Clematis with deep blue, nodding, fragrant flowers. It actually dies to the ground every fall so pruning is not an issue. New stems jump into action the next spring and cover themselves with flowers. This one works especially well as a scrambler amongst Hosta and other shade perennials. All Clematis enjoy alkaline soil with a pH around 7.0 or slightly above. If needed, work some lime into the soil around the roots in fall. Zones 4 - 8

Climbing Hydrangea (Hydrangea anomala petiolaris) 20' - 30' Sun - Part Shade. Early summer bloomer. White flowers. This vine climbs by aerial roots. I have mine climbing up a huge oak tree. Climbing Hydrangea is breathtaking when in bloom with its white, lacy flowers running 20' up the trunk. The only care I give it is in spring. I prune out some climbing stems at their base to allow more airflow to the tree's bark. I don't want insect or disease problems caused by too much captured moisture. Climbing Hydrangea's leaves turn a golden yellow in fall before dropping. Then peeling bark carries the show through winter. This is not the plant to buy if you are not a patient person. It can take up to seven years for a plant to bloom. When buying Climbing Hydrangea, buy the biggest, most mature one you can for a quicker return on your investment. Zones 4 - 9

False Hydrangea Vine (Schizophragma) 40' - 50' Part Sun - Part Shade. Early summer bloomer. White or pink flowers. This vine looks similar to Climbing Hydrangea but it blooms at a younger age. It will push out flowers after three or four years of growth.

'Roseum' is a pink flowering cultivar and 'Moonlight' has white flowers and bluish leaves. False Hydrangeas climb by aerial roots. Zones 5 - 9

Dutchman's Pipe (Aristolochia)
6' - 30' Sun - Shade. Spring bloomer. Yellowish brown flowers. The large, heart-shaped green leaves grow closely together, making Dutchman's Pipe a super shade and privacy vine. The flowers are insignificant. They hang under the leaves and look like a Dutchman's pipe (whatever that looks like), hence its common name. This is usually grown on a trellis, pergola or latticework to provide a natural shade awning. It climbs by twining. Zones 4 - 8

Fiveleaf Akebia, Chocolate Vine (Akebia)
12' - 20'' Sun - Part Shade. Late spring bloomer. Purplish flowers. I fell in love with this interesting vine a few years ago. It has five leaflets positioned in a circular pattern that meet at a central point. The leaves have a waxy appearance. The flowers are fragrant and smell a bit like chocolate. It is a very 'enthusiastic' vine and can be trimmed to keep it in line. Please note that in warmer regions (Maryland, Virginia, Kentucky, New Jersey, Pennsylvania and Washington D.C.) this vine is considered invasive. It is a twiner. Zones 4 - 9

Artic Kiwi, Tricolor Vine (Actinidia)
25' - 30' Sun - Part Shade. Late spring, early summer bloomer. White flowers. Small fragrant flowers appear in late spring but it's the leaves that are the main attraction. The leaves are variegated white, pink and green. The color becomes more pronounced after several years of growth, as well as when they get more sun. There are male and female plants. You need both to get the fuzzy fruit. Males are the showiest with the greatest variegation. Don't get me started. 'Kolomikta' is hardy to Zone 5. 'Artic Beauty' can handle zone 3 but has smaller leaves. Use minimum fertilizer for best leaf color. A twiner it be. Zones 3 - 8

English Ivy (Hedera helix)
Up to 50' Sun - Shade. Foliage vine. This beauty scrambles its way across the ground and up structures by aerial roots and remains evergreen in winter. In some regions, English Ivy is noted as an invasive thug. Zones 4 - 9

Boston Ivy (Parthenocissus tricuspidata)
Up to 50' Sun - Part Shade. Foliage vine. This is a rapid grower that differs from English Ivy in that it is deciduous. The shiny, green foliage turns a pretty red and scarlet in fall. Boston Ivy climbs by aerial roots. Zones 4 - 8

PerennialResource.com

Silver Lace Vine (Polygonum aubertii) 20' - 30' Sun - Part Shade. Summer bloomer. White flowers. This is a very, very fast grower. To give you an idea, it can scramble up to 20' in a season. Don't turn your back on it! Of course, in shadier areas it doesn't get as much speed up. It is best used to cover up unsightly objects quickly or flow over slopes, choking out any competition. To regain control when needed, prune it hard in spring. A very fast twiner. Zones 4 - 7

'Ramblin' Red' Climbing Rose Sun - Part Shade. Summer, fall bloomer. Red flowers. I know. You think I've been dippin' into the hooch when I included a rose on this list. I've found that Knockout roses do okay in part shade. Agreed, there are not as floriferous but they still add appealing color in shade, especially the double red roses. 'Ramblin Red' is from the Knockout line so you know it is a winner. It has medium red flowers on 6' to 10' canes. 'Ramblin Red' boasts the same great flowering habit as its siblings as well as their ability to resist black spot and other fungal diseases. But one difference is that 'Ramblin Red' is hardier than the others. It can handle Zone 3 just fine whereas most Knockouts are geared for Zone 4 or warmer. Zones 3 - 7

CHAPTER FOUR

Flowering Shrubs, Trees, Bulbs and Annuals for Shade

Top Ten Flowering Shrubs

Bottlebrush (Fothergilla) 2' - 5' Sun - Part Shade. Spring bloomer. Creamy-white flowers. This native shrub has bottlebrush flowers that emit a delightful, honey-like fragrance. The flowers appear before the green foliage leafs out. The flowers get a jump-flowering; an encore takes place in fall when the shrub explodes into a brilliant orangey-red-yellow glowing spectacle. Burning Bush, which is overused in my opinion and is now listed as an invasive plant, has found its rival in Fothergilla. Not only does Fothergilla cook up brilliant fall color but it also serves fragrant flowers in spring and requires far less pruning to stay at a desirable size. 'Blue Shadow' (frosty blue leaves, 3' - 4'), 'Blue Mist' (frosty blue leaves, 2' - 3'), gardenii (green leaves, 2' - 4') and 'Mount Airy' (green leaves, 4' - 5') are all highly acclaimed cultivars. 'Blue Shadow' and 'Blue Mist' prefer part sun or part shade. Zones 4 – 8

Bush Honeysuckle (Diervilla) 2' - 5' Sun - Shade. Late spring, summer bloomer. Yellow flowers. I discovered this shrub at Estabrook's Nursery in Maine. 'Cool Splash' has bold green and white variegated leaves and masses of small, sassy yellow flowers. It looks like a compact, fuller bodied variegated, red-twig Dogwood. 'Butterfly' has bright green leaves and 'Copper' features coppery-red spring growth and stays the shortest at 2' - 3'. Hummingbirds enjoy dining on the yellow flowers. Zones 4 - 8 but 'Copper' handles Zone 3.

Rhododendron (Rhododendron) 3' - 12' Sun - Shade. Spring bloomer. White, pink, red, purple or lavender flowers. There are small-leaved and broad-leaved varieties of Rhododendrons. In general, the smaller-leaved Rhododendrons prefer full to part sun while the broad-leaves prefer part sun to shade. Broad-leaved cultivars include 'Roseum Elegans' (pink flowers, 6' - 8'), 'Nova Zembla' (red flowers, 4' - 6') and catawbiense album (white flowers, 6' - 8'). Maximum, also known as Rosebay, is one of the most shade tolerant with white to pale pink flowers, growing to 8' - 12'. All large-leaved cultivars prefer a cool, moisture-retentive soil and protection from winter winds. Zones 3 - 8

Abelia (Abelia) 24" - 6' Sun - Part Shade. Spring, summer bloomer. Pink or white flowers. Abelias have nose-twitching fragrant flowers and glossy green leaves. Most are only hardy to Zone 6 but A. mosanensis, at 5' - 6' tall, can muster Zone 4 winters. It has rich pink flowers plus foliage that turns reddish-orange in fall. The Anniversary series are all hardy to Zone 6. 'Bronze Anniversary' at 3' - 4', has bronze-orange spring foliage that changes to a golden color in summer with white flowers. 'Ruby Anniversary' features ruby-red new growth and white flowers with dark pink bracts (bases). 'Golden Anniversary', 24" - 28", has green and gold leaves while 'Silver Anniversary' displays shimmering white and green leaves. Both have white flowers. Zones 4 - 9

Smooth Leaf Hydrangea (H. arborescens) 3' - 6' Sun - Shade. This group of hydrangeas has pink or white flowers and set their flower buds in spring on new wood. All can be pruned hard in late winter or early spring before new growth begins. 'Annabelle' (3' - 5') and 'Grandiflora (3' - 7') have white, ball-shaped flowers and have been around for years. 'Annabelle' is one of the most shade tolerant of all Hydrangeas. 'Incrediball' (4' - 5') is marketed as an improved 'Annabelle' with larger white flowers and stiffer stems. 'White Dome' (4' - 6', white dome-shaped flowers) and 'Invincibelle Spirit' (3' - 5', pink ball-shaped flowers) are newer selections. A portion of all plant sales from 'Invincibelle Spirit' goes to breast cancer research. Zones 3 - 9

Spring Meadow Nursery

Elderberry (Sambucus) 5' - 10' Part Sun - Part Shade. Summer bloomer. White flowers. The gold leaved Elderberries are the best pick for lower light areas. 'Sutherland Gold' and 'Aurea' have large, lacy yellow leaves and flat white flowers that ripen to darker red berries. The fruit of all Elderberry shrubs are prized by both birds and people. Elderberries need good drainage or they will rot (trust me, I speak from experience). Zones 4 - 8

Japanese Kerria (Kerria japonica) 3' - 5' Sun - Shade. Spring bloomer. Yellow flowers. Kerria's cheerful yellow flowers are carried on bright green stems and herald in spring like Forsythia. Flowers can be single-petaled or double that look like roses. There is some rebloom through the summer. Some. 'Golden Guinea' and 'Honshu' have single flowers, 'Plenifora' has double blooms. 'Picta' has variegated white and green leaves with single yellow flowers. Zones 5 - 8

Redvein Enkianthus (Ekianthus campanulatus) 5' - 15' Sun - Shade. Spring bloomer. Pink and white flowers. Dangling clusters of pink and white flowers that look a tad like Lily-of-the-Valley flowers are absolutely charming. Ekianthus c. 'Red Bells' and c. 'Summer Hill' stay compact at 5' while the species, campanulatus, gets up to 15'. Foliage is green through summer and turns varying degrees of yellow, orange and red in fall. Enkianthus is similar to Rhododendrons in that it prefers a moisture-retentive soil. Zones 4 - 7

Bigleaf Hydrangea (H. macrophylla) 2' - 6' Sun - Part Shade. Summer bloomer. Blue, purple or pink flowers depending on soil pH. This is the Hydrangea group that drives gardeners crazy. There are mophead and lacecap varieties in this group. The reason that most Bigleaf Hydrangeas bloom little, or not at all, is usually related to when they set their flower buds and to your hardiness zone. Many Bigleaf cultivars bloom on old wood. This means flower buds are formed in late summer and need to make it through the winter to bloom the next year. In colder zones, siting the shrubs on the east side of the house or in other sheltered areas, creates pretty good odds that you'll be smiling at summer flowers. If not, well, you know..... Thankfully there are now mophead Hydrangeas on the market that set flower buds on old and new wood. Translation: it doesn't matter how many buds freeze off in winter, there will be a whole new round of reinforcements in spring. Another perk of these newer offerings is many are repeat bloomers. After the first round of flowers, more buds will appear through summer into fall. Some great Bigleaf cultivars that bloom on old and new wood are: 'Endless Summer' (4'- 5'), 'Blush-

ing Bride' (3' - 6'), 'Let's Dance Moonlight' (2' - 3'), 'Let's Dance Starlight' (2' - 3', lacecap) and 'Twist-N-Shout' (3' - 5', lacecap). Bigleafs will be blue in acid soil (pH 6.0 or lower) and pink in alkaline soil (pH 7.0 or higher). Sometimes 'Blurple' is the result of pH's between 6.0 - 7.0. As far as pruning Bigleafs, you only need to prune if the shrub has gotten bigger than you want. Don't prune just for the sake of pruning. For Hydrangreas that bloom on new and old wood, prune lightly in the fall or late winter. For those that bloom only on old wood, prune right after they flower in late summer or early fall. Most Bigleafs do best in part sun to part shade. In full sun they usually wilt miserably by the afternoon. I've found Lacecap varieties can handle full shade and still flower pretty well. Zones 4 - 8

⁜Summersweet (Clethra) 3' - 8' Sun - Part Shade. Summer bloomer. Pink or white flowers. The name is so accurate. Their flowers perfume the summer air with their sweet fragrance. Summersweet is one of the few shrubs that can handle wet soil as well as average soil. They stress out in dry soil. Flower buds are set on new wood so prune in late winter or early spring. 'Sixteen Candles' (28", white flowers), 'Ruby Spice' (3' - 6', pink flowers), 'Pink Spires' (6', pale pink flowers), 'Hummingbird' (30", white flowers) and 'Vanilla Spice' (3' - 6', white flowers) are all butterfly magnets with showy golden foliage in fall. Zones 3 - 9

Top Ten 8' - 20' Ornamental Trees

Some trees make fetching focal points in a garden and are easier to plant beneath than others. All of the following, with the exception of Paperbark Maple and Tricolor Beech, also have enchanting flowers. Most trees are quite drought tolerant once established.

As with most flowering shrubs, periodic pruning is helpful in maintaining a tree's shape and branching habit, especially when the plant is young. Limbing up and/or thinning branches allows more filtered light to reach plants below.

Witchhazel (Hamamelis) 8' - 20' Sun - Part Shade. Winter, early spring bloomer. Yellow or red flowers. Witchhazel's flowers look like finely shredded paper. They dangle from leafless branches when little else is happening in the landscape. The green leaves turn an exquisite yellow, orange and red in fall. The more sun the shrub or small tree gets, the more striking the display. All Witchhazels tend to have a vase-shaped growth habit. 'Diane' has dark red flowers and stays more compact than some at 8' - 12'. 'Arnold Promise' has yellow flowers and can get up to 20'. Both of these are hardy to Zone 5. H. virginiana, Common Witchhazel, is hardy to zone 4 (maybe even 3). It has fragrant yellow flowers and is native to eastern and central US. Zones 4 - 9

Eastern Redbud (Cercis canandensis) 6' - 10' Sun - Part Shade. Spring bloomer. Rosy-mauve or white flowers. This exquisite plant is covered with flowers in spring before its foliage appears. It can be grown as a multi-stem shrub or a single trunk tree. All Redbuds have pretty, heart-shaped leaves. 'Forest Pansy' (rosy-mauve flowers) has lush purple leaves in spring that green up in summer but change to purple-red in fall. 'Covey', also know as 'Lavender Twist', has a contorted trunk and a weeping nature. It is a crowd-stopper in spring when covered with pink flowers. Some resources list Redbuds as Zone 5 plants, other as Zone 4. Gardeners in northern climates should site these out of the path of winter winds for best results.

Serviceberry, Shadblow (Amelanchier) 4' - 25' Sun - Part Shade. Spring bloomer. White flowers. Serviceberry can be a multi-stemmed shrub or be grown as a single trunk tree. All have yummy fruit you'll love if you can get to it before the birds do. Glowing orange and red fall leaf color is another bonus. The smooth, light gray bark is also striking. 'Rainbow Pillar' is narrower growing than others, reaching 14' - 20'. 'Autumn Brilliance' grows fuller and maxes between 15' - 25'. Zones 3 - 9

⚜Magnolia (Magnolia) 10' - 20' Sun. Spring blooms. White, pink or yellow flowers. Tree Magnolias make stunning focal points. Their tulip-like blooms take your breath away, especially soft yellow flowering specimens like 'Butterflies' , 'Elisabeth', 'Yellow Gardland' and 'Yellow Bird'. Do not confuse tree forms with Star Magnolias that are densely branched bushes. Sometimes their buds are prone to early frost damage so site out of the path of cold winds. 'Henry Hicks' is more shade tolerant than other Magnolias. It gets' 10 - 20' with white flowers that smell like lemons. Zones 5 - 8

Dogwood (Cornus kousa, pagoda and mas) 8' - 30' Sun - Part Shade. Spring bloomer. White, yellow or pink flowers. There are three types of tree form Dogwoods. They all develop a nice horizontal branching habit (some more than others) as they mature and even more so if planted in less light. Cornelian Cherry (Cornus mas) is a striking Dogwood that is definitely underused in my area. Cornelian Cherry, hardy to Zone 4, has showy yellow flowers that burst open before its leaves appear. Fast out of the gate, it blooms even before Forsythia! The flowers then turn to small, bright red fruit in summer, followed by rich burgundy-red leaves in fall. It is usually grown as a multi-stemmed tree reaching 8' - 15'. 'Golden Glory' is a popular cultivar. Korean or Kousa Dogwood (Cornus Kousa) has white or pink flowers with four distinct petals. The leaves turn a pretty red in fall and the trees are hardy to Zone 5. I planted kousa 'Wolf Eyes' several years ago just for the wonderful green and white variegated leaves. The white flowers are icing on the cake. Pagoda Dogwood (Cornus alternifolia) is a hot seller in colder climates, given its hardiness to Zone 3. It has white flowers that cover side-sweeping branches. 'Golden Shadows' is in this group and it has eye-popping sizzling yellow and green leaves. It does best in part sun or part shade and grows between 8' - 12'. Zones 3 - 8

⫶Weeping Cherry (Prunus subhertilla) 8' - 15' Sun - Part Sun. Spring bloomer. Pink or white flowers. This is a top selling flowering tree, especially when color-starved gardeners in colder climates see it in bloom in spring. Add to this display long, swaying branches and it's sure sale! I have only listed here smaller trees that are better for planting beneath. Some Weeping Cherries can get 20' - 30' over time. 'Snow Fountains' has pure white flowers and grows to 8' - 15'. 'Pink Showers' and 'Pendula' are its twins but they have pink blooms. Many folks are 'confuddled' when it comes to pruning these trees. If you want a more natural look, prune the weeping branches at different lengths. A more formal look occurs when all the limbs are sheared at the same length. If any 'nonconforming' branch starts growing straight up, prune it off. Irrational behavior will not be tolerated. Zones 5 - 9

Beech (Fagus sylvatica) 6' - 15' Sun - Part Sun. Foliage. Two cool trees to use as garden focal points are Weeping Purple Beech and Tricolor Beech. 'Purpurea Pendula' has rich purple leaves adorning long weeping branches that touch the ground. It grows between 6' - 10' tall. This is one tree that you do not plant directly beneath. Locate ornamentals at a slight distance from its long 'locks'. Tricolor Beech is one of the most asked about woodies in my yard. It has pink, green and white leaves with a very delicate branching habit. I have pink and red Knockout roses circling beneath it and the combination is a 'knockout'! Tricolor Beeches can grow 15' - 20' tall and do best in part sun. Zones 3 - 7

⁜ Paperbark Maple (Acer griseum) 10' - 15' Sun - Part Shade. Foliage. Ooh la la. Everything about this tree is to die for. It has rich green, tri-foliate leaves that turn brilliant red, orange and yellow in fall. The bark is a sensual reddish-cinnamon that peels in large sections from the trunk. Striking. Plus it has a divine branching habit and overall form. Zones 4 - 7

⁜ Dwarf Flowering Crabapple (Malus) 8' - 20' Sun. Spring bloomer. Pink or white flowers. For use in a garden setting, I am focusing on shorter growing cultivars that are more disease resistant to apple scab or rust. 'Adirondack' only gets 8' - 10', grows in a vase shape, and covers itself with white flowers. 'Louisa' is a weeping crabapple with rich pink flowers, golden-yellow fruit and tops out between 8' - 12'. 'Camelot', at 10', has pink flowers with burgundy- red fruit; 'Molten Lava', a weeper at 12', sports white flowers and red fruit, and 'Sargent', also has white flowers but is upright at 8'. Zones 3 - 8

⁜ White Fringe Tree (Chionanthus virginicus) 12 - 20' Sun - Part Shade. Spring bloomer. White flowers. In addition to writing about plants that make good garden specimens, I like to introduce folks to underutilized beauties. White Fringe Tree is one such plant. Lush, white flower tassels drip from branches in spring, perfuming the air. Blue-black berries, enjoyed by birds, follow in fall as well as golden leaf color. Zones 3 – 9

Bailey Nursery

Top Ten Evergreen Shrubs

Evergreens are essential for winter interest plus they add great bones to a garden. The majority on this list also have attractive flowers or berries plus remarkable leaves.

Many ornamental evergreens grown in colder climates prefer to be sheltered from blasting winter winds. Don't you? Deciduous shrubs are not as stressed by these conditions. They discard their leaves in fall and 'abandon ship' (go dormant) until warmer weather returns. The leaves of evergreens 'stay with the ship'. The leaves continue to transpire water, day in and day out, that cannot be recovered from frozen ground. Spring flowering shrubs like Rhododendrons and Japanese Andromeda are especially taxed. They do double duty by supporting both leaves and flower buds (that blossom in spring). Evergreen leaves can also get sunburned by the winter sun, resulting in 'tanning'. And this 'tan' is not a healthy one.

Protect evergreen shrubs from wind and sunburn with an anti-transpirant like Wilt-Pruf. This liquid coating is like a winter jacket, insulating vulnerable leaves from nasty weather. Apply anti-transpirants in late November or early December when the temperature is above 40 degrees. Wilt-Pruf will last three to four months and is organic.

Other ways to protect evergreens is to site them out of the path of winter winds, like on the east side of the house. Or set up a burlap wall to block assaulting winds. You can also wrap shrubs in burlap, creating winter 'meatballs'.

Evergreen flowering shrubs are ideal around a home's foundation, especially in the front of the house and near entrances. The sturdy leaves block 'embarrassing' views of the cement foundation, plus they contribute lovely floral displays. Just make sure that crashing snow or ice is not a factor or else the benefits will be compromised, to say the least. Use shrub tents to protect their posture and good looks.

Now on with the show:

✢**Mountain Laurel (Kalmia)** 3' - 10' Sun - Shade. Spring bloomer. White or pink flowers. Mountain Laurel is a close relative to Rhododendron. Both are shallow-rooted, flowering evergreens that prefer acidic soil. Mountain Laurels remain more compact in sunnier locations. The shadier it is, the more open-branched and gracefully 'stretchy' they become. Most Mountain Laurels grow between 6' to 10' but there are dwarf cultivars such as 'Elf' (3' - 5', white flowers), 'Minuet' (3' - 5', light pink buds open to white flowers with maroon markings), 'Tiddlywinks (2.5' - 3', pink flowers), and 'Little Linda' (3' - 4', red buds open to white flowers that age to pink). A few of my taller favorites are 'Olympic Fire' (5' - 8', red buds opening to pink flowers) and 'Carola' (5' - 6', white flowers). In colder climates it is key to keep these beauties in a protected spot, far from drying, winter winds. Zones 4 - 9

✢**Boxwood (Buxus microphylla)** 2' - 6' Sun - Shade. Foliage. Boxwoods are always one of my first picks for shady spots frequented by deer. There are globe shaped as well as pyramidal varieties. They add a formal feeling to gardens when kept neatly clipped. And they are a natural for cottage gardens. Many cultivars are only hardy to zone 5 but thankfully a few push through Zone 4 winters. These are the Korean Boxwood bunch. Check out 'Green Gem' (2', globe), 'Green Mountain' (4' - 5', pyramidal) and 'Green Velvet' (3', globe). 'Verdant Hills' (3', globe) was introduced from the University of Vermont in Burlington, VT and it can live through Zone 3 winters. Let's give it a hand! If you want an eye-catching, globe-shaped Boxwood for Zone 5 or warmer, look for 'Wedding Ring' with rich green leaves edged in gold. Zones 4 - 8

⁜Drooping Leucothoe (Leucothoe fontanasiana) 18" - 24" Sun - Shade. Spring bloomer.
White flowers. Leucothoe has arching branches with glossy green leaves and dangling white flowers in late spring. The leaves of some varieties turn burgundy-red in fall. 'Compacta' and 'Nana' remain shorter at 18" - 24" while 'Rainbow' reaches 3' - 4' and has creamy-white, pink and red leaf variegation in early spring that turns solid green by summer. It also has red stems. Zones 5 - 9

Euonymus (Euonymus fortunei) 18" - 24" Sun - Shade. Foliage. Some Euonymus can
get large and ratty looking. I promise I will not recommend any of these. My picks are 'Blondy' (bold, creamy yellow centers with dark green margins, 18" - 24"), 'Gold Splash' (wide, golden-yellow margins surrounding green centers, an improved sport of 'Emerald n'Gold', 18") and 'Moonshadow' (gold centers with green margins, 2'). Euonymus scale can be a problem. This insect attaches itself to the leaves and stems. Brown, oval-shaped shells and a sticky, 'honeydew' substance are indicators that all is not well in Dodge. Horticultural oil and registered pesticides are typically the weapons of choice. Zones 4 - 8

Broad-Leaved Rhododendron (Rhododendron) 3' - 12' Part Sun - Shade. Spring bloomer.
White, pink, red, purple or lavender flowers. There are small-leaved and broad-leaved varieties of Rhododendrons. In general, the smaller-leaved Rhododendrons prefer full to part sun while the broad-leaves prefer part sun to shade. Obviously for shade gardening, the larger leaved rhodies are the best choice. Some popular picks include 'Roseum Elegans' (pink flowers, 6' - 8'), 'Nova Zembla' (red flowers, 4' - 6'), 'Minnetonka' (purple flowers, 4' - 6') and catawbiense album (white flowers, 6' - 8'). Maximum, also known as Rosebay, is one of the most shade tolerant with white to pale pink flowers, growing to 8' - 12'. Zone 3 - 8

⁜Russian or Siberian Cypress (Microbiota decussta) 8" - 3' Sun - Part Shade. Foliage.
Russian cypress has soft, sweeping foliage that always looks good. In the summer the foliage is medium green and then in winter the leaves turn bronze-copper. 'Celtic Pride' is a popular pick and matures to 3' tall and 4' wide. New to the plant shelf is 'Fuzz Ball'. It is more rounded versus spreading and tops out at 12". 'Jacobsen' hugs the ground at only 8" - 12" in height. The species, decussta, will tolerate full shade. Zones 2 - 6

Blue Holly (Ilex X meservae) 5' - 15' Sun - Shade. Summer bloomer. White flowers. Hollies are beloved for their showy red berries and shiny green leaves. They can grow in a mounded shape or grow more pyramidal. You need a male and female Holly to have 'baby' berries. Both have white flowers. One male can fertilize twenty females within a 50' + range. Don't get me started. But not all males will do the 'mating dance' with all females. You need to make sure the varieties are pollen compatible. Usually it is pretty easy to make the match. For example, 'Blue Prince' is compatible with 'Blue Princess'. 'China Boy' and 'China Girl' are partners. You get the drift. Zones 5 - 9 (many resources say Zone 4)

Yew (Taxus) 4' - 15' Sun - Shade. Foliage. Yews are commonly used in landscapes because of their forgiving nature. Their only negative trait is their tastiness to deer. Some Yews are much more tolerant of full shade than others. 'Hicksii' is a good pick for darker areas. It has a narrow, upright shape with dark green needles and grows slowly to 10' + . 'Hatfieldii', another Yew tolerant of low light, has bright green needles. It is slow growing as well, eventually reaching 20' in many, many, many years. Zones 4 - 7

Creeping Barberry, Creeping Hollygrape, Creeping Mahonia (Mahonia repens) 6" - 12" Sun - Part Shade. Spring bloomer. Yellow flowers. This is a happy, slow spreading groundcover. It maneuvers by setting roots from underground stems. Fragrant lemon-yellow flowers in spring decorate the blue-green leaves. Edible bluish-purple berries are the result of pollinating insects. The foliage turns a coppery-purple in winter, is leathery and sort of like a Holly's, with pointy edges. Creeping Mahonia prefers acidic soil, making it perfect as an evergreen groundcover under pines. Zones 4 - 9

Andromeda (Pieris japonica) 4' - 12' Sun - Shade. Spring bloomer. White or pink flowers. This graceful shrub has eye-catching flowers and neat, shiny green leaves. 'Mountain Fire' struts bright red, new foliage after flowering. Most Andromeda have dangling white flowers but 'Valley Valentine' has rosy-pink blooms and 'Dorothy Wycoff' blushes softer pink. Zones 4 - 9

photo courtesy of Daniele Ippoliti

Flowering bulbs are an easy way to 'supersize' color in your garden. Granted, not as many bulbs can handle lower light conditions, but those that can step up to the challenge are super heroes. Before introducing you to this elite group, let's go over some general bulb planting and design tips.

As a rule, a bulb's planting depth is three times its height. Plant bulbs with the pointy side up. If you're not sure of where the point is, no problem. A neat attribute of most bulbs is the ability for an emerging stem to find the surface despite its orientation in the ground. You can always plant bulbs sideways for added insurance. Plant bulbs in multiples; the more the better. And please, not in straight lines. Create sweeps; 5's, 7's and 9's work nicely.

Most bulbs demand good drainage or they rot. After spring flowering bulbs are finished blooming, remove the spent flowers and stalks so that energy is directed back into the bulb instead of seed formation. Wait until the leaves are brown before cutting them back. Ideally, you should be able to gently pull them off. The one exception to this rule is Daffodils. Their foliage takes a long time to cry 'Uncle'. So when I can't stand their scrappy look, usually in early July, I shear the foliage back to a 6" tall clump. If you're the type that impatiently taps your fingers waiting for the foliage to ripen, then select dwarf or miniature varieties, those that top out at 10". After these flower, usually earlier in the spring, the foliage goes dormant pretty quickly.

For summer blooming bulbs such as Asiatic, Oriental and Trumpet lilies, wait until the flowers have finished blooming and then remove the spent stalks as noted above. Now some of you may be thinking, what is she talking about? Those are sun-loving bulbs. Yup, but many of them will still bloom in part shade. To compensate for less sunlight, they stretch for the sun and grow taller than usual. Allow for this 'extension' by planting them farther back in the garden. You can always plant other sun loving bulbs, including spring bloomers, in shade but just treat them as annuals. When you bought these they already had enough energy stored in the bulb from the prior growing season. They will bloom just fine their first year. But after flowering they cannot conduct the same level of photosynthesis in lower light, so the following season's blooms will be sorely compromised, if at all.

Spring blooming bulbs do better under deciduous trees than evergreens. After flowering they can catch some sun before the leaf canopy shuts down the party. When digging holes, save your back and wrists by using a bulb auger and power drill. Steel augers make digging spring, summer and fall blooming bulbs fun. Really. I used to dread this project but now I'm a fan. I'll even drill in my neighbor's bulbs. Simply place the auger into an electric or battery-operated power drill and feel the power. You can also use it for digging in annuals, smaller perennials and for aerating soil as well as compost piles. Heck, I bet it would even work in the kitchen.

If bulb-chomping critters are a problem you can:

- Plant bulbs an inch or two deeper that standard protocol.
- Drench bulbs in taste repellents like Invisible Fence or Plantskydd.
- Use chicken grit (crushed oyster shells) from farm and feed stores (i.e., Agway) or crab shells from Coast of Maine (www.coastofmaine.com). These sharp fragments feel nasty on tender noses and paws.
- Plant bulbs in large pots. Sink the pre-planted pots in the ground in fall and remove them after they've finished blooming in spring. You can fill the empty spot with annuals or better yet, replace with them with similar-size containers of tender tropicals, such as Cannas or Elephant Ears, that you've overwintered inside.
- Use wire cages to protect bulbs, although I find these a drag to fiddle with. Plus I smack into them when installing new plants or dividing perennials.
- Finally, you could simply use poisonous bulbs such as Daffodils, Fritillaria, and Colchicums. Although this sounds cruel, it's not. The 'muncher' takes one nibble of the bulb and realizes it's bad for tummies and then moves on, unharmed.

Many times mail-order companies are some of the best sources for getting unusual bulbs. Some of my favorite 'candy stores' are John Scheepers (www.johnscheepers.com), Brent and Becky's Bulbs (https://store.brentandbeckysbulbs.com) and Old House Gardens Heirloom Flower Bulbs (www.oldhousegardens.com).

⊹Checkered Lily (Fritillaria meleagris) 8" Part Sun - Shade. Spring bloomer. Maroon and white flowers. Charming, just charming. Checkered Lily has slender blue-green foliage topped by nodding flowers. Flowers can be maroon-purple with white checks or solid white. Checkered Lilies naturalize at a polite pace and can tolerate moist soil, unlike many bulbs. Fritillarias are detested by munching critters, including deer. Zones 3 - 8

⊹Trout Lily, Dogtooth Violet (Erythronium Pagoda) 8" - 12" Part Shade. Spring bloomer. Yellow flowers. These cheerful flowers, resemble miniature turk's cap lilies, are born on airy stems above broad green, low growing leaves. Zones 4 - 8

⊹Narcissi (Daffodils) 5" - 20" Sun - Shade. Spring bloomer. Yellow, white or bicolor flowers. I used to think there were basically two choices for Daffodils, white or yellow and that they were all around 12" tall. Times are a'changin'. Now you can select daffs that are miniature (5" - 6" tall), double cupped (pom-pom looking centers), dou-

John Scheepers.com

◖drought tolerant ⊹deer resistant

ble petaled, all different cup lengths from petite to those that look like Pinocchio's lyin' nose), and those with orange, pink and 'red' cups. There is a common misconception that all Daffodils can handle shade. Per Brent and Becky's Bulbs (a specialty mail-order bulb company in Virginia) only the Cyclamineus group of Daffodils are up to this challenge. Zones 3 - 7

⚜ Allium (Allium)
6" - 24" Sun - Part Shade. Spring, summer bloomers. White, rosey-violet, pink or yellow flowers. Alliums are always great accents. Most varieties require full sun but there are a few that perform on the shadier side of the tracks. Allium karataviense blooms in May and June with ball-shaped white flowers above broad, blue-green, ground-hugging leaves. It gets 8" tall. Nodding Onion (A. cernuum) has pink, dangling flowers in mid-summer that reach 10" - 12". Blooming around the same time is Allium moly. 'She' screams for attention with bright yellow umbrels topping out at 12" tall. The latest blooming Allium is thunbergii 'Ozawa'. This one doesn't begin the show until late September and parades its rosey-violet blooms into November. It grows between 6" - 12" tall. Zones 3 - 8

⚜ Quamash (Camassia)
24" - 30" Sun - Part Shade. Spring bloomer. White, lavender, blue or violet flowers. Quamash is a tall spring bloomer with an airy look. It does best in moisture-retentive soil. I love tucking them among Astilbes and Ligularias for early color. Quamash is a native that is rarely bothered by deer. Zones 4 - 8

English and Spanish Bluebells (Hyacinthoides)
12" - 15" Sun - Part Shade. Spring bloomer. Blue-violet, pink or white flowers. These deer-proof plants have hanging, bell-shaped flowers. English Bluebells (non-scripta) are very fragrant while Spanish Bluebells (hispanica) are not. Both naturalize well and are long-lived. Zones 3 - 8

Martagon Lily (Martagon)
3' - 6' Sun - Part Shade. Early summer bloomer. White, pinkish-purple or burgundy-red flowers. These are rarely seen in gardens, one reason why you want people oogling them in yours. Martagons have small, downward facing flowers with reflexed petals. They are slow growers but once they get established, they're breathtaking. Mine are six years old and have at least eight nodding flowers per stem. Martagons are harder to find at garden centers. It is easier to purchase them online at www.vanscheepers.com, www.plantdelights.com or www.oldhousegardenscom. But be forewarned. These beauties come at a price: $10 or more per bulb. Zones 3 - 7

⚜ Winter Aconite (Eranthis hyemalis)
4" Part Sun - Shade. Spring bloomer. Yellow flowers. Tiny, sweet flowers nestle atop dark green, fringed 'plates'. Being petite, they look best when planted in masses. Over time they will happily naturalize. Winter Aconite will bloom right through the snow. Zones 4 - 8

⚜ Wood Squill (Scilla)
4" - 6" Sun - Part Shade. Spring bloomer. White, blue or light pink flowers. Wood Squill will gladly keep marching forward and carpet your gardens. If you

feel they crossed the line, just dig 'em out where you don't want them. Most folks gravitate to the rich blue varieties but there are soft pink (bifolia rosea) and white (siberica alba) flowers as well. Zones 3 - 8

✛Grape Hyacinths (Muscari) 6" Sun - Shade. Spring bloomer. Blue, purple, white or soft pink flowers. This is another bulb that will rapidly spread, or naturalize if you prefer that description. The flowers are mildly fragrant. Deer tromp right on by these 'grape clusters'. Zones 4 - 8

Even though I am a 'passionate perennialist', I rely on workhorse annuals, especially in shade, to provide nonstop color May through October. Of course, being a low-maintenance gardener, I insist these annuals require little or no deadheading. It doesn't matter if they are in my garden, window boxes, hanging baskets or patio containers. The same rules apply. I will also not tolerate bi-weekly fertilizer applications with products like Miracle-Gro. I refuse to do this for my perennials and shrubs, so why should annuals get this special attention? The only time I fertilizer annuals is at planting time. I use Plant-Tone, a time-released organic fertilizer or Osmocote 14-14-14. This feeds them for three to four months. And by the time the fertilizer runs out, I'm just about to pluck the annuals out and toss them in the compost pile.

Here are a few more tips when working with annuals:

- Pinch the tips off at planting time. This promotes a fuller, more compact flowering plant instead of a spindly one.
- To reduce how often you have to water containers, work water retentive crystals such as Stockosorb into the potting medium. But be careful, a little goes a long way. Some potting mixes already have these incorporated so check the label first. These crystals can also be dug into the soil around a plant's roots (annuals, perennials, shrubs). They have a 'lifespan' of up to five years.
- To increase drama, build in shade annuals with striking foliage such as Coleus, Caladiums, Angel Wing Begonias, and Elephant Ears.
- When planting decorative containers or window boxes, I mix approximately ½ topsoil (amended with compost) and ½ potting soil together. This mix does not need to be watered as much and is less expensive that 'top shelf' bagged mediums. The trade off is that my recipe is heavier. So for all but the smallest containers, I incorporate packing peanuts, chunks of Styrofoam, plastic Easter eggs, pine cones, crunched up annual packs or plastic soda bottles to fill air space. This reduces the amount of potting medium needed and the overall weight of the container. Another approach is to fill larger containers with space-filling material and then set smaller pots of annuals on the 'fill'. Camouflage the flower-filled pots with some potting soil or spanish moss.
- When selecting containers, remember that pots made out of plastic, fiberglass and metal hold water longer than clay pots, unless the pot is glazed. Also, the larger the pot, the less often it needs watering.
- To keep thirsty shrub and tree roots from stealing water and nutrients from annuals planted nearby, place the annuals in pots in the ground so their space is protected from foraging roots of woodies.

The following annuals are no fuss, high scoring 'beauty queens'.

Browallia (Browallia) 10" - 14" Sun - Shade. Rich blue, soft blue, or white flowers. Browallia receives the MVP award in my garden, not only for its exceptional performance but also for its ability to trick folks into believing it's a perennial. This 'Energizer Bunny' blooms in sun or shade from May through the first heavy frost. Browallia is quite drought tolerant, making it a great substitute for thirsty Impatiens in dry shade. 'Endless Flirtation' sports crisp white flowers, 'Endless Sensation' has rich blue-purple flowers and 'Endless Celebration' has soft blue flowers.

Wax Begonia (Begonia) 6" - 16' Sun - Shade. White, pink or red flowers. Wax Begonias are a great pick for dry shade, especially those with white flowers that reflect light. Their leaves can be green or bronze-mahogany. In shadier spots I steer clear of the darker leaves because they are harder to see. No deadheading required.

Rex or Angel Wing Begonias 15" - 18" Part Sun - Shade. Pink, red, white or orange flowers. I love these plants for their distinctive leaves that fan out like angel wings. They add a wonderful tropical feel to the garden. When colder temperatures approach, I cut my favorites back, dig them up, spray the leaves with an insecticidal spray and bring them inside as houseplants. Dragon Wing Begonias, a cross between Angel Wing and Wax Begonias, can get 12" - 15" tall and have a sweeping habit with shiny green leaves.

Tuberous Begonias 10" - 12" Part Shade – Shade. White, pink, orange, yellow, salmon or bicolor flowers. Bright colored Tuberous Begonias add 'pop' wherever they're planted. They can be upright or trailing. Probably my favorite Tuberous Begonias are those in the Mandalay™ series. I trialed Mandalay 'Mandarin' in my gardens a few years ago and it was a showstopper. It reached 12" and was covered with dangling, bell-shaped, single-petaled, orange flowers spring through fall with no deadheading. There are also pink and white varieties. These also work well in hanging baskets and window boxes because of their arching posture.

Coleus (Solenostemon) 8" - 3' Sun - Shade. Foliage. Striking foliage colors, leaf shapes, forms and textures have made Coleus a top seller, surpassing many heavy flowering annuals. Coleus can grow upright or be trailing. The Kong Series has massive leaves. There are now cultivars available that are tolerant of full sun. Some of my favorites for shade include 'Freckles' (chartreuse and orange, 24" - 30"), 'Pink Chaos' (brilliant pink, white and green, 6" - 12"), 'Sedona' (burnished bronze, 18" - 24"), 'Gay's Delight' (screaming yellow with rich red veins, 24" - 30"), 'Saturn' (chocolate-maroon with splashes of chartreuse, 12" - 18"), 'Strawberry Drop' (petite red, chartreuse, burgundy and green leaves, 8" - 12") and Fishnet Stockings (sexy black lines throughout lime-green leaves). Coleus are great mixed with other annuals in containers but can make an eye-catching statement by themselves. They also jazz up shaded perennial beds that can become monopolized by Hosta. When combining Coleus, be careful not to mix too many different variegations or the effect can be overwhelming. And please, pinch off emerging flowers. This is one of those times when flowers play second fiddle. Being a tight wad, I like to save my favorite Coleus from Old Man Winter's death blow. I simply pinch them back to within 4" - 5", plant them in colorful glazed containers, spray their leaves with insecticidal soap and bring them inside to a brightly lit room.

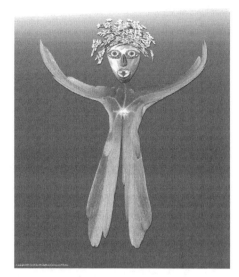

⚜Lobelia, annual Cardinal Flower (Lobelia) 4
- 10" Sun - Part Shade. Blue, white or blue and white flowers. True blue is a hard color to find in flowers but this annual group has a number of cultivars that deliver this mesmerizing hue. 'Techno Heat Blue' is stunning with intense cobalt blue flowers growing between 4" - 10" tall. 'Lucia Dark Blue' is a darker blue. All in the Techno series are more heat tolerant than others that usually flower less when the heat increases. There are more compact, edging plants as well as trailing varieties.

Impatiens (Impateins) 6" - 10" Part Sun - Shade. Pink, white, red, orange, apricot, yellow, salmon, purple and other colors. Impatiens walleriana (commonly referred to simply as 'Impatiens') and New Guinea Impatiens are the annuals that most folks associate with shade gardening. Impatiens walleriana requires consistent watering to look good, otherwise it mopes miserably. On the other hand, New Guinea Impatiens are more drought tolerant. This is good to keep in mind when planting in dry shade. New Guineas also have larger leaves and flowers. Variegated leaves are available in both groups.

⚜Wishbone Flower (Torenia) 2" - 16" Sun - Part Shade. Purple, blue, yellow, white or pink flowers. Wishbone flowers look a little like snapdragons. They bloom all season and are self-cleaning, requiring little or no deadheading. Their tubular flower shape makes then attractive to hummingbirds. 'Yellow Moon' is particularly showy with glowing canary-yellow flowers that are easy to spot in shade.

✿Flowering Tobacco (Nicotiania) 12" - 36" Sun - Part Shade. Red, pink, white, yellow, lime green or maroon flowers. These have to be one of the most fragrant annuals for scenting the night-time air. Flowers are carried on long stems with most of the foliage staying near the base. The blooms are star-shaped, tubular and nodding. Because of their, dare I say gangly, growth habit, they look best planted in tight groups or interplanted among perennials. Flowering Tobacco is a magnet for hummingbirds and hummingbird moths.

Elephant Ears (Colocasia) 36" - 60" Part Sun - Part Shade. Foliage. Ba-boom! Elephant Ear's massive leaves scream 'tropical'. They also scream water. As with any large leaved plant, adequate soil moisture is essential to replace water lost through transpiration. 'Illustris' (black leaves with lime-green veins), 'Mojito' (lime-green leaves splashed with black), 'Black Magic' (jet black leaves), and my favorites, 'Elena' and Xanthesoma 'Lime Zinger' (brilliant chartreuse leaves) create dramatic statements. In colder climates you can overwinter Elephant Ears in one of two ways. Treat it as a houseplant. When the temperature drops in fall, bring it inside to a brightly lit room. Or allow Elephant Ears to go dormant in your basement in a pot. Water it occasionally in winter. After danger of frost, relocate the pot outside in a sunny spot, water and enjoy another season.

🍂drought tolerant ⫶deer resistant

CHAPTER FIVE

Foliage Plants for Shade

Top Ten Ornamental Grasses

Please don't be fooled into thinking that ornamental grasses are only for sunny gardens. There are some that prefer cooler, shadier retreats over scorching sun. And their wispy blades provide a pleasing contrast to fuller figured plants like Hosta. Couple this with the fact that deer leave ornamental grasses alone and you'll be singing the Halleluiah Chorus.

When buying ornamental grasses, make sure you select 'clumpers', not those that spread rapidly by renegade roots (rhizomes) or above-ground stems (stolons). If the tag does not clearly state its mode of advance, ask. If you have fallen in love with a 'spreader', unless you want it to be a groundcover, sink it in the ground in a large pot to imprison the roots.

Grasses provide terrific winter interest. Leave them be in fall. Taller grasses benefit from staking so they keep a better posture when blasted by winter winds and snow. Once spring arrives, whack taller grasses to within a few inches of the ground. A power hedge trimmer comes in handy. To save time from raking up fallen blades, tie twine, bungee cord or duct tape around the grass's 'waist' before shearing. Some grasses have razor-sharp blades so use protective gloves. Shorter grasses like Black Mondo Grass can be 'deadleafed' by simply running your fingers through the clump and pulling out ratty or brown foliage.

The best time to divide grasses is in late winter or early spring after you've cut them back or 'combed' them. Depending on the grass, you may need a saw, ax, machete or chainsaw to slice the dense root mass.

⁙Gold Sedge (Carex elata 'Bowles Golden') 2' - 3' Part Sun - Part Shade. The bright yellow blades of this delicate grass are skinny and slightly arching. It looks terrific paired with fuller figured plants as well as those with yellow variegation in their leaves. Although many resources state this Carex likes to be planted near a water's edge, I have it in the middle of a dappled shade bed and it does fine. Could it do a tad better with more consistent moisture? Probably. Do I care? No. Zones 5 - 8

⁙Carex 'Ice Dance' (Carex morrowii) 12" - 16" Part Sun - Part Shade. 'Ice Dance' flows gracefully with its rich green leaves edged in crisp white margins. It forms tufted clumps that slowly spread. 'Evergold' has a similar habit but its blades are slightly narrower, and creamy-yellow and green. Zones 5 - 9

⁙Carex 'Treasure Island' (Carex ciliato-marginata) 6" - 10" Part Shade - Shade. I love this broad-leaved Carex! Green and white variegated leaves make a bolder display than its thinner siblings. You'll hit the jackpot when you pair it with Hosta and ferns. Zones 5 - 9

⁙Northern Sea Oats (Chasmanthium) 2' - 3' Sun - Part Shade. Late summer, fall blooms. Tan flowers. Northern Sea Oats has a bamboo look with arching seed heads. 'River Mist' is a green and white variegated variety. Northern Sea Oats is a clump former but it can seed aggressively where comfortable. I reduce its fertility by sheering off the flowers (seed heads) before they ripen. This plant is very versatile. I have planted it in dappled shade, full sun and in the water at the edge of my pond. Zones 3 - 8

⁖Black Mondo Grass (Ophiopogon p. 'Nigrescens')

6" - 12" Sun - Part Shade. Jet black, narrow blades swishing in the breeze are simply seductive. You can't help but want this 'little black dress' in your garden. It has pinkish-purple flowers in summer that turn into a 'necklace' of black beads in fall. Even though this grass is tagged as a Zone 6, I have grown it for years in my borderline Zone 5 garden. I plant it out of the path of winter winds, on the east side of my house. I also allow some fallen oak leaves to snuggle with it in fall. As with all black or dark leaved plants, surrounding them with gold or silver foliaged partners helps dark leaves 'pop'. Zones 6 - 9

⁖Wood Rush Grass (Luzula) 18" - 24" Part Sun - Shade. 'Ruby Stiletto' is a looker. She struts green blades with red tips and edges. It resembles Japanese Blood Grass. 'Ruby Stiletto' is compact and grows to 12". Zones 3 - 8

⁖Ribbon Grass (Phaleris) 2' - 3' Sun - Part Shade. Before I go any farther, this spreader must be contained or you will never see the end of it. Thankfully, shadier sites slow down its enthusiasm. 'Picta' is probably the most commonly sold, with green and white striped blades to 3'. 'Strawberries and Cream' (who wouldn't buy a plant with that name?) is similar to 'Picta' but has narrower blades with pink flushes on new growth. Zones 4 - 8

⁖Clump Bamboo (Fargesia) 8' - 10' Part Sun - Shade. Because I have a conscience and enjoy sleeping peacefully at night, I will only focus on clumping Bamboo. Clumpers spread several inches per year versus running Bamboos that can cross State lines. Fargesia n. 'Juizhaigou' will reach 10' in warmer zones but stays shorter 'up north'. It has small green leaves carried on canes that turn burgundy-red and then yellow as it matures. Fargesia rufa grows to 8' or less and has orangey-red canes. For a complete list, visit the American Bamboo Society's web site at www.americanbamboo.rog. And remember to look for the word, CLUMPING. Zones 5 - 8

⁖Gold Leaved Japanese Forest Grass, Hakone Grass (Hakonechloa macra) 12" - 24" Part Sun - Shade. Gold grasses really show well in low light. Two favorites are 'Aureola' with gold and green striped blades and 'All Gold' that has....guess. In my garden 'All Gold' stays quite a bit shorter than 'Aureola', topping at around 10" - 12" 'All Gold ' also

doesn't have the same sweeping arched blades but does stand out more because of its solid gold leaves. 'Aureola' was the Perennial of the Year in 2009. Zones 5 - 8

·ᴛ·Green Leaved Japanese Forest Grass, Hakone Grass (Hakonechloa macra) 12" - 24" Part
Sun - Shade Hakonechloa macra has sold green, arching leaves reaching 2' while 'Albo Striata' pulls the pinstriped look with white lines in 1' - 2' tall blades. Zones 5 - 8

·ᴛ·Multi-Colored Japanese Forest Grass, Hakone Grass (Hakonechloa macra) 8" - 16" Part
Sun - Part Shade. Several years ago I picked up a small pot of 'Nicolas' at a garden center. It looked pretty anemic but I felt sorry for it. What a great decision on my part! Now its lush arching green leaves turn a magical orange, red and light yellow in late summer. 'Naomi' does a similar trick, with her creamy-yellow and green leaves taking on shades of purple-red in fall. 'Beni Kaze' is another trickster with green blades that redden in cooler weather. Bravo! Zones 5 - 8

Top Ten Fine or Lacy Foliage Perennials

Lace and leather. Don't they make an intriguing pair? A similar effect can be made between lacy leaves that dance gracefully in the slightest breeze and large, full-bodied leaves that are not ashamed of their commanding figures.

Pairing these contrasting 'body types' creates a positive tension that turns heads. You can also create illusions with leaves. For example, if you place tall, lacy plants in the back of a border, the garden looks bigger than it really is. Fine-foliaged perennials can also soften or veil a vignette. Visualize looking through a long stemmed, Shredded Umbrella Plant's leaves to see a large, frosty blue Hosta surrounded by wispy, gold blades of Carex 'Bowles Golden'. Riveting.

First we will take a look at some fine-boned perennials and the next list will introduce you to 'Big Berthas'.

⁙**Maidenhair Fern (Adiantum pedatum)** 8" - 24" Part Shade - Shade. Foliage. There are many great ferns with delicate fronds. My pick for the easiest and most delicate is Maidenhair Fern. It has soft green fronds set in a circular pattern held up by jet-black, wiry stems. Maidenhair Fern has a mystical appearance as it emerges in spring. Himalayan Maidenfern (A. venustum) is a petite fern (8" - 10") with coppery-pink fronds on black stems in spring that change to soft green in summer. Zones 3 - 8

⁙**Fern-Leaved Bleeding Heart (Dicentra)** 8" - 15" Part Sun - Shade. Late spring, summer bloomer. White or pink flowers. All Fern-Leaved Bleeding Hearts have lacy foliage, many with a frosty blue hue. I am a big fan of the Heart series: 'King of Hearts' (rich rosy-pink), 'Ivory Hearts' (white), 'Candy Hearts' (medium pink) and 'Burning Hearts' (deep pink with white edges). An unusual cultivar, 'Spring Magic', has silver foliage and soft pink flowers. This was found in Adrian Bloom's Foggy Bottom garden in England. All Fern-Leaved Bleeding Hearts resent being divided but if you are feeling adventurous, do so in spring before they set bloom. Zones 3 - 8

Corydalis (Corydalis) 6" - 16" Part Shade - Shade. Late spring, summer, fall bloomers. White, blue, yellow, pink or purple flowers. These are relatives of Bleeding Heart and act as 'Ever-Ready Bunnies' in shade. They bloom May through September with no deadheading. They can be short-lived and reseed if happy. C. lutea has cheerful yellow flowers with ferny-green leaves. Less common but as impressive is the white corydalis, ochroleuca. C. bulbosa has purple flowers and gets 6" - 8". Be wary of C. sempervirens, a pink and yellow flowering lady that gets very leggy and is a biennial, not a perennial. The blue flowering Corydalis ('Blue Panda' and 'China Blue') go dormant in warmer temperatures and can be short-lived. 'Berry Exciting' is a relative newcomer with screaming yellow foliage and purple flowers. Zones 4 - 9

⊹Ornamental Grasses Part Sun - Shade. Narrow bladed, sweeping grasses are always safe matches with big partners. Please see the Top Ten list for winners in shade.

⊹Jacob's Ladder (Polemonium) 6" - 36" Sun - Part Shade. Spring bloomer. White, blue, apricot or lavender flowers. Jacob's Ladder can have solid green, bronze-purple or variegated leaves. It looks like a lacy fern. P. reptans only gets 6" - 8" tall and covers its green leaves with violet flowers. The variegated varieties are the rage. 'Stairway to Heaven' has pink, white and green leaves, 'Touch of Class' and 'Snow and Sapphires' have mint-green leaves with crisp white margins. 'Apricot Delight' has apricot flowers and green foliage. 'Purple Rain' has bronze-purple leaves with blue blooms. 'Northern Lights' is getting a lot of attention with its fragrant, bright blue flowers and rich green leaves. I suggest staying clear of 'Brise D'anjou'. It has a weaker constitution than others. Zones 3 - 8

Meadowsweet (Filipendula) 8" - 4' Sun - Part Shade. Summer bloomer. White or pink flowers. My top pick for shade is Filipendula ulmaria 'Aurea'. It has glowing, deeply serrated, gold leaves with white flowers and grows between 2' - 3'. Its only peeve is dry, sandy soil. 'Venusta', sometimes called 'Queen of the Prairie', has fluffy pink plumes that remind me of cotton candy. It and 'Elegans' (very pale pink flowers) can reach 4' or more in rich soil. Their exuberance is also displayed in how quickly they spread, although the less sun they get, the slower their stride. 'Variegata', on the other hand, at 3' has variegated green and yellowish-white leaves with white blooms and is a behaved clumper. 'Kahome' is also well mannered and the shortest of the Meadowsweets at 15" with medium pink flowers. Zones 4 - 9

❦Shredded Umbrella Plant (Syneilesis) 12"- 24" Part Sun - Shade. Summer bloomer. Pinkish-white flowers. This sassy plant always catches people's eyes. It pushes through the soil in spring like a closed umbrella covered with white fuzz. Then it spreads its wings and opens up to deeply divided, flat green leaves. Small, pinkish-white blooms emerge on thin stems above the foliage in summer. Plant Delight's Nursery (www. plantdelights.com) offers a variety called 'Kikko' with creamy-yellow and green leaves in spring before fading to green in summer. Very unusual. Because Shredded Umbrella Plants have long, leafless 'legs', I like to put 'foliage slips' in front of them like Astilbe and Jacob's Ladder. All Umbrella Plants are quite drought tolerant and gentle spreaders. Zones 5 - 8

⊹Goat's Beard (Aruncus) 10" - 5' Sun - Part Shade. Spring, early summer bloomer. White flowers. This family has members that barely reach 10" and others that soar to 5' or more. They all are long-lived and have delicate, astilbe-like white flowers that sway above ferny, mounded foliage. The 'baby' in the group, aethusifolius, has tiny, extremely ferny green leaves and puffy white flowers. Aruncus dioicus is the big boy at 5' in bloom. 'Misty Lace' and 'Kneiffii' fill in the gap at 24" - 3' tall. Zones 3 - 9

⁜Astilbe (Astilbe) 6" - 4' Sun - Part Shade. Summer bloomer. White, pink, purple, lavender or red flowers. All Astilbes have handsome, ferny foliage. Most cultivars have solid green leaves but some have a burgundy cast, others change colors in cooler weather ('Colorflash'), and then there is 'Color Flash Lime' with limey leaves that turn orange-red in fall. Two of the most petite Astible are 'Lilliput', (pink, 6" - 8") and 'Perkeo" (rosy-pink, 6"). Both have dark green, crinkly leaves and bloom in July. Check out the Top Ten Astilbes list for more on these ferny wonders, including early, mid and late season bloomers. Zones 3 - 8

photo courtesy of Daniele Ippoliti

✎Chocolate Bugbane, Snakeroot (Cimicifuga)

2' - 6' Part Sun - Part Shade. Late summer, fall bloomer. White or soft pink flowers. I am torn about what I love more about this plant; the lacy, chocolate leaves or the flowers. The elegant flower spires are incredibly fragrant and are also a nectar source for honeybees. But the leaves, oh the leaves are magnificent and draw attention long before the flowers appear. 'Brunette', 'Hillside Black Beauty', 'James Comton' and 'Atropurpurea' all get 4' to 5' tall. And how could you say no to 'Black Negligee'? 'Chocoholic' is the shortest at 2' to 3'. All have creamy white flowers. 'Pink Spires' has very soft pink blooms. Zones 3 - 8

Top Ten Perennials with Honkin' Big Leaves

Having looked as some petite, fine-leaved perennials now it's time to turn our attention to 'monster trucks'. The pairing of these 'unlikely couples' makes them intriguing. You know, like Beauty and the Beast; Shrek and Princess Fiona, and The Thing and Alicia Masters in The Fantastic Four (can you tell I'm a kid at heart?)

Part of what makes a captivating garden is contrasting foliage. Contrast can come from color as well as a leaf's size, shape and texture. Leaves entertain the eye before, during and after bloom. We should take greater advantage of this easy, low-maintenance way to add pop to a garden.

The only needy dimension of 'big kahuna' leaves is their thirst for water. With larger leaf surfaces comes greater water loss through transpiration. If you do not naturally have a wet area in your yard then plant these near downspouts (if you are not using water barrels), or work water retentive polymers into the soil around the roots, or build a mini-bog. Mini-bogs are easy to make and can be as small or large as you want them. For a single plant you can simply dig a hole about twice as the width of the container; place a plastic bag inside the hole as a liner; puncture a few holes in the bag to allow some drainage; put a few inches of soil on top of the plastic; insert plant and backfill with more soil. Ta da!

⁙Comfrey 'Axminster Gold' (Symphytum) 24" - 4' Sun - Part Shade. Late spring, early summer bloomer. Pinkish-blue or lavender flowers. I first saw this spectacular plant in one of my client's gardens. I was awestruck. Its huge, sweeping, banana-shaped, gray-green and gold leaves are incredible. It produces nodding lavender-blue flowers in spring. 'Axminster Gold' demands sharp drainage and enjoys a nutrient rich soil. It is primarily grown for its leaves. After flowering, whack it back hard to encourage a fresh new foliage display. Zone 5 - 7

⁙Pig Squeak (Bergenia) 8" - 18" Sun - Part Shade. Spring bloomer. White, pink or ruby-red flowers. You will either squeal with delight at Pig Squeak or turn your 'snout' at it. It has a very interesting architectural form. Kind of like a big cabbage. Pig Squeaks have large, leathery, green leaves that turn reddish-burgundy in fall. 'Bressingham Ruby' has rosey-pink flowers and stunning bronze-maroon leaves in spring and fall. Pig Squeaks have flower clusters that pop open in spring on top of 6" - 12" burgundy stems. Individual blooms don't last more than a few weeks, but if spent stalks are removed, more will come. And why is it called Pig Squeak? If you take a wet leaf between your fingers

❦drought tolerant ⁙deer resistant

and rub it, you'll hear a noise that sounds like a squealing pig (imagination required). Zones 3 - 8

⊹Purple Stemmed Angelica (Angelica gigas) 4' - 6' Part Sun - Part Shade. Summer bloomer. Purple flowers. Here is another funky plant. Purple Stemmed Angelica has huge, unusual leaves and fascinating, dome-shaped purple flowers. Large, tropical looking, leaves extend from bright burgundy stems. Angelica is usually tagged as a biennial or short lived perennial. Although not a long-lived specimen, it is worth every penny. Zones 4 - 7

⊹Giant Japanese Butterbur (Petasites) 36" - 42" Sun - Part Shade. Spring bloomer. Pink or white flowers. This is not a shy plant. It is the 'Big Papa' of leaves. Massive leaves up to 3' - 4' look a bit like Rhubarb's on steroids. It will overtake anything in its path if not restrained. Because of its sensational leaves, it is best used in wet areas or along the water's edge. There is a variegated variety, j. 'Variegatus' with creamy-yellow splotches on the leaves. Another interesting one is Yellow-leaved Butterbur (Petasites palmatus). It has enchanting golden leaves up to 1' across with pink flowers. This one is hardy only to Zone 6. All of these can be invasive, but the green leaved Butterbur will be the one leading the takeover. Zones 4 - 9

⊹Astilboides (Astilboides tabularis) 3' Part Shade - Shade. Summer bloomer. White flowers. The round leaves of Astilboides are gently notched on the edges and can reach 3' across and float 2' to 3' above the ground. White, plumy flowers that resemble Astilbe, soar on long stalks above the leaves. Yes, the flowers are impressive, but your eyes will always return to oogle the foliage. Zones 5 -7

⊹Rodger's Flower (Rodgersia) 30" - 4' Part Sun - Shade. Early summer bloomer. Creamy white to pink flowers. We need more Rodger's Flowers in our gardens. They prance large, heavily textured, '5-fingered' palmate leaves that are green or bronze. The flowers look like giant Astilbe plumes. R. aesculifolia has greenish-bronze leaves with very soft pink flowers. The foliage of 'Chocolate Wings' starts out chocolate and changes to bronze. 'Die Shone' has deep pink flowers while 'Fireworks' sports bright red-pink flowers echoed by a reddish tinge in the leaves. 'Dark Leaf' has burgundy-red leaves in spring, turning to green in summer. Zones 4 - 7

⊹Ligularia (Ligularia) 20" - 4' Part Sun - Part Shade. Summer bloomer. Yellow or orange flowers. All Ligularias have dramatic leaves. 'The Rocket' has thrilling, ragged edged, heart-shaped leaves; 'Little Rocket' echoes these but is one notch smaller in height. L. przewalskii is similar to 'The Rocket' but its leaves are more dissected and the stems are almost black. 'Othello' and 'Desdemona' have chocolate-green scalloped leaves; 'Britt-Marie Crawford' is an absolute knockout with rich chocolate, rounded leaves with purple undersides. 'Japonica' looks like a tender tropical with is deeply lobed, green

leaves. 'Osiris Fantaisie' and 'Osiris Café Noir' have large, leathery, serrated leaves with colors that vary from dark chocolate to bronzy green. Zones 4 - 9

🌿**Hosta (Hosta)** 2' or larger. Part Shade - Shade. Summer bloomer. White, lavender or purple flowers. Hosta is one of the first grandiose plants that gardeners think of for shade. And well so. Check out the Top Ten List for Monster Hostas. Zones 3 - 9

⚜**Ornamental Rhubarb (Rheum palmatum)** 6' - 8' Sun - Part Shade. Summer bloomer. Red flowers. These dramatic, deep green to dark red leaves with purple undersides, are meant for staring at, not eating. No pies here. The leaves are poisonous as with all Rhubarbs. This is not a shy wallflower. Give it room and a stage. R. palmatum can grow up to 5' and has green, palmate leaves and crimson flowers. R. Alexandrae has shiny green leaves and yellowish-white flowers. Zones 5 - 8 (Zone 6 for Alexandrea)

⚜**Ostrich Fern (Matteuccia struthiopteris)** 3' - 6' Part Shade - Shade. Foliage. Large, rich green, tapering fronds look like they should be fanning an emperor. Ostrich Ferns lend a tropical presence wherever they are planted. When happy, they can spread at a good pace from underground rhizomes. Other large ferns include Cinnamon Fern (Osmunda cinnemonea), Royal Fern (Osmunda regalis), and Interrupted Fern (Osmunda claytoniana). Zones 3 - 8

Top Ten Blue or Silver Foliage Perennials

Blue is a favorite color of many. It is a calming, serene color. Unfortunately blue is not as common in the floral world as other colors. Think about it. How many blue flowered perennials can you name compared to yellow or pink? Let's make it one step harder. How many blue fall blooming flowers can you name? See? And the task is just as hard with blue foliaged perennials. But oh, how gardeners covet this rich, calming hue in the garden.

Silver is another prized color. It drapes a garden in elegance. Silver, as well as gray, are the best colors to use as buffers between hot, contrasting colors, such as fuchsia and orange. They make great 'peacemakers'.

The first five perennials on this list 'sing the blues' with style, while the last five are the silver lining.

Hosta (Hosta) 6" - 4' Part Shade - Shade. Summer bloomer. White, lavender or purple flowers. Frosty blue Hosta are standouts in shade gardens. There are smaller cultivars like 'Blue Mouse Ears' (6"), 'Popo' (4" - 6"), 'Baby Bunting' (10") and 'Blue Cadet' (15") and then there are the big boys like 'Big Daddy' (36"), 'Blue Angel' (36"), 'Blue Umbrellas' (32"), 'Blue Mammoth' (34'), and sieboldiana 'Elegans' (32"). 'Fragrant Blue' (18") has sweet-smelling lavender flowers. All blue Hosta need as much shade as you can give them. The blue is actually caused by a wax coating on green leaves that 'melts-off' in sun and heat or gets washed off by dripping water. Zones 3 - 9

Fringed-Leaved, Fern-Leaved Bleeding Heart (Dicentra) 8" - 15" Part Sun - Shade. Late spring, summer, early fall bloomer. White or pink flowers. There are medium green, or gray-green leaved Fringed Bleeding Hearts but it's the icy, frosty blue foliaged knockouts that create excitement: 'King of Hearts' (deep pink); 'Ivory Hearts' (white), 'Candy Hearts' (medium pink), and 'Burning Hearts' (rosy-red with white edges). Zones 3 – 9

Japanese Bluebells (Mertensia pterocarpa var. yezoensis) 6" - 12" Part Shade - Shade. Spring, early summer bloomer. Blue flowers. This is a challenging plant to find for sale but when you do, grab it! It has blue-gray leaves that do not go dormant in summer like its cousin, Virginia Bluebells. It also stays much shorter but still has an arching nature to its stems. Zones 4 - 9

Chives (Allium flavum) 6" - 12" Sun - Part Shade. Summer bloomer. Yellow flowers. Rich blue, slender leaves send forth yellow flowers in early summer. The small dangling umbrels are a nice contrast to blue leaves. You need a cluster of three of more to make a nice show. I have these in dappled shade next to Coral Bell 'Citronelle' (yellow leaves), Japanese Painted Fern and dwarf Astilbes. Zones 4 - 9

Japanese Fan Columbine (Aquilegia flabellata) 3" - 5" Sun - Part Shade. Spring bloomer. White, blue and white, or plum and yellow flowers. These petite beauties have gray-blue leaves that are larger than other Columbine leaves plus they're fan shaped, hence the word 'fan' in their common name. Because of their diminutive size, it is good to place 3 or 5 together to make a statement. 'Alba' (white), 'Blackcurrant Ice' (plum and yellow), 'Ministar' (blue and white) and 'Blue Angel' (blue and white) are four in the flabellate group. Leaf miners can be an issue with all Columbines. You know you've got visitors when you see white, squiggly lines on the leaves. These insects are actually inside the leaf. The easiest way to deal with disfigured leaves is to prune them off. If a lot of the leaves have been munched, I cut the entire plant to within a few inches of the ground. This stimulates a new batch of fresh leaves that remain clean for the rest of the season. This approach is much better than reaching for a systemic insecticide. Zones 2 - 9

PerennialResource.com

⚜Lungwort (Pulmonaria) 8" - 12" Part Shade - Shade. Spring bloomer. Pink and blue flowers. 'Majeste' has solid silver-white leaves. 'Silver Bouquet', 'Silver Shimmers', and 'Diana Clare' look similar to 'Majeste' but have occasional blotches of green on their leaves. 'Samurai' flashes silver centers with narrow green margins. All Lungworts can get powdery mildew or ratty looking foliage after flowering. Don't tolerate this. Whack the leaves back to within a few inches of the ground and they will respond with a nice new set that remain captivating the rest of the season. Zones 3 - 9

⚜Dead Nettle (Lamium maculatum) 4" - 8" Part Sun - Shade. Spring, summer bloomers. Pink, white or rosey-purple flowers. Lamiums can have silver; green and white; green, gold and white; and gold and white leaves. But for this list we are focusing on the silver ladies. In my opinion the silver ones are the best. Silver foliage is choice for reflecting light in shady beds. Top performers include 'Pink Pewter' (pink flowers), 'Purple Dragon' (rosy-purple), 'Pink Chablis' (soft pink) and 'Cosmopolitan' (pink). 'Ghost' (rosy-purple flowers) breaks the stride of other Lamiums in that it gets taller (up to 14"). It makes quite a showy groundcover around trees. Whack it back in late winter to refresh the leaves and create a denser cover. 'White Nancy' with white flowers has failed my appreciation test. It tends to get leggy and die out in sections. 'Beacon Silver' is another one that gets low marks. It frequently gets fungal problems on its leaves later in summer. Zones 3 - 8

⚘drought tolerant ⚜deer resistant

⚜Siberian Bugloss (Brunnera) 10" - 15" Part Shade - Shade. Spring bloomer. Blue flowers. Siberian Bugloss has shapely, heart-shaped leaves in many color 'patterns'. The 'silveriest' cultivar in the family is 'Looking Glass'. Completely silver leaves that seem to shimmer are hard to miss in shade. 'Jack Frost' comes in next with silver leaves marked with green veining. 'King's Ransom' looks like 'Jack Frost' but has creamy-yellow margins. All have delicate blue, Forget'-Me-Not like flowers in spring. Sometimes in mid-summer, older leaves can get brown edges on them. Clean up their act by removing these and fresh new leaves will appear. Zones 3 - 7

⚜'Ghost' Lady Fern (Athyrium filix-femina X niponicum) 2' - 3' Part Shade - Shade. Foliage. 'Ghost' is an arresting fern with a very upright, narrow habit and silver, gray-green fronds with a burgundy stem. It looks quite different from one of its parents, Japanese Painted Fern, that has more sweeping, arching fronds and darker coloring. Zones 3 - 8

⚜Coral Bell (Heuchera) 12" - 18" Part Shade - Shade. Summer bloomer. Creamy-white or pink flowers. 'Checkers', 'Geisha's Fan', 'Mint Frost', 'Persian Carpet', 'Pewter Veil', 'Pewter Moon', 'Paris' and 'Prince of Silver' all display silver in their leaves, some more than others. I usually cut the flowers off Coral Bells (unless they are bright pink or red) so the attention is on the leaves. All of these listed have wishy-washy 'dirty' white or pale pink flowers (in my opinion) except 'Paris' that has large, deep rose blooms that last for weeks. Zones 4 - 9

Top Ten Yellow or Gold Foliage Perennials

Glowing yellow and gold-leaved perennials illuminate gardens, especially shady ones. Many such plants actually do better in part shade, even if they are listed for full sun. Their foliage doesn't bleach out or brown at the edges in light shade. Experiment for yourself. Plant a gold-leaved perennial or shrub in less sun and see what happens. You will most likely be impressed.

On the other hand, many of these 'glowing embers' will turn limey-green in full shade. If this happens, grab you spade and move the 'turncoat' to a spot that gets a tad more sun. This could even be an area where dappled light shines a little longer through the tree canopy. Bingo!

Hosta (Hosta) 6" - 4' Part Shade - Shade. Summer bloomer. White, lavender or purple flowers. Dwarf gold Hosta include 'Gold Drops' (6", lavender flowers), 'Maui Buttercups' (6", violet flowers), 'Cheatin Heart' (8", lavender flowers), 'Fire Island' (12", red stems, lavender flowers), 'Little Miss Sunshine' (11", lavender flowers on burgundy-red stems), and 'Gold Edger' (7", white flowers). Medium sized golds are 'August Moon' (16", white flowers), 'Choo Choo Train' (24", white flowers), and 'King Tut' (18", white flowers). Large golds are 'Sum and Substance' (36", white flowers), 'Parhelion' (32", a sport of 'Sum and Substance' that has a narrow, white leaf margin, lavender flowers), 'Gold Standard' (mostly gold with dark green margin, 24", lavender flowers) and 'Sun Power' (26", lavender flowers). Zones 3 - 8

Bleeding Heart (Dicentra) 24" - 34" Part Sun - Shade. Spring bloomer. Pink flowers. 'Gold Heart' makes you want to put on sunglasses. Screamin' yellow leaves and bright pink flowers get your blood pumpin'. 'Gold Heart' stays shorter and grows wider than green-leaved, spring blooming Bleeding Hearts. Another difference is its ability to hang on and not go dormant as early (or at all) as other spectabilis cultivars. 'Spring Gold' is a new yellow-leaved, ever-blooming (Fern-Leaved) Bleeding Heart that grows around 15" and has light pink flowers. Zone 3 - 8

Spiderwort (Tradescantia) 12" Part Sun - Part Shade. Summer bloomer. Violet flowers. 'Sweet Kate' is one of the few Spiderworts that is a 'behaved young lady'. She doesn't roam all over the place. Her brilliant gold blades can easily be mistaken for an ornamental grass. As with other Spiderworts, shearing it back by half or three quarters in mid-summer results in a neater clump. Occasionally 'Sweet Kate' will send up a green shoot. She is trying to return to her native roots, a sold green Spiderwort. Stop her. Otherwise the entire plant will eventually revert back to a green Spiderwort. Pinch off, or dig out, these naughty shoots. Zones 3 - 9

Coral Bell (Heuchera) 6" - 14" Sun - Shade. Summer bloomer. White, cream or pink flowers. 'Lime Rickey' (8", white flowers), 'Key Lime Pie' (8" - 10", pink flowers), 'Lime Marmalade' (10", cream flowers), and 'Citronelle' (12", cream flowers) glow in shady beds. 'Citronelle' has silver undersides, a fuzzy surface and remains a gold beacon even in heavier shade. 'Electra' (8" -10", white flowers) has bright chartreuse leaves marked by stunning red veins in spring. It loses the red color as the heat rises. 'Tara' (8" - 14", white flowers) is similar to 'Electra' as far as how it colors, but the red is more of a blush across the entire leaf. Zones 4 - 9

Meadowsweet (Filipendula ulmaria 'Aurea') 2' - 3' Part Sun - Part Shade. Early summer bloomer. White flowers. 'Aurea' has ferny yellow foliage with misty white flowers in early summer. I prune the flowers off to put the spotlight on the delicate foliage. Removing the flowers also stimulates lusher foliage. 'Aurea' looks especially nice next to Hosta 'June' (blue and chartreuse), purple Coral Bells and violet-blue flowering Geranium 'Rozanne'. It is easy to divide anytime in spring or summer. Zones 4 - 9

Deadnettle (Lamium) 8" Part Sun - Shade. Spring, summer bloomer. White or pink flowers. 'Aureum' and 'Beedham's White' have gold leaves with white center stripes and white flowers. 'Golden Anniversary' has the same leaf but lavender-pink flowers. All Lamiums look super placed along paths, retaining walls and at the front of borders. They also work well in containers and window boxes but remove the plants in fall and winter them over in the ground. Lamiums can be propagated by division or stem cuttings, spring through summer. The running stems (called stolons) form roots at various intervals. Use a sharp knife to cut stem pieces from the 'mother plant' and replant. Zones 3 - 9

Japanese Forest Grass (Hakonechola macra) 12" - 24" Part Sun - Shade. Foliage. 'All Gold' has solid gold, slightly wider blades with a less cascading nature than other Japanese Forest Grasses. 'Aureola' has thinner, gold and white variegated leaves but appears mostly gold. These clump-forming grasses are pricey so divisions are the way to go. They can be divided at any point before September. Zones 5 - 8 (although they can handle Zone 4 if planted in a sheltered area)

Columbine (Aquilegia) 11" - 18" Sun - Part Shade. Spring bloomer. White, pink, blue or purple flowers. I love these bright yellow-leaved Columbines! 'Mellow Yellow' has very lacy leaves and gets up to 18" while 'Woodside Gold' has broader leaves and produces pink, white or blue flowers. 'Leprechaun Gold' mixes it up with gold leaves splashed by green blotches. It gets 10" - 12" with purple flowers. All Columbines can be short-lived let some go to seed. I have been thrilled that my gold-leafed Columbines have seeded true and not reverted back to green leaves. Zones 3 - 8

⊹Sedge (Carex) 10" - 3' Sun - Part Shade. Foliage. 'Bowles Golden' is a snappy perennial for shade. Its thin, spaghetti-strap, golden blades look fetching near puckered-leaved Hostas, Japanese Painted Ferns, and burgundy flushed Astilbe foliage. It gets 2' to 3' tall. 'Evergold' has yellow blades with narrow green margins. Its tufts max out at 10" to 12". Zones 4 - 8

Bellflower (Campanula carpatica, persicifolia)

4" - 18" Sun - Part Shade. Summer bloomer. Blue flowers. I have glowing, golden domes of 'Dickson's Gold' at various intervals on both sides of a shade garden path. They act like runner lights on an airplane runway. Petite golden leaves with 'pinked' edges are decorated with blue, bell-shaped flowers in summer. I would be fine without the flowers. That's how great these 4" - 6", upside down bowls look. 'Blue-Eyed Blond' is a yellow-leaved, peach-leaved Bellflower with a narrow, upright habit, growing between 12" - 18". It has blue flowers as well. Zones 4 - 9

Top Ten Black, Burgundy or Chocolate Foliage Plants

These sultry colors can add 'sex appeal' to a garden but a little goes a long way. You can overdo it with too many chocolate leaves, unlike chocolate candy. Dark colors help companion plantings to jump to the foreground as stars while they play a quiet backup role. Too many dark foliaged perennials elicit a somber mood or can get totally lost in full shade. Surrounding them with bright colored flowers or leaves is the ticket. For example, Black Mondo grass or 'Obsidian' Coral Bell standout when surrounded with Creeping Yellow Jenny (tiny yellow, button leaves) or 'Beedham's White' Lamium (yellow leaves with narrow white stripes). Also, brown, bronze or black foliaged perennials are challenging to see against dark mulches. Bottom line, when planting these sultry colors, think who is next to, or under them, in the bed.

The following list features mostly perennials but there is an annual and tropical that I couldn't resist adding. They just were too delicious to resist.

⚜Ligularia (Ligularia) 20" - 4' Part Sun - Part Shade. Summer bloomer. Orange or yellow flowers. The large dark, glossy leaves of Ligularias create great drama. 'Desdemona' and 'Othello' have a purple tone to their leaves in spring that slowly fades to brownish-green in summer. I find it difficult to tell the two apart but 'Desdemona' has a slighter richer substance and darker stems. On the other hand, 'Britt-Marie Crawford' leaves no guesswork. Her huge, scalloped leaves are seductively dark and shiny. All three shoot up orangey-yellow, daisy-shaped flowers on long stalks in August. As with other large leaf plants, Ligularias need a moisture-retentive soil to handle the amount of water lost through their leaves. For those of you with sandy soil, move to the next plant on the list. Zones 4 - 9

⚜Coral Bell (Heuchera) 5" - 24" Part Sun - Shade. Late spring, summer bloomer. White, pink, red or creamy-white flowers. Dark leaved Coral Bells sizzle. And many of the names sound as delicious as they look: 'Brownies' (24", olive-brown leaves, white flowers), 'Cherries Jubilee' (7", chocolate-purple leaves, red flowers), 'Mocha' (16", chocolate leaves, white flowers), 'Beaujolais' (12", burgundy-bronze leaves with a silvery overcast, white flowers), and 'Chocolate Ruffles' (10", chocolate leaves with burgundy undersides and curly edges, creamy-white flowers). 'Petite Pearl Fairy' is remarkable for the punch it gives for such a small plant (6", burgundy-chocolate leaves, pink flowers). The 'black sheep of the family' include 'Obsidian' (10", very shiny leaves), 'Blackout' (12" - 18"), and 'Black Beauty' (10", curly leaves). All have black leaves and creamy-white flowers. Zones 4 - 9

⚜Bugbane, Snakeroot (Cimicifuga) 2' - 6' Part Sun - Part Shade. Late summer, fall bloomer. White or soft pink flowers. Rich chocolate and sublime perfume are a girl's best friends. The dark leaved Bugbanes provide both. 'Brunette', 'Hillside Black Beauty', 'Atropurpurea', 'Black Negligee' 'James Compton' and 'Chocoholic' are all 'womanizers'. They have long, slender, fragrant flowers that dance in late summer breezes. Zones 3 - 8

⚘⚜Bugleweed (Ajuga) 3" - 6" Sun - Shade. Spring bloomer. Violet-blue flowers. 'Black Scallop' makes you want to eat it right up. Big, black, shiny, crinkly leaves matt the ground, eliminating any hope for weeds to press through. The spiky rich flowers bloom for three weeks or more in spring. I like using 'Black Scallop' around yellow and marmalade Coral Bells for a striking foliage combo. I have also combined it with Geranium 'Rozanne' for three seasons of divine violet-blue flowers coupled with attractive black leaves. Zones 4 - 10

⚘Foamy Bells (Heucherella) 10" Sun -Shade. Summer bloomer. Pink flowers. I fell in love with 'Burnished Bronze', a glossy, bronze, mounded perennial from the moment I laid eyes on it. The individual leaves are nicely dissected and good size. Soft pink flowers finish the look. A tough love, drought tolerant perennial that works well in groups. 'All Gold' Japanese Forest Grass looks fantastic next to it. Zones 4 - 9

⚜Black Mondo Grass (Ophiopogon p. 'Nigrescens') 6" - 12" Sun - Part Shade. Jet black, narrow blades swishing in the air are simply seductive. Black Mondo Grass has pinkish-purple flowers in summer that turn into a 'necklace' of black beads in fall. Even though this grass is tagged as a Zone 6, I have grown it for years in my Zone 5 garden. I plant it out of the path of winter winds, on the east side of my house. I also allow some fallen oak leaves to snuggle with it in fall. One of my favorite combos is sweeps of Black Mondo Grass and 'Bowles Golden' Carex surrounded by 'Purple Dragon' silver Lamium. Zones 6 - 9

⚜Cardinal Flower (Lobelia) 24" - 5' Sun - Part Shade. Summer bloomer. Red flowers. Many gardeners are familiar with native Cardinal Flower that has jolting red flower stalks in midsummer and hummingbirds competing for sipping time. 'Queen Victoria' has the same stately flowers but reddish-bronze foliage instead. She grows to 3' - 5'. Slightly shorter is 'Fan Scarlet' with the same dark foliage and red flowers but a mere 24" tall. All of the catalogs list these two as perennials but I have found them to be short-lived perennials at best. And even though I have tried to get them to reseed, I've met total failure. So I simply treat these as annuals and buy them in 4" pots. They are so striking, I am willing to make these accommodations. I'm a pushover. Zones 5 - 9

⚜Chocolate Joe Pye Weed (Eupatorium rugosum) 3' - 5' Sun - Part Shade. Fall bloomer. White flowers. 'Chocolate' grows in dry shade and features billowy white flowers covering textured, chocolate leaves. A bonus is its shiny, purple stems. Sometimes I like to pinch the stems back by 1/3 their height in June for a more heavily flowering, compact plant in September. The flowers are great for cutting and last a long time in a vase. It also makes a pretty cut flower. Zones 3 - 7

Elephant Ears (Colocasia) 3' - 60" Part Sun - Part Shade. Foliage. Here is the tropical on this list. Even though Elephant Ears is native to warmer climates you can still winter it over inside, either as a houseplant or in a dormant state in a cool basement. Elephant Ear's massive, heart-shaped leaves scream 'Bahama Mama'. Accordingly, as noted in other sections, adequate water is a necessity for such impressive leaves. 'Illustris' (black leaves with lime-green veins) and 'Black Magic' (jet black leaves) are outstanding specimens. Another topical worth exploring is New Zealand Flax (Phormium). These look like super-sized grasses with very wide blades. 'Purpureum' has purple-red leaves (3' - 4') and 'Platt's Black' has deep, reddish-brown leaves (2' - 3'). *Tropical*

Sweet Potato Vine (Ipomoea) Sun - Part Shade. Foliage. And here is the annual. 'Black Heart' has big, heart-shaped, nearly black leaves while 'Midnight Lace' has the same rich coloring but finely cut leaves. 'Sweet Caroline Sweet Heart Red' features smaller, heart-shaped, reddish-purple leaves and her twin, 'Sweet Caroline Bronze' has lacy, copper leaves. All Sweet Potato Vines have wonderful trailing habits that makes them perfect for flowing onto paths, over retaining walls, and in hanging baskets. *Annual*

Top Ten Bicolor or Tricolor Foliage Perennials

Multi-colored leaves add a fun, psychedelic dimension to a garden. Of course you don't want too many different combinations together or you may be reaching for Pepto Bismal. Break up 'stripes and plaids' with some solid-colored leaves. Splish, Splash. Fizz, Fizz. You'll feel better.

I did not include Hosta on this list even though there are many bicolor and even some tricolor winners. See the Top Ten Hosta lists for great picks.

⊹Athyrium niponicum (Japanese Painted Fern) 8" - 24" Part Shade - Shade. Foliage.
Japanese Painted Ferns are the lush 'painted ladies' of the shade garden. The silver, burgundy-red, and green fronds make all 'bed partners' look good. 'Silver Falls', 'Ursula's Red', 'Regal Red', 'Red Beauty', 'Pewter Lace' and 'Burgundy Lace' have richer coloring than 'Pictum'. These ferns look especially lovely near heavier substance perennials like Hosta, Ligularia and Rodger's Flower. Japanese Painted Ferns are easy to divide in spring. Zones 4 - 9

Toad Lily (Tricyrtis) 24" - 28" Part Shade - Shade. Late summer, fall bloomer. White,
raspberry or lavender flowers. 'Tricolor' has pink, white and green mottled foliage with white and purple spotted flowers. The description may make you queasy but its appearance is unique. If you can't handle the 'plaids and stripes' look, pinch off the flowers. 'Gilt Edge' has soft green leaves edged in creamy yellow with white flowers. 'Blonde Beauty' struts bright, chartreuse-yellow leaves with some green streaks in spring. The leaves tone it down a notch with summer heat. Flowers are raspberry with some chocolate mixed in. Zones 5 - 8

⍦⊹Coral Bell (Heuchera) 9" - 12" Sun - Shade. Summer bloomer. Creamy-white flow-
ers. There are oodles of bicolor Coral Bells available so for this list I focused on tricolor picks. 'Green Spice' is a showy Coral Bell that thrives in sun or shade. It has large green, silver and red leaves. 'Sonic Smash' is a knockout with 5" - 6" leaves that are green and silver with burgundy veins. 'Tiramisu' and 'Miracle' are like chameleons. In cooler weather (spring and fall) they have pinkish, red and chartreuse leaves but in summer they change to a chartreuse, green and silvery wardrobe. Interesting. Zones 4 - 9

Painter's Palette (Persicaria virginiana) 24" - 30" Part Sun - Part Shade. Late summer,
fall bloomer. White or light rosy-red flowers. 'Painter's Palette' was a gift to me from another perennial collector. I cherish it. It has creamy yellow and green, triangular leaves with a burgundy-red 'V' in the center. The airy, rosy-red flowers are interesting but less so than the leaves. 'Red Dragon' has even showier leaves but I have not been able to winter it over even though it is rated Zone 5 in some catalogs. 'Silver Dragon' displays

silver leaves with a soft green 'V' and a bronze center and edge. Both 'dragons' have white flowers and most resources list these two as only hardy to Zone 6. Zones 5 - 9

⊹ Woods Phlox (Phlox stolonifera) 8" Part Sun - Shade. Spring bloomer. Pink flowers. All of the ground-hugging Phlox in the stolonifera group are remarkable. Don't be confused and think I am talking about Moss or Creeping Phlox (Phlox subulata). Moss Phlox drives me nuts with how often grass seeds in it. Phlox stolonifera has low growing, matted leaves that easily choke out weeds. Delicate stems shoot forth from this weed mat in spring, topped by starry flowers that bloom for weeks. Phlox s. 'Variegata' has creamy-white leaves with green centers and bright pink flowers. Fabulous! Zones 4 - 8

⊹ Foamflower (Tiarella) 6" - 8" Part Sun - Shade. Late spring, summer bloomer. White or pink flowers. Foamflowers have green leaves with chocolate-black beauty marks. The leaves vary in size and shape. Some standouts are 'Black Snowflake' (white flowers), 'Crow Feather' (soft pink flowers), 'Mint Chocolate' (creamy-white), 'Iron Butterfly' (white flowers), 'Sugar & Spice' (pink and white flowers) and 'Neon Lights' (pink and white flowers). 'Heronswood Mist' has fuzzy, creamy-green leaves and white flowers. Most Foamflowers are clump formers but 'Cascade Creeper', 'Eco Running Tiger', and 'Running Tapestry' spread slowly and make magnificent groundcovers. For more on Foamflowers, see the Top Ten 'Ellas' list. Zones 3 - 9

🍂 Foamy Bells (Heucherella) 6" - 18" Sun - Shade. Early summer bloomer. White flowers. 'Stoplight' will stop you in your tracks. The leaves have glowing red centers surrounded by bright yellow margins. Forget the flowers. 'Alabama Sunrise' looks similar to 'Stoplight' but it is marketed as more tolerant of heat and humidity. And then 'Golden Zebra' entered the traffic circle. Its red center is so large that the yellow leaf margin is dwarfed in comparison. 'Sweet Tea' had me ordering more the minute I planted one. It has three leaf colors; apricot, orange and burgundy in spring that shifts to cinnamon, orangey-yellow and russet in summer and fall. All Foamy Bells have neat, compact foliage mounds. These Foamy Bells can be pricey so propagate what you have. They divide easily anytime from spring through late summer. For more on Foamy Bells, see the Top Ten 'Ellas' list. Zones 4 - 9

⊹ Jacob's Ladder (Polemonium) 1' - 2' Sun - Part Shade. Spring bloomer. Lavender flowers. 'Stairway to Heaven' is the most reliable variegated Jacob's Ladder I've grown. It has green, white and pink flushed leaves in spring and grows to 2' in flower. After blooming, shear off spent flowers to create an impressive ferny mound that transitions to green and white in summer. Other solid performers are 'Touch of Class' and 'Snow and Sapphires' with mint-green leaves surrounded by crisp, white margins. Zones 3 - 8

PerennialResource.com

❦✛Cushion Spurge (Euphorbia) 12" - 20" Sun - Part Shade. Spring bloomer. Yellow flowers. This family has a lot of funky members with foliage that is much showier than the flowers. 'First Blush' (pink, white and green leaves) and 'Bonfire' (burgundy-red and orange leaves) are attention getters. Both have yellow flowers and benefit from a hard shear after blooming to promote a neat, tight mound. Don't be timid when whacking these. I shear them by one third to half their height. If you have sensitive skin, wear gloves as the sap may cause a rash. I left the best for last. 'Ascot Rainbow' blew my muck boots off. It is taller than the others at 20" with bold yellow and green variegated leaves that take on a pinkish-orange hue in cooler weather. It is very stiff-stemmed and looked great all year without any shearing. Zones 5 - 9 ('First Blush' handles Zone 4)

❦✛Dead Nettle (Lamium) 4" - 8" Part Sun - Shade. Spring, summer bloomer. White, pink or purple flowers. These are workhorses for dry shade. Bicolor cultivars include 'Beedham's White' (chartreuse leaves with a white stripe); 'Purple Dragon', 'Orchid Frost' and 'Pink Pewter' (silver leaves with green margins); 'Friday' (green and yellow leaves) and 'Shell Pink' (green leaves with white stripe). 'Anne Greenaway' is a tricolor with green, gold, and white leaves. Zones 3 - 9

✛Siberian Bugloss (Brunnera) 10" - 15" Part Shade - Shade. Spring bloomer. Blue flowers. Siberian Bugloss has rich blue flowers that look like Forget-Me-Nots. Brunnera macrophylla, the species, has green leaves and can self seed a lot. You can decide if this is a good or bad trait. The bicolors are much handsomer and more behaved. 'Jack Frost' has silver leaves with green veins, 'Variegata' and 'Hadspen Cream' have green leaves with bold white margins, and 'Emerald Mist' is a bolder version of 'Langtrees' (green leaves with white flecks rimming the margin). Zones 3 - 7

CHAPTER SIX

The Photo Gallery

Welcome to the shade family's wall of portraits. Similar to my first book, *The Ultimate Flower Gardener's Top Ten Lists*, this book was written to introduce fascinating plants as well as tips for designing and caring for showcase gardens. Obviously it is not a glossy, coffee table book meant for decoration. I want you to use it as a resource for shopping at garden centers and online. The pictures on the following pages are teasers for other beauty queens mentioned in this book. There are also a few snapshots of my gardens for plant combination possibilities. Some great web sites for photographs of plants in this book are PerennialResource.com (www.perennialresource.com); Proven Winners (www.provenwinners.com); Plant Delights Nursery (www.plantdelights.com); Estabrook's Nursery (www.estabrooksonline.com); Cold Climate Gardening (www.coldclimategardening.com); Dave's Garden (www.davesgarden.com); Terra Nova Nurseries (www.terranova.com) and Perry's Perennial Pages (www.uvm.edu/~pass/perry) hosted by horticulturist Dr. Leonard Perry from the University of Vermont.

One of my shade beds in spring

Astilboides
Part Shade – Shade
Summer bloomer

Coral Bell 'Electra'
Sun – Shade; Late spring,
summer bloomer
Photo courtesy of PerennialResource.com

Browallia 'Illumination'
Sun – Shade
Annual
Photo courtesy of ProvenWinners.com

Campanula 'Dicksons Gold'
Part Sun – Part Shade
Summer bloomer
Photo courtesy of PerennialResource.com

Siberian Bugloss 'Jack Frost'
Part Shade – Shade
Spring bloomer
Photo courtesy of PerennialResource.com

Corydalis 'Berry Exciting'
Part Sun – Shade
Summer, fall bloomer
Photo courtesy of Terra Nova Nurseries

Athyrium filix-femina
'Frizelliae'
Part Shade – Shade
Photo courtesy of PerennialResource.com

Campanula 'Blue-Eyed Blonde'
Sun – Part Shade
Summer bloomer
Photo courtesy of Terra Nova Nurseries

Checkered Lily
Sun – Part Shade
Spring bloomer
Photo courtesy of JohnScheepers.com

Purple Coral Bell surrounded
by Creeping Yellow Jenny

Cushion Spurge
'Ascot Rainbow'
Sun – Part Shade
Spring bloomer
Photo courtesy of PerennialResource.com

Geranium macrorrhizum
'Bevan's Variety'
Sun – Shade
Spring bloomer
Photo courtesy of BluestonePerennials.com

Athyrium 'Dres Dagger'
Part Shade – Shade
Photo courtesy of PerennialResource.com

Japanese Painted Fern 'Ursulas Red'
Part Shade – Shade
Photo courtesy of Terra Nova Nurseries

Mukdenia 'Crimson Fans'
Sun – Part Shade
Spring bloomer
Photo courtesy of Terra Nova Nurseries

Clematis 'Comtesse de Bouchaud'
Sun – Part Shade
Late spring, summer bloomer
Photo courtesy of PerennialResource.com

Japanese Forest Grass 'Nicolas'
Part Sun – Part Shade
Photo courtesy of PerennialResource.com

Japanese Forest Grass 'Aureola'
and Corydalis lutea
Part Sun – Shade; Summer, fall bloomer

Toad Lily 'Imperial Banner'
Part Sun – Shade
Fall bloomer
Photo courtesy of Terra Nova Nurseries

Hellebore 'Raspberry Ripple'
Part Shade – Shade
Spring bloomer
Photo courtesy of Barry Glick

Fern-Leaved Bleeding Heart 'King of Hearts'.
Part Sun – Shade
 Summer, fall bloomer
Photo courtesy of PerennialResource.com

Foam Flower 'Neon Lights'
Part Sun – Shade
 Spring bloomer
Photo courtesy of Terra Nova Nurseries

Foamy Bells 'Sweet Tea'
Sun – Shade; Spring bloomer
Photo courtesy of PerennialResource.com

Hosta 'Empress Wu' Part
Shade – Shade; Summer bloomer
Photo courtesy of PerennialResource.com

White Shooting Star
Part Shade – Shade
Spring bloomer

Lousiana Iris 'Black Game-
cock' Sun – Part Shade
Summer bloomer
Photo courtesy of Niels Mulder

Pink Cardinal Flower
Sun – Part Shade
Summer Bloomer

Winter Aconite
Part Shade – Shade
Spring bloomer

Rodger's Flower 'Chocolate
Wings' Part Sun – Part Shade
Summer bloomer
Photo courtesy of Sunny Border Nurseries

Solomon's Seal 'Grace Barker'
also called 'Striatum'
Part Shade – Shade
Spring bloomer
Photo courtesy of Plantdelights.com

Coral Bell 'Georgia Peach'
Sun – Shade; Late spring,
summer bloomer

Photo courtesy of PerennialResource.com

Trout Lily Part
Sun – Shade
Spring bloomer

Photo courtesy of JohnScheepers.com

Foamy Bells 'Golden Zebra'
Sun – Shade; Spring bloomer

Photo courtesy of PerennialResource.com

Xanthosoma 'Lime Zinger'
Part Sun – Part Shade

Photo courtesy of Terra Nova Nurseries

Bugbane 'Hillside Black
Beauty' Part Sun – Shade
Late summer, fall bloomer

Photo courtesy of PerennialResource.com

Shredded Umbrella Plant
Part Sun – Shade
Summer bloomer

Photo courtesy of Plant Delights Nursery

Martagon Lily
Part Sun – Part Shade
Early summer bloomer
Photo courtesy of WaysideGardens.com

Lady's Slipper
Part Shade – Shade
Spring bloomer
Photo courtesy of Plantdelights.com

Phlox g. 'Triple Play'
Sun – Part Shade
Spring bloomer
Photo courtesy of Sunny Border Nurseries

Barrenwort 'Amber Queen'
Part Sun – Shade
Spring bloomer
Photo courtesy of Plantdelights.com

Happy Trails shade container
Photo courtesy of PerennialResource.com

Summersweet 'Ruby Spice'
Sun – Part Shade
Summer bloomer
Photo courtesy of Bailey Nurseries

shade side bed in spring

Hosta 'Praying Hands'
Part Shade – Shade
Summer bloomer
Photo courtesy of PerennialResource.com

Red fruit of Jack-in-the-Pulpit
and Trillium in late summer

Monkshood and Liliums.
Sun – Part Shade
Summer bloomer

My shade bed with
blue gazing ball

Redbud canadensis
Sun – Part Shade
Spring bloomer
Photo courtesy of Bailey Nurseries

Bleeding Heart 'Gold Heart'
Part Sun – Shade. Spring bloomer

Variegated Jacob's Ladder, blue Hosta and
Fern-Leafed Bleeding Heart

Comfrey 'Axminster Gold'
Sun – Shade. Spring bloomer
Photo courtesy of Dr. Leonard Perry

One of my shade gardens

Woodland Peony, Japanese Forest Grass
and Primrose

Happy gardening from
Sergio, Evan and Kerry Mendez

CHAPTER SEVEN

Garden Design Tips

Top Ten Design Tips for
Sensational Shade Gardens

The steps for designing a glorious garden in shade echo many of the same for sunny spaces. Light assessment, plant selection and layout, and bed preparation are essentials for both. Sure, there are some different considerations, but for the most part the below recommendations are applicable to sound garden design in general.

❧ Seeing is believing. Be honest about the amount of sunlight, or lack thereof, that your garden actually gets. No fair pushing the 'light meter' and baptizing your garden part sun simply because that is what you want it to be. Buying the right plants for the right light brings great results. Doing otherwise may have you pulling your hair out. Review the notes on assessing shade in Chapter 1.

❧ For mesmerizing gardens spring through fall, plant a mix of flowering perennials and shrubs that peak in different seasons. Of course, additional standout foliage plants will be constant contributors all three seasons. Here are some tips for making sure you have waves of colorful blooms April through October:

- Get a comprehensive mail-order catalog like Bluestone Perennials (www.bluestoneperennials.com) that has over 1,000 perennials and shrubs for zones 3 - 8. A great perennial and shrub reference book is good too.
- Thumb through the pages and create a list of plants that meet your garden's conditions (light, hardiness zone). For listing purposes, make three columns on a piece of paper (or a computer spreadsheet if you are more computer literate than I am). The columns are sorted by a plant's mature height: tall (over 3'), medium (1' - 3') and short (1' or under). Write the names of the plants you would like to have in your garden in the appropriate column. Include the plant name (including cultivar), flower color, bloom time, spacing requirements, and any special features (i.e., fragrant, striking foliage, foliage goes dormant in summer)
- On a piece of graph paper, use a scale of one foot equals one inch for simplicity sake. Draw the dimensions of your garden.
- Think of the garden in three *broadly defined* rows for beds 5' or wider (two rows for beds 3' to 4' in width).
- When placing plants from your columns into the design, start with plants in the tallest column. Then place the mid-border plants (1' - 3') and finally the front of the garden plants (1' or less).
- Don't be too rigid when placing plants in the design. Allow some taller plants to come forward, giving the garden a more natural look.
- The larger the plant, the fewer you need to make an impact.
- Make sure you have spring, summer and fall bloomers in the back, middle and front of the garden for continuous color

✌ Because the majority of shade blooming perennials and shrubs bloom in spring and early summer, it is important to incorporate no-fuss annuals for continuous flowers all season. Check out the Top Ten Annuals list for winners.

✌ Many folks can be impatient when it comes to enjoying lush, mature shade gardens. I'm no different. We want *Better Homes and Gardens* NOW…no…yesterday! But with shade gardens it is important not to ignore a plant's spacing recommendations. If we cram plants closer together than recommended, the plant's roots are competing for a limited amount of nutrients and water. We set them up for slower growth and compromising results. Better to abide by the spacing recommendations and plant annuals as fillers for the first year or two.

✌ Foliage is the backbone of gardens, especially shade gardens. For bewitching shade gardens, include a mix of foliage colors, shapes, textures and overall plant forms to anchor the show.

✌ Pleasing, 'eye-candy' gardens are the result of planting multiples of the same plant versus the 'gum drop' look. 'Gum drop' gardens feature one of everything from the plant buffet table. This can cause upset stomachs. Plant in groups of threes, fives, sevens…you get the gist. This doesn't mean you cannot have single specimens or even numbered groupings. Just don't do so with abandon. Place plants off-center from each other when digging them in. Think triangles and zig-zags, not straight lines.

✌ Repetition is another key to beautiful gardens. Incorporate the same plants at various intervals throughout the garden. Repeated plants don't necessarily have to have same flower color, as long as they're in the same (genus) family and look similar. Also, when repeating plant groups in the garden, try to site them at different depths in the bed. Pull some forward and place others farther back. This looks more natural.

✌ Anchor larger gardens with flowering shrubs, evergreens or smaller trees. This reduces maintenance and provides structure. Larger gardens also benefit from incorporating paths that breakup the space and allow access to plants for maintenance. You should never be stepping directly on garden soil to do your 'handiwork'.

✌ Plant spring, summer and fall blooming bulbs, as well as spring ephemerals, to add another layer of flower color to shade beds. Bulbs can be drilled (I use a bulb auger and power drill) in the narrow channels between perennials and shrubs. This layering effect works wonders for creating color-jammed gardens.

✌ When planting under trees where root competition for water and nutrients is a factor, use plants that are drought tolerant. Review the Top Ten list for drought tolerant shade perennials. When purchasing these 'camel-like' beauties, buy smaller pots. These are easier to dig into tough planting sites than larger pots with more mature root systems. Not to worry. These young'uns will wiggle their little roots in between tree roots and do just fine. Be sure to give them some supplemental watering their first year or two to get them off to a good start.

Top Ten Design Tips for Dry Shade

For some reason many folks shudder at the thought of gardening in dry shade. I'm here to comfort you with proven ways to transform these barren spaces to lovely panoramas. Simply select plants from the Top Ten Perennials for Dry Shade list and follow the below recommendations.

✿ Tree roots are 'big bullies' and notorious for stealing water from thirsty perennials. When prepping a garden under trees, please don't rototill. Tree roots are a drag to tear through plus the process can be stressful to trees. Rather, prepare the bed by shoveling 1" to 2" of loamy soil over the existing grass, weeds or sad-looking soil and rake smooth with a landscape rake. Do not put down a thicker soil layer. This can stress underlying tree roots. Also be careful not to build up soil against a tree's trunk. Now place 6 to 8 pages of newspaper over the thin layer of soil, wet the paper and shovel 2" of mulch on top. Mulch can be compost, aged manure or finely shredded wood. Allow this to sit for four to six weeks for easier planting through the paper. If you are itchin' to get going, you can dig plants right through the mulch and slice holes in the paper.

✿ To make installing plants easier, purchase smaller containers (4" or 6" pots) instead of one or two gallon containers. The less mature roots don't need as large a planting hole.

✿ When digging in plants, add some slow-release fertilizer to the holes. Plant-Tone is a great organic choice; Osmocote 14-14-14 is a synthetic option.

✿ Remember that even drought tolerant perennials need extra watering initially to overcome transplanting stress and for developing great roots. Water every second or third day (taking into account natural rainfall) for two, preferably three weeks and then ease off.

✿ In those instances when you can't help yourself and you want to plant thirstier plants in drier spots, create a man-made bog to retain water or use water retentive crystals around their roots.

✿ If planting closer than 18" from a tree trunk, use perennials with smaller root systems to minimize stress to both tree and perennial.

photo courtesy of Daniele Ippoliti

๛ Many gardeners pay little heed to spacing recommendations on plant tags. We assume suggested spacing applies to others, not ourselves. We want lush looking gardens right from the get go. Let me urge you to 'follow the rules', especially when planting under trees. These shade plants already have tougher conditions that perennials planted in shade created by a building or fence. They're competing against trees for light, water and nutrients. Planting perennials closer together just makes it tougher.

๛ Apply a nutrient-rich mulch such as compost, aged manure or finely shredded wood to shade gardens once a year. This provides nutrients as the material breaks down, reduces evaporation and reduces weeds (another competitor for light, water and nutrients).

๛ Dry shade can be caused by overhangs. Consider putting in a stone drip line below eaves or make sure you have a watering system to reach thirsty roots stuck there. Soaker hoses under mulch are a good solution.

๛ Dry shade can be in areas where irrigation systems or sprinklers can't reach. For example, the back of my large shade gardens remain relatively dry after watering due to the limited reach of sprinkler heads. Use drought tolerant plants in these hard to water spots.

Top Ten Tips for Designing with Foliage

Admit it or not, leaves are the backbone of perennial gardens, and especially in shade. Leaves play an invaluable, and usually thankless, role. When interviewed by a national gardening magazine about how I design sensational, three season gardens, I gave foliage much of the credit. Great leaves complement flowers and bring out their best. Leaves can also hide eyesores and carry the interest when there are no blooms in sight. And because the majority of shade perennials bloom in spring and early summer, foliage is the star for the second half of the 'show'.

When designing gardens in sun, I count on at least one out of three perennials to contribute striking leaves. But in shade, this ratio increases to two out of three. Now don't panic and think I've blackballed flowers. There are many exquisite shade plants that have both intriguing foliage and flowers. After all, shade plants need to 'have sex in the garden' too to produce baby seeds, and flowers are essential for this!

If you need more convincing that leaves are the stars in shade, consider that they:
- are attractive spring, summer and fall (and some in the winter as well)
- require very little care. Less maintenance is good!
- can enhance the beauty of neighboring flowers
- can dramatically 'set the mood' of a garden
- contribute a range of artful shapes and textures unmatched by flowers
- are easier to design with then their flowering counterparts. You don't have to consider when they bloom and how their flower colors work together
- can capture our attention in a way few flowers can. A foliage garden's beauty is more subtle, intriguing, and invites longer gazes than sunny borders

Below are ten tips for creating a foliage tapestry second to none, and certainly not to flowers.

Don't plant too many dark-foliaged plants together. The resulting feeling can be very somber plus dark colors are harder to see, especially in shade. When using chocolate, black, brown or bronze leaves, place yellow, gold or silver foliaged bedmates near them. These colors play off each other and make a striking statement. For example, put two or three vase-shaped, 'Sun Power' Hosta (bright yellow, deeply ribbed leaves, 24") in front of one large Cimicifuga 'Hillside Black Beauty' (lacy, chocolate-black leaves, 4' - 5'). Now you have the tango.

Cascading or sweeping branches generate a serene feeling. Working some of these throughout a garden, or along a path, or at the top of a wall, adds a relaxing touch. Any of the Japanese Forest Grasses are exceptional choices for this effect.

In contrast to the above, bold, upright foliage leads your eye upward and adds a vertical dimension to the garden. Now a lush leaf canopy, gracefully stretching tree branches, or flickers of blue sky become part of the picture. Think of how your eye follows the tall, rich green fronds of Ostrich Fern (4' - 5') or slender, slightly arching stalks of Giant Solomon's Seal (5' - 6').

❧ Ephemerals are breathtaking in spring. But when they dive underground in summer, the celebration party ends. Take their disappearing act into consideration when planting them. Either plant annuals in their empty 'seats' or site perennials nearby that have large, unfurling leaves to fill their void. Hosta, Astilbes, and Japanese Painted Ferns are good partners.

❧ Don't group too many different variegated plants together or motion sickness can occur. When placing a variety of variegated plants together, one way to create an interesting combo is to placing plants with 'reverse' variegation near each other. For example, separate a gold margined, green leaved Hosta from a green margined, gold leaved Hosta with a solid leaved plant that repeats one of the variegated colors.

❧ Let ferny, delicate leaves play with the big boys. The contrast is electrifying. If finer leaves are placed behind large, broad leaves, the garden appears deeper than it really is. The opposite if you reverse the playing field.

❧ Take pictures of your foliage garden in black and white. This can be an eye-opening exercise to see how interesting foliage shapes, textures, and forms can be without the benefit of color.

❧ Use foliage to unify a garden and to build continuity among all the beds in a landscape. For example, use yellow foliaged plants periodically down the length of a garden bed. Place some at the front of the bed, some mid-border, and others in the back. This repetition of the same color carries the eye along. Now repeat that same color in other gardens. Now the landscape works together as a whole with individual beds being tied together by a 'common thread'. Make sure the foliage color you pick as the 'connector' is a bright one that can easily be seen from a distance. Yellow, caramel or white are all good choices.

❧ Allow foliage plants to grow close together. This 'melts' the design into one harmonious picture. Plus overlapping leaves shade the soil, minimizing the number of weeds that can grow. Another benefit of foliage plants is they don't have the same nutrient-rich soil requirements as their heavy flowering counterparts. This means more foliage plants can happily coincide in tighter spaces because they're satisfied with being on a 'diet', less available food per square foot.

❧ Include shade tolerant evergreens for winter interest. Boxwood, Holly, Pieris, Rhododendron and Yews all make strong statements. Ornamental Grasses are also nice winter ornaments. See the Top Ten lists for shade loving evergreens and ornamental grasses.

Top Ten Tips for Designing with Hosta

There are hundreds of impressive Hostas. Why not quilt a garden of just these? You couldn't ask for a more low-maintenance, drought tolerant, luxurious display. Here are some tips for starting your masterpiece.

🌿 When selecting Hosta don't just consider the leaf color, size (height and width), and flowers. Also think about the overall plant shape. Some Hosta are vase-shaped. They are narrow at the base and the leaves are upright and slowly fan out at a higher point. 'Krossa Regal', 'Praying Hands' and 'Sagae' fall into this group. Some Hostas have rippling leaf edges such as 'Stiletto', 'Medusa' and 'Pineapple Upsidedown Cake'. There are those with cup-shaped leaves like 'Love Pat', 'Abiqua Drinking Gourd' and 'Big Daddy'. Leaves can be very puckered, ribbed or smooth; shiny or dull; and narrow or wide. Most petioles (stems) are green or red. Red-stemmed cultivars include 'Red October', 'Designer Genes', and 'Fire Island'. There are so many 'faces' to Hostas!

🌿 If you have ever designed a garden around one flower color (monochromatic), you know that the small addition of one other color really makes the design pop. This strategy also works with Hosta beds. But instead of a 'non-conforming' flower color, add plants with ferny, delicate, or airy foliage to offset bold leaves. Japanese Painted Fern, Maiden Hair Fern, Filipendula 'Aurea' and Astilbes are all possibilities. Another angle is to use inanimate objects tucked next to, or barely underneath, Hosta leaves. I love decorating Hosta beds with shiny, blue gazing balls. I tuck various sizes at random points among the leaves. The change of texture plus the ball's reflection are magical. I also place fun little statutes, small birdbath basins and other artsy pieces in the Hosta garden. Amuse yourself. I do.

🌿 Create a 'mini-Hosta village' as a cute focal point. By definition miniature Hostas are 4" - 6" tall. You can mix gold, blue, green and variegated gems at the front of garden or at a path's entrance. Decorate with little fairies, gnomes or even toy train sets. Use your imagination. PerennialResource.com is a super web site that provides information about thousands of perennials, including miniature Hosta.

🌿 Don't plant too many different, variegated Hosta together. Break up the patterns with solid-colored Hosta leaves.

🌿 Plant ephemerals between Hosta for great spring color. Ephemerals are woodland perennials that bloom in spring and then go dormant as the temperature rises. They finish their 'flower dance' before Hosta leaves unfurl. Hostas gracefully 'drop the curtain' to cover up the spring bloomers' exit. Check out the Top Ten Ephemerals list for possibilities.

🍃 When gardening in full shade, reach for blue-leaved Hosta. These thrive in darker locations. The frosty blue color is caused by a waxy coating on the leaves. This 'melts away' in sun, revealing green leaves beneath. I prefer blue Hosta with white flowers. These flowers show better than lavender or purple in low light.

🍃 Plant low growing, shady groundcovers around Hosta as colorful 'stitching' to the quilt. These also contribute weed-smothering action. To appreciate the colorful leaves and/or flowers of these groundcovers, space Hosta farther apart. Some lovely groundcovers include Lamuim, Creeping Yellow Jenny, Yellow Star Flower (Chrysogonum) and Bugleweed (Ajuga).

🍃 Keep Hosta leaves looking nice by saying no to chomping slugs and snails. Leaves disfigured by holes or shredded sections are particularly distracting in a Hosta theme garden. Thick leaved Hosta and those with puckering are least bothers by 'slimers'. For effective ways to wage war on snails and slugs, check out the Top Ten list for keeping them in line.

🍃 If you insist on putting Hosta in full sun, then at least use varieties that tolerate this insult. Some sun-resistant Hosta include 'Patriot' (green leaf with white margin, lavender flowers), 'Royal Standard' (green leaves, fragrant white flowers), 'Honey Bells' (green leaves, fragrant lavender flowers), 'Francee' (green leaf with white margin, lavender flowers) and 'Striptease' (dark green leaf with gold center and white strip, light lavender flowers). In fact, all green leaved Hosta are very sun tolerant as is the commonly used 'Undulata Albomarginata' (green centers with white edge).

🍃 Hosta with fragrant flowers are highly desirable around patios, porches, entrances, entertainment areas and below windows that are kept open to catch lovely summer breezes. As a general rule of thumb, I usually cut Hosta flowers off to direct attention to their leaves. Not so with these 'perfume bottles'. There is a Top Ten list of my favorites. By the way, it does not hurt Hosta to remove their flowers. All this does is funnel more energy back into lush leaves.

Top Ten Design Tips for Flowering Shrubs

There are so many pluses for adding flowering shrubs to your landscape. By definition a shrub is a woody plant that branches at its base. They come in a tremendous range of sizes from only several inches tall to those that stretch up to 15 feet. They can be deciduous or evergreen.

- They provide lovely color from flowers, fruits and/or foliage
- Most shrubs are quite hardy, need minimal care, and demand less water compared to 'thirstier' annuals or perennials
- They add interest and 'bones' to the landscape. They are good under-story plantings for taller trees
- Certain varieties make pleasing hedges for privacy
- They can make striking focal points. A few 'strutting peacocks' are Daphne 'Carol Mackie'; Hydrangea 'Little Honey'; Weigela 'My Monet'; and Sambucus 'Sutherland Gold'
- Shrubs can hide eye-sores. Use evergreens for yearlong cover-up
- They help 'tie' a house, or other strong vertical objects, to the rest of the landscape
- Shrubs can unify a landscape by using some of the same varieties in different areas around the property
- Shrubs act as erosion-control mechanisms for steep areas

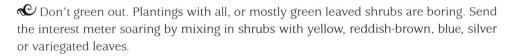

- Shrubs quickly dress-up a new home's foundation since most are fast growers versus trees that typically mature more slowly. Plus shrubs are usually less expensive than trees
- They can help reduce noise pollution

❧ Don't green out. Plantings with all, or mostly green leaved shrubs are boring. Send the interest meter soaring by mixing in shrubs with yellow, reddish-brown, blue, silver or variegated leaves.

❧ Create tension. I'm not talking the tension from telling my teenage son for the umpteenth time he cannot have the car that afternoon. I'm referring to pairing delicate-leaved shrubs next to heftier ones.

❧ Incorporate a mix of evergreen and deciduous shrubs. This is especially important at the front of the house where it makes sense to hide some of the foundation during winter months.

❧ Allow proper spacing between shrubs. Don't be fooled by young plants in small pots. Shrubs planted too closely eventually grow into a tangled mass, become misshaped, and are more prone to insect and fungal diseases. To calculate where to dig the holes for adjacent shrubs, take half the measurement of each mature shrub's width and add these together. This is the planting distance apart, measured from the center of each planting hole. If you prefer to see more space between the shrubs, then add additional footage between planting holes.

❧ Buy plants that mature to fit their allotted space (height and width). Don't try to force (prune) shrubs to fit into a size 6 when they are really a size 12. There are many great compact shrubs available that resemble their bigger brothers but remain petite.

❧ Allow adequate space between the shrub and the foundation (and other structures). One way to calculate the planting distance from the foundation is to take half the diameter of the mature shrub's width and add two feet to this. Also take into consideration drip lines, overhangs, and crashing winter snow and ice. The plants need adequate space to branch out and room for their roots to spread in all directions. Good air circulation is also important.

❧ Use drought tolerant shrubs in sandier soils or where watering is an issue. And apply the same approach to wet areas by planting shrubs that love playing in the mud.

❧ Remember to consider Bambi and friends. If you live in an area besieged by munchers, plant lower browse plants. A deer's eating preferences can change by region. The best bet is to get a list of low browse plants from your local cooperative extension office.

❧ In general, smaller shrubs look better planted in groups of 3, 5, 7 – odd numbers – just as most perennials do.

❧ Choose shrubs that will not block windows, entrances or infringe upon walkways when mature. Also don't plant shrubs with messy fruits or flowers next to sidewalks or driveways.

Top Ten Perennial Combinations

Obviously this list is very subjective but many of the combinations listed are those that hundreds of visitors have asked about in shade beds. There are so many fabulous combinations; please do not assume this is an exclusive list. Have fun mixing up your own favorites.

As a general rule, when creating combos in shade I try to include two plant with great foliage or form to carry the show for three or more seasons. I grouped three different perennials in each vignette. Typically, the smaller the plant's size, the greater the number I plant to balance the display. I also used color echoing to unify the grouping and create more drama. Color echoing is when a color is repeated in two or more plants. The color could come from flowers, foliage or stems. Finally, I noted the range of light conditions with each vignette and its zone.

Part Shade - Shade. Zone 4 (possibly 3). Astilbe 'Montgomery' (burgundy-red flowers, July); Japanese Painted Fern (foliage plant, silver and green leaves with burgundy veins) and Lamium 'Pink Pewter' (soft pink flowers, May-June-August, silver leaves)

Part Shade - Shade. Zone 5 (possibly 4). Hosta 'June' (foliage plant, frosty blue and chartreuse leaves); Japanese Forest Grass 'Aurea' (foliage plant, variegated gold and green, cascading blades) and Fern-Leaved Bleeding Heart 'King of Hearts' (pink flowers; June-September, frosty blue, delicate leaves).

Part Shade - Shade. Zone 4. Coral Bell 'Caramel' (creamy white flowers, June-July, large caramel leaves); Jacob's Ladder 'Stairway to Heaven' (lavender-blue flowers, May-June, pink, white and green variegated, ferny leaves) and Astilbe 'Veronica Klose' (rosy-lavender flowers, June-July)

Part Shade - Shade. Zone 5. Black Mondo Grass (foliage plant, narrow black blades, listed as a zone 6 perennial but I've found it tougher); Creeping Yellow Jenny (foliage plant, ground-hugging yellow leaves, insignificant white flower), Lenten Rose 'SP Sally' (soft yellow, nodding flowers, April-May, rich green, leathery leaves).

Part Shade - Shade. Zone 5. Carex 'Bowles Golden' (foliage plant, narrow, yellow blades); Yellow Wax Bells (soft yellow flowers, September-October, maple-shaped green leaves); and Hosta 'Fragrant Blue' (light lavender, fragrant flowers, June-July, frosty blue, ribbed leaves).

Part Shade - Shade Zone 3. Bleeding Heart 'Gold Heart' (pink flowers, April-May-June, bright yellow leaves); Bugbane 'Brunette' (creamy-white, fragrant flowers, August-September, chocolate ferny leaves); and Ligularia 'Little Rocket' (yellow flowers, July-August, green heart-shaped leaves with ragged edges).

⨏ Part Shade. Zone 4. Astilbe 'Peach Blossom' (soft peach, fragrant flowers, June-June, medium green foliage); Coral Bell 'Georgia Peach' (creamy-white flowers, June-July, glowing peach leaves with a silvery overlay); Woodland Peony (white flowers, April-May, great seed pods with blue-black berries in pink shell, green leaves).

⨏ Part Shade - Shade. Zone 3. Goat's Beard 'Misty Lace' (white astilbe-like flowers, June-July, ferny, green leaves); Siberian Bugloss 'Variegata' (gentian blue, forget-me-not flowers; May-June, heart-shaped green leaves with bold white margins); and Fern-leaved Bleeding Heart 'Luxuriant' (dark pink flowers, May-September, blue-green leaves).

⨏ Part Shade. Zone 5. Rodger's Flower 'Chocolate Wings' (soft pinkish-white, astilbe-like plumes, July, bronzy, highly textured leaves), Cardinal Flower cardinalis (red flowers, July-August, dark green leaves); and Japanese Forest Grass 'Nicholas' (foliage plant, green and yellow-green blades turn orange-red in late summer and fall).

⨏ Part Shade - Shade. Zone 3. Maidenhair Fern (delicate, light green, swirled fronds carried by jet black stems); Coral Bell 'Obsidian' (cream flowers, May-June, shiny black leaves); and Foamflower 'Neon Lights' (pink and white flowers, June-July with rebloom, light green leaves with dark chocolate centers).

Top Ten Annual
Combinations for Shade Containers

Container gardening has become the rage. You can transform a blah entrance into a magnificent focal point with some well appointed, lushly planted urns or add a dash of color and fragrance to a shady retreat. Creating your own masterpiece is a fun way to express the Picasso in you and it doesn't have to be an expensive 'painting'. Just get your hands in the potting soil and let it fly!

There are three design components when creating containers: thrillers, fillers and spillers. Sounds like an out of control party. The thriller plant is for vertical interest and is positioned in the center or back of the container. It makes a bold statement. Fillers are thriller 'want-to-be's. They cluster around the foot of the thriller. Fillers are usually 'full bodied' and billowy in nature. Then the spillers finish the masterpiece by cascading over the container's edge. When designing your container, go wild and pack in lots of plants that will make a spectacular statement. This is not the time to be shy. Rarely do pots bursting with bodacious color disappoint; it is the anemic, skimpy looking ones that sadden. There are too few opportunities in life to pull out all stops and go wild; let potting containers be one of them.

As noted in the Top Ten annuals list, use a time-released fertilizer to provide a slow feed for three to four months. Plant-Tone and Osmocote (14-14-14) are two time-released products. You can also use a liquid fertilizer at half strength once a week, in addition to the time-released fertilizer, if the urge hits you. It's never hit me!

As I began creating this list of annual combinations, I knew I had to go to the expert, Proven Winners. Proven Winners has eliminated the guesswork for great annuals and they also provide opulent shade container designs (as well as those for sun). Any annual that wears the coveted 'PW' label has passed Proven Winners unforgiving 'muck boot camp'. These 'warriors' passed rigorous control tests conducted at trial stations across the United States, Canada, Europe, South Africa, and Japan. The plants had to have superior flowering and be disease resistant. If an annual made it through this challenge, it should make it in my container.

The following design combinations are from Proven Winners. Some are more mounded displays, without the soaring thriller. Those with theme descriptions are diagrammed on Proven Winners' web site, www.provenwinners.com. Each plant is labeled as a thriller (T), filler (F), or spiller (S) in the combinations. The number of each plant needed will depend on the container's size. Remember, the more, the merrier. Trust your time-released fertilizer and potting medium to fuel their needs in cramped quarters.

๛ Banana Split: (T) Red Banana (Ensete), green leaves with dark red undersides, 36" - 96" tall; (F) New Guinea Impatiens 'Infinity Scarlet', red flowers, dark green leaves, 10"

- 14"; (S) Sweet Potato Vine (Ipomoea) 'Sweet Caroline Purple', black/purple leaves, 6' - 8"; (S) Swedish Ivy (Plectranthus) 'Troy's Gold', yellow leaves, 10" - 12"

ᴥ Dots with Dash: (T) New Guinea Impatiens 'Infinity Dark Pink', dark pink flowers, 10" - 14"; (F) Lungwort (Pulmonaria, perennial) 'Gaelic Spring', pink flowers, lime-green, spotted leaves, 8" - 14"; (S) Wishbone Flower (Torenia) 'Summer Wave Amethyst', amethyst flowers, 8" - 10"

ᴥ Fascination: (T) Carex 'Orange Sedge', bronze blades, 12" - 16"; (F) Osteospermum 'Melon Symphony', salmon flowers, 8" - 14"; (F) Spurge (Euphorbia, perennial zone 6) 'Efanthia', yellow flowers, burgundy and green leaves, 14" - 20"

ᴥ Happy Trails: (T) Coleus 'Freckles', yellow and orange leaves, 24" - 30"; (F) New Guinea Impatiens 'Infinity Orange Frost', soft orange flowers, black/purple leaves, 10" - 14"; (S) Creeping Yellow Jenny (Lysimachia, perennial) 'Goldilocks', yellow leaves, 2"; (S) Vinca (Vinca minor, perennial) 'Illumination Vinca', yellow leaves with dark green margins, 3" - 6"

ᴥ Silver Anniversary: (T) Dwarf White Striped Sweet Flag (Acorus, perennial) 'Variegatus', green and white striped blades, 6" - 15"; (T) New Guinea Impatiens 'Infinity White', white flowers, 10" - 14"; (F) Coral Bell (Heuchera, perennial) 'Green Spice', creamy-white flowers, green and silver leaves with burgundy/purple veins, 8" - 14"; (S) White Licorice Plant (Helichrysum), silver leaves, 8" - 12"

Provenwinners.com

ᴥ (T) ColorBlaze Coleus 'Dark Star', dark purple leaves, 12" - 24"; (F) New Guinea Impatiens 'Infinity White', white flowers, 10" - 14"; (F) Coral Bell (Heuchera, perennial) 'Dolce Blackcurrant', coral flowers, purple leaves with silver accents, 8" - 16"; (S) Wishbone Flower (Torenia) 'Summer Wave Blue', true blue flowers, 8" - 10"

ᴥ (T) Begonia 'Big Rose', pink flowers, 12" - 24"; (F) Shamrock (Oxalis) 'Charmed Wine', light pink flowers, dark plum leaves, 12" - 16"; (S) Dead Nettle (Lamium, perennial) 'Pink Chablis', pink flowers, silver leaves, 8" - 12"; (S) Browalia 'Endless Flirtation', white flowers, 10" - 14"

❧ (T) ColorBlaze Coleus 'Dipt in Wine', burgundy-red and yellow leaves, 20" - 36"; (F) Tuberous Begonia 'Nonstop Fire', orange flowers, 8" - 12"; (F) Shamrock (Oxalis) 'Charmed Velvet', light pink flowers, black leaves, 12" - 16"; (S) Browalia 'Endless Flirtation', white flowers, 10" - 14"

❧ (T) Golden Variegated Sweet Flag (Acorus, perennial), 'Ogon', yellow and green blades, 6" - 14"; (F) Double Impatiens 'Rockapulco Orchid', double orchid flowers, 10" -20"; (S) Browallia 'Endless Sensation', lavender-blue flowers, 10" - 14"; (S) Dead Nettle (Lamiastrum, perennial) 'Herman's Pride', yellow flowers, silver and green leaves, 8" - 12"

❧ (T) ColorBlaze Coleus 'Dark Star', dark purple leaves, 12" - 24" ; (F) Coral Bell (Heuchera, perennial) 'Dolce Mocha Mint', coral flowers, silver-laced leaves, 8"- 16"; (S) Browalia 'Endless Illumination', lavender-blue flowers, 10" - 14"; (S) Licorice Plant (Helichrysum) 'Licorice Petite', silver leaves, 8" - 12"

Top Ten Tips for Accessorizing Shade Gardens

Shade gardens have a quiet, seductive beauty. Dressing them up with a few, well-placed accessories can make them beauty queens.

❧ Create a focal point. Focal points direct the eye and have a commanding presence. Perfect for an 'understated' shade garden. Focal points can be objects such as a decorative urn, armillary, unique piece of artwork, water fountain, wind spinner, gazing ball on a stand, statuary, trellis, obelisk, or a handsome birdhouse on a support. Here is a different idea. How about a wire-framed topiary covered with Boston or English Ivy? Gardener's Supply Company (www.gardeners.com) sells labrador, poodle, pug and jack russell frames. Modify these as you like to create your own pooch or cat.

❧ Use flower-filled containers for color accents. There are many super, no-fuss annuals for shade that will add boisterous blooms 24/7. Containers can be grouped together on a patio or set right in the garden among lush leaves. You can super-size the show by making the container itself eye-popping as well.

❧ Infuse colors less commonly found in shade plants with the help of garden accents. For instance, gentian blue is one of my favorite colors but there are few shade perennials with this flower color. Orange is my teenage son's color preference, and one I have surprisingly acquired a taste for. Yet, once again, it is pretty uncommon in the shady world of flowering shrubs, perennials and annuals. Solution? Place a garden piece of your pleasure decorated in that color. You can make the effect as bold or as subtle as you like depending on the size of the piece. Another way to inject your underrepresented color is with spray paint. Simply spray dried flower heads of Astilbe, Hydrangea, Hosta, Goatsbeard and others with your prized color. It is okay to be silly!

❧ Gentle outdoor lighting in the shade garden can be magical at night. Of course, solar lighting is not a great choice in shade. Low voltage or battery powered outdoor lighting are the best options. There are many different lighting styles to choose from.

❧ Paths provide grace and functionality. A path leads you somewhere. Either to a quiet sitting area, focal point, water feature, into another garden room, out of the garden, you name it. There should always be a purpose for a path. It should not lead you to a dead end with nothing to look at or accomplish (I know that is the type A in me talking). A path can be straight or curvy. Sinuous paths make the garden seem bigger and less formal. Paths can be made from a variety of material. Pine needles, shredded wood chips, brick, pea gravel, flagstone or other solid materials. Turf is not the best choice in shade. Allow plants along a path's edges to periodically sweep onto the surface. This softens edges and creates a more relaxed feeling. As far as a path's width, 12" to 18" is manageable for one person's stroll. If two people are strolling together, then 3.5' to 4' is better (unless one is riding piggy back). Paths through gardens also allow access to plants for maintenance purposes versus tromping on the soil (please don't do that). Paths also can lead you past charming features (birdbath, stone bench, gurgling fountain) and 'hidden treasures' (a garden gnome peaking out from under large Hosta leaves, a stone plaque inscribed with a special message, a small water garden container).

♻ Fragrance adds a powerful dimension to shade gardens. Shade gardens tend to be still areas with light breezes at best moving through them. This is the perfect setting for capturing fragrance. For maximum pleasure, place seats near these 'airwicks', many of which are aromatic at night. Check out the Top Ten list of fragrant shade plants for great choices.

♻ Add arbors, arches, pergolas or trellises to a shade garden for a vertical element. These can stand alone or they can be draped in 'living scarves' (climbing plants). These make striking entrances to a garden.

♻ Water features are great additions. The sound of running water is very soothing, unless it is from a plumbing problem. You needn't have a large in-ground water feature to get this melodic effect. There are battery operated and plug-in, recycling water fountains that can be easily positioned for the perfect touch. Remember solar-powered fountains are useless in shade. Even petite fountains designed for tabletops can provide a surprising amount of sound from such a small object (like some children). Many larger fountain replicas are made of lightweight materials, such as resin, that can be easily moved without the aid of large muscles.

♻ Introduce another sensory stimulant with sound. Perhaps like me, you enjoy listening to soothing classical music when in the garden. Unfortunately, this is periodically interrupted by a crass rapping 'song' if my teenage son switches the station. Or maybe chirping tree frogs or tweeting birds are more your style. Check into weather resistant indoor/outdoor wireless speakers (that can receive transmissions from inside a house) or portable, weather-resistant stereo systems that can be set in outdoor entertainment areas or a secret retreat. "The world is alive, with the sound of music....."

♻ Where better to have a sitting area than in a shade garden? You are protected from the hot day sun and surrounded by lush, soothing foliage of shade plants. The space can be designed for only one comfy chair or it can accommodate a number of seats and a table. Whatever the size, make sure the 'floor' is created from a material that keeps feet dry and clean. The surface should also be smooth and level.

CHAPTER EIGHT

Garden Care

Top Ten Tips for Jump-Starting Shade Gardens in Spring

One of the reasons my perennials gardens are so lush and healthy is from how I ramp them up in spring. A little helping hand early on pays huge rewards and saves me time and money in the long run.

Here are some of my tried-and-proven tricks for jump-starting beautiful shade gardens. By the way, many of these also work for their sunnier counterparts.

Espoma

In late March or April, after the snow has melted (if you are 'lucky' enough to have it) and the ground is starting to soften, cast 5-5-5, 5-10-5, 5-10-10 or 10-10-10 granular fertilizer on gardens before, or immediately after, the foliage starts to emerge. You can use synthetic or organic products. I choose organic and use a 5-5-5 blend of alfalfa, plant meal, and naturally occurring minerals. This early feed encourages strong root growth and development. Many of these fertilizers are applied at the rate of approximately 2 pounds per 100 square feet but follow label instructions. Everything in my yard, except the lawn, gets this early snack: perennials; spring, summer and fall blooming bulbs; climbing vines; roses; shrubs; evergreens and groundcovers. Granular fertilizer will burn foliage so by applying it before plants emerge, you reduce this risk and save time in getting it down. If foliage is already up and at'em by the time you have a chance to do this, make sure to wash off any fertilizer that landed on the leaves. Easier yet, wait to apply fertilizer right before it's supposed to rain.

In late winter cut back ornamental grasses. There are not many grasses that tolerate shade so this should not take long. Cut back clumps to within an inch of the ground. Smaller grasses like some of the sedges and Black Mondo Grass can be hand-combed versus whacked. Simply pull the brown, weather-beaten blades out with your fingers.

Some perennials are more prone to heaving (out of the ground, not getting sick) with swinging spring temperatures. Shade plants that get pushed up from the soil, exposing roots, are Coral Bells, Foam Flowers (Tiaralla), Foamy Bells (Heucherella), and Astibles. When you see this uprising, press them back down into the soil. Plants in clay soil are more likely to heave.

Perennials that are evergreen or semi-evergreen show wear and tear after making it through Old Man Winter's playground. Cut off any dead or weather-beaten foliage on

Ginger (Asarum), Pigsqueak (Bergenia), Lenten Rose (Helleborus), Barrenswort (Epimedium) and Coral Bells.

❧ Apply a time-released fertilizer like organic Plant-Tone (5-3-3) or synthetic Osmocote (14-14-14) five to six weeks after you applied the above-mentioned granular fertilizer. I am chintzy with my time and money so I don't use these time-released fertilizers on every plant in the garden; only on heavy-feeding perennials that quickly deplete nutrients from the soil. Plants that 'wolf down their food' benefit from a slow, steady release of fertilizer over three to four months. Follow directions for the application rate, scratch it into the soil around the plant, and water in. Shade perennials that benefit from this extra serving of fertilizer include Astilbe, shade-tolerant Clematis and bulbs in the Lilium family (i.e. Martagons).

❧ Shovel mulch on the gardens to reduce weeding, conserve moisture, supply nutrients and make the gardens look nicer. Don't make the mistake of mulching too early. You need to allow the soil to warm up and dry out. Timing will vary depending on your hardiness zone and if you have sandy or clay soil. My 'green flag' for swinging the mulch shovel is when perennials are about 4" tall. For perennial gardens I recommend nutrient rich, organic mulches such as aged compost, manures, shredded leaves and finely shredded wood. Spread mulch approximately two to three inches thick around plants, being careful not to build it up against perennial stems.

❧ Squash problems with chomping slugs and snails by employing defensive strategies in spring. Refer to the Top Ten tips for winning the battle against slimers.

❧ Start dividing summer and fall blooming plants when shoots are 3" to 4" tall. Hosta can be divided just as the pips (stem tips) are coming through the ground. This is an ideal time for those that have intimated you by their size. You are a lot bigger than they are at this point. Go for it.

❧ Prune spring flowering shrubs right after they bloom. Shade tolerant shrubs include Rhododendrons, Pieris, Azalea, Kerria, Abelia and Enkianthus.

❧ Prune back spring blooming perennials that get ratty looking foliage after flowering or ephemerals that are going dormant. Unlike spring flowering bulbs, these do not need to store energy in a bulb for next year's flowers. Old-fashioned Bleeding Heart (D. spectabilis) is one perennial that can really try your patience after blooming. It's an eyesore by early summer. Stop the silliness and whack back the foliage to within 3" to 4" of the ground. Fill the cavity with some colorful annuals or plant perennials nearby with foliage or flowers that will expand into this space. Some good companion perennials include Astilbe and Hosta. Now is also the time to divide your Bleeding Heart if it has outgrown its spot.

Top Ten Tips for Preparing the Gardens for Winter

As the days get shorter and leaves start to fall, gardeners begin having sweet thoughts of cutting back their perennial beds, especially if our gardens' wardrobe has become drab. That's when I let it rip! ZZZZZZZzzzzzz. That's the sound of my hedge trimmer roaring to life as I head out to the gardens to say 'Hasta luego baby!' Once the hedge trimmer is back in the shed, I'll grab my power drill and bulb auger, hit the 'on' switch, and dart about making holes for spring blooming bulbs to the beat of my buzzing drill. Finishing this task quickly and easily, I'll then move inside to my kitchen and grab the blender for the soothing whirling sound of a margarita in the making. I love fall.

Here are some things I do to 'gently' tuck my gardens in for winter.

❧ Cut perennial foliage in shade beds down to within 2" or 3" of the ground. Yes, that includes Hosta and Ferns. Leave ornamental grasses alone and cut these in late winter or early spring. Semi-evergreen perennials such as Lenten Roses and Coral Bells can also remain unscathed. Also leave Astilbes alone for winter interest. Remove all other foliage with a hedge trimmer, weed whacker, pruning shears, hand pruner or even a lawn mower (raise the blade height). Remove all foliage from the garden and compost it. Do not put diseased foliage in the compost pile, especially leaves infected by mildew or aphids.

❧ Do you like a drink of water before going to bed? So do your gardens. Sending plants to bed with well hydrated roots will improve their odds for making it through the winter and performing well the next season. Deep water gardens and flowering shrubs before the ground freezes. I water my gardens until mid-November, even after I have cut them back.

❧ Most shrubs can make it through winter without a lot of handholding. But there are a few things you can do to show kindness.

- ❖ Keep flowering shrubs properly watered in fall. As noted above, they need to be well hydrated before the ground freezes and shuts off their water supply. This is especially important for spring blooming shrubs that have flower buds already formed on their branches. If the plant is 'parched' going into winter, the buds are compromised and this could lead to poor, or zippo, spring flowering.
- ❖ In November place chicken wire around shrubs that are targets for possible winterkill, stress or frozen flower buds. Pack the interior of the hooped cage with raked leaves. Shrubs that benefit from this protective measure include Hydrangeas that bloom on old and borderline hardy woodies that you couldn't resist

buying. Another option is to wrap them with burlap or set-up 'burlap screens' protecting them from wind as well as Bambi.

❧ In late November or early December spray anti-dessicant (Wilt-Pruf) on broad-leaved evergreens like Rhododendron, Holly, Boxwood and Pieris (Andromeda).

❧ Ramp up the color next season by planting spring, summer and fall blooming bulbs. Most people only plant spring blooming bulbs in fall but don't stop there. Hand dig or drill (using a bulb auger) summer and fall bloomers too for three seasons of color. Check out the Top Ten flowering bulbs list. I like planting a few pockets of bright colored, *sun-loving* bulbs (like tulips) in shade beds. I treat these as annuals. A 24" steel bulb auger and power drill help me zip through this easy project. After flowering you can pull these bulbs out of the shade bed and plant them in sunnier spot to ripen and bloom there the following season or give them to a friend. Another approach is to simply cut the bulb's foliage off at soil level. In the fall when you drill more sun-loving, colorful bulbs in the shady spot where you cut off the foliage, you'll hit the existing bulbs and they become compost. The fresh bulbs take their place.

❧ If you want to recycle tender 'bulbs' for the following season, dig and store them in fall. Some shade tolerant ones to winter over include Tuberous Begonias and Caladiums. Wait until right after the first frost, dig, cut back foliage, remove soil from bulbs, allow to air dry for a few days and store in a cool, dry place. They can be stored in peat moss, vermiculite, newspaper, brown bags or onion bags. Many gardeners grow tropicals such as New Zealand Flax (Phormium), Shield Plant (Alocasia), and Elephant Ear (Colocasia) in large containers. These can be brought inside and grown as houseplants or allowed to go dormant in a cool, dry place like the basement. If you treat these as houseplants, make sure to wash off leaves with an insecticidal soap or soapy water to kill bugs before setting them near other houseplants.

❧ If you have not done a soil pH test in years, fall is a great time to do this. Follow the instructions in Chapter 1. If a correction is needed, apply lime or sulfur after cutting back the gardens. This makes the job go more quickly since you don't have to work around a lot of foliage.

Rapitest

❧ To save a bundle of money, purchase marked-down perennials in containers. If it is too late to plant or you don't have the time to do this, over-winter them in their pots. Be sure to keep the potted plants consistently watered while they are still in active growth. In late October, cut back the plants in their pots. In late November give all pots a good drink of water and then cover with small squared chicken wire. This keeps voracious wildlife like chipmunks, voles and squirrels from eating the roots. If you want to further protect the plants, place mice bait between some pots. After securing the chicken wire, cover everything with tarp. Uncover in early April, depending on weather. If you have an unheated garage, shed or barn, then winter them there and skip the tarp step.

🔗 If your soil needs improvement, apply nutrient-rich mulch such as compost or aged manures around the plants after cutting them back. This will start breaking down and enrich the soil through fall, winter and spring.

🔗 The flowers of Bigleaf Hydrangeas will be pink, blue or 'blurple' based on the soil's pH. As noted in the Top Ten Flowering Shrubs list, Bigleafs are blue in acid soil (pH 6.0 or lower) and pink in alkaline soil (pH 7.0 or higher) or 'Blurple' between 6.0 - 7.0. Since an adjustment to soil pH takes three to six months from the time lime or sulfur is applied, I treat the soil in fall. This results in the blooms being the color I want the following year. Because I want blue Hydrangeas and the bushes are next to my home's foundation, the addition of sulfur is an annual activity to compensate for the leaching lime from the foundation.

🔗 Many upright Arborvitaes, especially 'Green Emerald', benefit from 'cinching' to reduce damage from snow and ice storms. I have a row of 'Green Emerald' that's the backbone to one shade bed. In November I circle twine around these Arborvitae, winding it from the base to the top, and then tying it off. This prevent splitting and deformation.

Top Ten Tips for Preparing New Perennial Beds

In Chapter 1 I talked about soil analysis, organic amendments, and soil pH tests (you remember, right?). These are all key elements in preparing a new bed or revitalizing existing gardens. Now on to tips for the actual 'dirty work', putting the shovel to the 'dirt'.

🌿 Many folks wimp out when it comes to digging beds deep enough. I empathize. It takes a lot more effort than reading this book (hopefully). But as my Mom always said, if it is worth doing, then do it well. You only get one chance to prep a mixed perennial bed, versus annual or vegetable gardens that are turned over every year. Loosen the soil to at least 8" deep and up to 12" for clay soil. Do this *before* adding organic amendments. As you dig, work backwards so you don't step on dug soil. Use flat boards to step on if necessary.

🌿 When creating a new garden, you cannot just spade under grass chunks and think out of sight, out of mind. These clumps will come back to haunt you as they sprout new shoots. You need to kill grass and weeds before turning them under. Some ways for accomplishing this include:

- ❖ BurnOut II (organic), Nature's Avenger (organic), Weed-Aside (organic), Herbicidal Soap from PlanetNatural (organic) and Round Up (chemical) are post-emergent weed killers that smite anything they touch. Be careful to follow label directions. Once the grass has browned, it can be turned under and worked into the soil.
- ❖ 'Smotherization' is my term for solarization (steaming grass to death under clear plastic in sunny areas) in shady spots. You 'smother' weeds and grass into submission by starving them of light and water. Cover the area with black plastic and pin down the edges with rocks, bricks or landscape pins. Keep the area covered for 4 to 6 weeks and presto, you should have killed most everything beneath. I say almost, because there are some incredibly persistent plants like Bishop's Weed (Aegopodium) that can survive pretty tough situations. If it does raise its ugly head, pull it quickly, even if you do not get the whole root. Because of its already stressed state, that should be the final, or second to last blow needed.
- ❖ 'Top spading' is another way to clear grass. Use a flat edged spade and slice under it about 2" to 3" deep. Peel back sections and throw pieces in the com-

post pile or use them to patch other lawn areas. Start from the back of the bed and work your way to the front so you do not step on already cleared ground. Looking for an easier solution? Rent a sod cutter that makes quick work of the job. Many rental centers have these. After removing the grass, prepare the soil at least 8" deep as noted above. Because you are removing several inches of root mass and soil, you will need to add additional soil so the garden does not become a 'sunken pit'.

᠕ Lasagna gardening is another way to build a new bed. Cover the grass with newspaper (6 to 8 pages), cardboard or rolls of landscape paper, and then top this with 3" to 4" of topsoil enriched with organic matter. In about 6 to 8 weeks you can dig right through the paper easily to install plants. If you want to start planting immediately, lay the paper down, cut X's or circles through it with a sharp knife, install the plants, water the area well, and then apply 3" of mulch on top of the paper and around the plants. My only caveat for this 'express' method (paper over grass and plant) relates to very poor quality or clay soils. These soils really need to be amended more deeply for long term, sensational results versus just a 'surface fix'.

᠕ After removing surface grass and loosening the soil to at least 8", now it's time to add organic matter. See the organic soil amendments chart in Chapter 1 for acceptable goodies. Depending on how deeply you dug the soil, add up to 1/3 of that depth in inches of organic matter. For example, if you prepared the bed to 8", then add 2" to 3" of organic matter. Then use a landscape rake to smooth out the bed. The final soil level should be a few inches higher than you ideally want it, as the soil will settle.

᠕ To accelerate great root development in a new bed, when preparing the soil work in a time-released organic fertilizer like Plant-Tone (follow package directions for amount). This will provide nutrients over a three to four month period. Or, you can use 10-10-10 granular fertilizer that is effective for 4 to 6 weeks. You can also fertilize existing flower beds with these fertilizers. Simply scratch the fertilizer into the soil around plants and water in. Apply this to your soil before putting down mulch or pull back mulch, apply, and then reset mulch.

᠕ Tree roots can stump many gardeners. You should not cut through large roots or rototill under trees. This kind of disturbance can quickly lead to a tree's decline. And remember, your goal is to create a shade garden. One way to deal with a very 'rooty' space is to spread a shredded mulch directly under the tree as far out as the tree's drip line. Start planting perennials outside this circle. Once perennials grow in, the mulched area will be less noticeable.

❧ When planting under trees, install perennials in smaller pots (i.e., 4" containers). These perennials have smaller root systems and are easier to dig into the soil and between roots. Be sure to keep the perennials well watered as they get established.

❧ If tree root competition is extensive, select shallow-rooted, drought tolerant groundcovers such as Bugleweed (Ajuga), Barenswort (Epimedium), Big Root Geranium (Geranium macrorrhizum), Dwarf Solomon's Seal, Lamium and Canadian Ginger that spread enthusiastically.

❧ When adding soil beneath trees on top of tree roots, it should be amended with organic matter and spread no deeper than three inches of soil. Also be sure the soil tapers off so it does not cover a tree's flare or trunk.

❧ After preparing the bed, water and allow the soil to settle for a week before planting. If you are the impatient sort (finger pointing at me) you can plant right away by using my 'tap dance' technique. Grab a big piece of plywood and set it on the prepared soil. Then step on the plywood and gently tap dance to lightly compact the soil. If done right, the soil will not be too fluffy, nor too compact, but just right for planting. Move the plywood along the bed, starting with the deepest part of the bed first and moving forward. Be careful not to step on the soil. If you need to use a plank or another piece of plywood to reach the deeper sections of the bed, do so.

Top Ten Tips for Pruning Flowering Shrubs

There are two primary seasons for pruning flowering shrubs. One is during a shrub's dormant season in late winter or early spring. At this time the plant is still 'asleep'; it doesn't even see you coming. The second opportunity is during its active growing season.

There is a misconception among some gardeners that all shrubs must be pruned every year, as if this is a golden rule. Not. Just because you plant a shrub doesn't mean the pruner must come. The following are reasons and tips for pruning (other than to maintain a shrub's size).

❧ To remove dead, damaged or diseased wood. Also remove any branches that are crossing and rubbing against the other.

❧ To promote a healthy, more vigorous shrub by thinning out older wood and allowing younger wood to replace it. This typically encourages more blooms since the plant's energy is channeled to fresh blooms instead of supporting older wood.

❧ To rejuvenate older shrubs and bring them back to a healthy state.

❧ To remove branches on shrubs that bloom on old new wood while the plant is still dormant. This way it doesn't waste energy directing food to limbs that will be cut off.

❧ Prune spring flowering shrubs right after blossoms fade. They bloom on old wood (wood that has gone through the winter). Many shrubs that bloom on prior year's wood benefit from an annual pruning to stimulate new growth for next year's flowers and to maintain size. Think of a common Lilac that has not been pruned for years. Soon the branches soar out of reach, the Lilac produces fewer and fewer flowers on old branches, it gets scraggly, and suckers abound.

❧ Prune summer bloomers in late winter or early spring before new growth starts. Most summer bloomers flower on new wood that comes off older wood. Some flowering shrubs rarely need pruning like Bottlebrush (Fothergilla) and Daphne 'Carol Mackie'.

photo courtesy of Daniele Ippoliti

❧ As a rule of thumb, don't prune flowering shrubs in fall. This can stimulate new growth and if the plant doesn't have time to harden-off this growth, damage can occur.

❧ If a shrub sends out suckers (new sprouts from the base that 'suck' energy from the main plant), remove these just below the soil surface. If the plant has been grafted, the suckers will outgrow the desired variety. Suckering shrubs include Lilac, Forsythia, Flowering Quince and Kerria.

❧ Prune non-variegated leaves that show up on variegated shrubs. The solid leaves are more vigorous and will eventually take over the plant if allowed to remain.

❧ Use hand pruners and loppers to prune flowering shrubs, not hedge shearers or hedge trimmers. Your goal is to carefully and selectively prune stems of flowering shrubs, not to shear off all of the stems at the same length as you would with evergreen Boxwoods and Yews.

❧ Shrubs grown for winter stem interest benefit from pruning. Examples are red and yellow stemmed Dogwoods. After stems get older than three years, their color fades. By removing the oldest stems each year and allowing younger ones to take their place, you have brilliant color every winter.

Top Ten Ways to Eliminate Weeds

Weeds are probably a gardener's number one enemy. They steal nutrients and water from our precious perennials and make gardens look unkempt. One terrific advantage of shade gardens is fewer weeds due to less light. And when we do have to weed, at least it isn't as bloody hot in the shade.

But since our goal is no weeds, here are some ways to squash them.

✺ A weed in time, saves nine. Pull weeds when they are small and before they go to seed. If you do a little weeding each time you stroll through the gardens, you'll be amazed at how this helps. Weeding becomes less and less necessary as gardens mature.

✺ Mulch miffs weeds. It is a great weed barrier. Shredded wood, aged compost or manure, leaf mold, and pine needles all help reduce weeds. Reapply mulch as it breaks down to maintain a 2" to 3" layer.

✺ A simple way to minimize weed seeds from sprouting is to stop disturbing the soil. Every time you dig or rototill, you unearth hidden seeds just waiting to germinate. Some seeds can live up to twenty years 'buried alive'. Now that's patience.

✺ One way to tackle taller weeds is to whack them off at the base and not pull them out of the ground, which disturbs soil. The weed will try to grow again from the remaining root. Cut it back another time. Eventually it will use all the stored energy in its root and give up the ghost. You win.

✺ Water beds well before weeding or weed after it rains. Moist soil makes it much easier to remove the renegades.

✺ Hoeing weeds with a stirup hoe (also called a scuffle hoe) is fun and efficient. This cool tool looks like a horse stirrup. It's sharp on both sides of the u-shaped blade. Simply pull it back and forth along the top inch of soil and it slices or uproots weeds without disturbing much soil. The hoes are designed with long handles that reduce stooping. I don't even bother to pick up the decapitated weeds. I let them compost right where they fell, unless they have a lot of seed heads and then I put them in the trash.

Gardeners Supply Company

To remove weeds in gravel or between stepping stones or sidewalk cracks, spray organic post-emergent products like Burnout II, Nature's Avenger or Weed-Aside. Simpler yet, use boiling water from your tea kettle. Many are fans of vinegar, either using it straight or mixing it with water and liquid dish detergent. I bet sauerkraut would work too.

Reduce weeding by allowing the leaves of shade perennials to slightly overlap, reducing the amount of light hitting the soil.

After cutting back your gardens in fall, weed one more time. I know, just make yourself. It will make a big difference next spring, especially eliminating perennial weeds in fall. I'm the first to admit I don't always know which weed is an annual or perennial. Just pull 'em all. You'll be smiling in the spring when you have a lot less weeding to do.

Post-emergents such as organic corn gluten or chemical Preen can be helpful in keeping weeds at bay by killing weed seeds as they germinate. But be aware that most of these products are non-discriminatory and will kill other seeds as well (biennials, annuals, perennials). I do not use these products (especially Preen) in my perennial beds for this reason. But the lawn is a totally different story. Every spring when the Forsythia is in full bloom, I apply corn gluten to the lawn at the rate of 20# per 1,000 square feet. It works as a great terminator for crab grass, dandelions and other invaders as well as a terrific fertilizer. Corn Gluten is high in nitrogen, just what grass blades are 'smackin' their lips for'.

Top Ten Deer Repellents and Strategies

They're out there. You know they're watching. The deer are just waiting for you to 'look the other way' so they can charge in for the 'kill'. And many are getting so bold, they'll march up to the buffet right in front of you. Is there no shame?

I'm the first one to say Bambi is cute, so is Thumper. But when they demolish my garden, they become monsters. I mean if they could wait until fall to 'cut back my garden', I'd be okay with that. But no. They target tender new foliage, plump tulip buds and the unfurling leaves of my prized Hosta. It's almost as if a green checkered flag is waved and the food frenzy begins each spring. I can deal with my teenage son and his buddies raiding my refrigerator, but the gardens are off limits. And yours should be too.

To win the battle, you need to understand what you are up against. How deer think. It's kind of like a chess game. Deer are very habitual. They tend to have the same browsing pattern. The goal is to not have your property on their dining route. One way to knock your garden off their 'commute' is to give them an unpleasant dining experience right from their first nibble. Once they associate your gardens with a yucky taste or sensation, you're headed in the right direction, and they are hopefully heading in your neighbor's direction. That doesn't mean they won't be back. Deer will eat almost anything if very hungry. Ditto teenage boys.

Another factor to keep in mind is that deer only have bottom incisors, no upper. So they tear or pull at leaves, leaving ragged edges. Rabbits, on the other hand, have upper and lower incisors and leave a smooth, clean cut. Deduce the offender and then create your strategy. Of course, if the culprit left its tracks, the mystery is over.

Here are some ways to create 'do not touch' boundaries for deer.

✿ Hosta are usually highly desirable in shade gardens. Deer find them highly desirable as well. It's deer lettuce. But even deer can be finicky. They tend to snub their little wet noses at thick (heavy substance) leaves. These leaves feel more substantive between your fingers and usually have puckering. And blue-leaved Hosta are particularly distasteful because, in addition to thicker leaves, they also have wax on their leaves that creates that lovely blue color.

✿ Commercial taste and smell repellents can slow deer down. Olfactory products work best in warmer weather; taste in colder temperatures. The most effective line of defense is a combination of both. Invisible Fence (www.invisiblefence.com), Bobbex (www.bobbex.com), Tree Guard (www.treeguard.com), Plantskydd (www.plantskydd.com), and Hinder have received praises from many gardeners. Hinder, Deer Busters, Deer Off, Deer Out, Deer

Gardeners Supply Company

and Pharm Deer are sprays that can also be used on edibles. Not Tonight Deer (www. nottonightdeer.com) has a great name but questionable results....on deer. Spray your weapon of choice on foliage and flowers per label recommendations. Even though most applications last six to eight weeks, spray more frequently in spring. Voracious deer, coupled with rapidly growing plants and untreated foliage, equal trouble. Switch products periodically during the season to confuse your opponent and keep deer from becoming desensitized to your defensive tactics. Plantskydd (www.plantskydd. com), with dried blood (from bovine or pigs) as its main ingredient, is reportedly very effective in winter when other odor repellants can be compromised due to cold temperatures. It seems the unnerving message of shed blood is not easily missed.

❧ Fencing is still one of the best ways to keep deer away. An 8' wall or fence is best. Even though deer could still jump this, they are less likely to do so when they can't see where they're landing. Double fencing, 3' apart, is very effective. Electric fencing also works but could be considered unfriendly in housing developments. A more feasible option is an individual, battery-operated, scent-charged electric post that gives tender noses a zap when they are attracted to the scent emitter. Black polypropylene mesh fencing is an option. It's virtually invisible from 20'. Many gardeners also swear by surrounding gardens with two fish lines; one at 1' and another at 3' from the ground.

❧ Home-made concoctions are entertaining to make. Forget baking cookies with your kids. Here is a whole new way of bonding in the kitchen. If you are a Julia Childs or Rachel Rae at heart, whip up your own nose-turning formula. Rotten eggs are always pleasant. Two eggs whipped into two cups of water and allowed to 'brew' a few days will do the trick. If this is too strong for your stomach, use one quart of water. Cayenne pepper and Tabasco sauce stirred into water and gently shaken also produces nice results. Add a few drops of vegetable oil or Murphy's Oil Soap to these mixtures so they stick longer to leaves. Fill a mister bottle with your favorite recipe and spray away. Irish Spring soap also works. You can spear bars onto 3' to 4' poles and place these soap torches around the yard. Leave the wrappers on so the bars last longer. Some folks enjoy making dried blood and hair sachets. Bloodmeal, sold by Espoma, mixed with some hair (from your last haircut) or fur from Fido's grooming, can make nice ornaments on trees and shrubs. These are just some of the incredible, swear-they-work recipes that one can find on the web.

❧ Recycled waste is always environmentally responsible. Dollops of Milorganite strategically placed around gardens works like a charm. Milorganite includes treated human sewage. Although it initially has a sharp smell, the vapors soon become imperceptible to the human nose but are still 'enjoyed' by four-footed marauders. Milorganite also works as a fertilizer but given its source, should not be used on edibles.

꿀 Predatory urine is prized by many. I've found 'yellow gold' to also be somewhat effective against chipmunks and squirrels. Popular 'dispensers' include wolves, bobcats, mountain lions, wolves, fox and coyotes. You can purchase this deterrent in a liquid, granular or powder form. A dab or shake will do around plants you wish to protect; not on plants. Leg Up Enterprises in Maine is one popular manufacturer.

꿀 Okay, for those of you with weak stomachs, move to the next suggestion. For those still reading, human urine is another tactic that some swear by. Yuck you say. Well, considering humans are at the top of the predator pyramid, it makes sense most wildlife would be cautious of us. Some imaginative gardeners have engaged the help of their husbands in marking gardens under the cover of darkness, although I doubt Emily Post would ever endorse such behavior. One of my friends routinely sends her husband out after he has polished down a few sodas or beers. They live in a rural area with a yard edged by woods. Unfortunately this approach is less appealing in my neighborhood where houses are side by side. I can just see my husband 'walking' around our yard in the evening, greeting our neighbors as he 'goes'. Now here's a hoot. When I told that story in one of my classes, a woman boldly blurted out, "I do the same thing." Silence. She explained she collects her urine and then puts it in a mister bottle and sprays her plants. Gasp! Then to my surprise, a woman at another of my lectures, one-upped her. She was dressed to the nines at a formal garden club annual event. Following my lecture, she marched up to me in her high heels and floral brimmed bonnet, and proclaimed "You know, you don't have to use straight urine. I dilute mine in half with water and it works just fine. I just didn't want to mention this in front of the others." And then she slipped off. You could have knocked me over with a feather!

꿀 Keep your eye out for Repellex systemic tablets scheduled to be released in 2011. These nontoxic tablets are placed in planting holes, or dug in around existing plants. The material is then absorbed by roots and distributed by the plant's vascular system. The plant will be fully 'inoculated' after a number of weeks (check the label for specifics and application details). It's predicted that these tablets will protect bulbs, perennials, annuals and shrubs for two to three years. Just don't place them around edibles designated for the dining room table. To learn more about their environmentally safe repellents and for an announcement on the release of this systemic product, visit www. repelleex.com.

꿀 Be smart about what you put on the buffet. Choose plants that are rarely browsed by deer or, better yet, are poisonous. The skull and crossbones approach may seem mean, but it isn't. One little nibble and deer move on. No harm done to the plant or Bambi. Poisonous perennials for shade include Monkshood, Foxglove, Hellebores, Colchicum, Lobelia, Lily-of-the-Valley and Daffodils. Some shade shrubs that are safe in deer territory are Enkianthus, Boxwood, Summersweet and Kerria. Deer's preferences can change by region so check with your local cooperative extension office to get a list of the least desirable. In general, most scented or silver leaved plants are Bambi turnoffs. To further protect plants at risk, 'barricade' them with borders of yucky tasting ones. If you are insanely desperate, you could always give deer 'bon-bon' plants to your neighbors as gifts. The deer will follow. Just don't overdo your generosity or the neighbors might get suspicious.

❧ Garlic clips are easy to use and highly effective. Simply clip the loaded mini-canisters to stems and nibblers are turned aside. Clips are effective for up to eight months and are usually sold in packages of 25. Many companies sell these including Gardener's Supply Company (www.gardeners.com).

Top Ten Mole, Vole, Chipmunk and Squirrel Deterrents

If you have already read my book, *The Ultimate Flower Gardener's Top Ten Lists*, you have seen some of these repellent lists already. The same tactics for dealing with these critters in sun, work in shade. Don't blame me.

Let me start by saying I am here to defend moles. It seems they get blamed for any 'trafficking' going on underground. Voles, chipmunks and squirrels are quick to point the furry finger. Unfortunately, moles are so ugly, they are easy scapegoats. Allow me to set the record straight. Moles are carnivorous. They eat grubs, beetles and earthworms. Actually, earthworms are almost 70% of their diet. Moles are not eating your plants. Yes, they tunnel, or should I say swim, through the ground with their big, clawed appendages but as they go they aerate the soil. Actually, some of their talents are fascinating. They can tunnel about 75' on a good day. Because their fur can lie flat in either direction, they can tunnel forward as fast as backward. Gold medalists can tunnel at over 16 feet per hour. Where are the mole cops when you need them?

In general, moles create two types of tunnels. Those close to the surface are used for feeding and the deeper ones connect the feeder tunnels. A soil mound at the surface is created from excavating deeper tunnels. Moles are very solitary creatures. Cornell Cooperative Extension states it is rare that more than one or two moles will reside in a half acre property. The only time moles gather is to reproduce and it is not pretty. Males are extremely aggressive and can fight for mating rights even unto death. Males....

Voles are field mice. Nasty little, voracious creatures that can rapidly reproduce and create a hungry, destructive army. Fertile little things, they can reproduce almost 50 babies in a year. To complicate matters, they do not hibernate in winter. They just keep munching on roots and bark. Voles create slightly smaller holes and tunnels than moles and the tunnels are closer to the surface. Voles can also 'tunnel' (chew) through taller grass. Above ground, they will also gnaw on bark and damage or kill trees. Wrap hardwire cloth around the base of susceptible trees in fall to protect them in winter. Remember to allow for snow and adjust for this additional height.

Chipmunks are not much better. Cuter, yes. My friend calls them rats with racing

photo courtesy of Daniele Ippoliti

stripes. Chipmunks create tunnels and will chew on plants and bulbs. If you have stonewalls or stone ledges on your property, chipmunks will come. You could be out in the middle of nowhere and they will find you. Eerie. Chipmunks are not as fertile as voles, but they do 'turn them out' at the rate of 8 to 10 a year. Sadly, voles and chipmunks will use mole tunnels to access and nosh on plant roots giving moles a bad rap. And not to burst your bubble of Alvin, Simon and Theodore, but chipmunks are omnivores and will eat young birds and eggs.

And squirrels. I'm really trying to come up with something good to say about them. I don't want to be known as a squirrel basher. But as many will adamantly agree, they are pests and a nuisance. They devour flowers and vegetables, strip bark off trees, hog the birdseed, create havoc in attics and sheds, and gnaw through plastic and wood. And they are quite the 'home bodies'. Once they make their home in your yard, they will be there for years. A gentleman in one of my classes trapped a squirrel in a Havahart trap and sprayed its tail blue. He then drove the cage miles away and let the squirrel go. The next week he looked in his backyard and there was the blue-tailed squirrel, angrily chirping at him. After telling the story, another person in the class suggested he should let it go on the other side of a body of water. Squirrels can't swim. Then another person eagerly piped in and suggested a busy highway. I stopped the discussion at that point as I saw others getting excited to pipe in with more ideas. I understand that squirrels have to eat, but sometimes they are just plain devious. Like the time they snapped off every one of my long-stemmed, purple tulips just as they were about to bloom. And to add insult to injury, they left each bud-topped stem on the ground by the plant.

I wish there was a single, humane 'bullet' that would handle all of these creatures, but there isn't. Sometimes patience is the best approach. The following are some tactics to defend your plants and lawns.

❧ Havahart traps can be used to capture critters without harm. The problem is what to do then. In many states, including New York, it is illegal to transport wildlife off your property. One of my clients had an interesting solution to this. After she had trapped a few squirrels, a raccoon and a groundhog she loaded the cages into her minivan and headed for a nearby park that had hiking trails through the woods. She let them go on one of the trails. Had she been asked what she was doing, she was prepared to say she was walking her 'pets' and they didn't come back. Creative.

❧ Mouse traps work well for voles. Now don't say ugh. Remember, they are mice! Simply bait the trap with peanut butter or go gourmet with Quaker Oats and peanut butter hors d'oeuvres balls. Place traps near the varmint's holes or grass 'tunnels'. To prevent cats, children or others from stepping into a trap, place it under a box with a 'Ben and Jerry' mouse door cut in the side. My friend, Roger Swain (with the red suspenders), suggests putting a large plastic pot from a prior plant purchase over the hole and trap.

Rat traps work the same for chipmunks. I know I am not making friends writing this but I did not make it up. You can read about this method on many web sites that state it's one way to deal with chipmunk infestations, especially if they are gnawing at your home. To each his own. You can always use Havahart traps. One word of advice from experienced trappers. Place food (apples pieces, dried fruit, nuts) in the trap of choice and leave it unset for a week. Allow the chipmunk to overcome its well-grounded fear of the trap. Then set it. Chipmunks are smarter and more cautious than mice, but eventually the stomach wins out. By the way, if you do choose to go with the rat trap approach, thankfully the animal's death is usually quite fast. Not like what happens when gardeners go the route of Juicy Fruit gum that slowly 'constipates' the poor creature to death.

Predatory urines can create unrest for voles, chipmunks and squirrels. There are many fragrances to choose from including coyote, fox and bobcat. You can purchase this 'extract' in liquid, granular or powder form. If you are using the liquid version, be careful not to spill this on yourself. Trust me. And here is a cute story from one of my clients. She was trying for weeks to get the 'bad smell' out of her first floor bathroom. Try as hard as she could, it remained. She finally approached her husband and asked he was having any urinary issues or just being more absent minded than usual in the lavatory. What a riot when they realized the smell was coming from outside their bathroom window where her husband had put down a large dose of coyote urine to protect prized Hosta. On a totally different note, some urine manufacturers also market predatory urine as a great tool for training dogs where to pee. A dog's natural territorial instinct is to mark over where an 'intruder' has been. Try it.

Hungry cats are an option. Unfortunately most cats are 'fat and happy' and not looking for snacks between meals. One of my neighbor's cats is a super hunter. Even though I hate cats using my garden as their litter box, at least one of the six felines is making 'other' contributions. Another angle is to plant Catmint (Nepeta) in your yard. Cats love Catmint to nibble and rub against. Even if the cats aren't hunters, they 'look' like hunters to little watching eyes.

Some folks reach for products like Poison Peanuts designed to be ingested by voles, chipmunks and squirrels. But there are several things that make these a poor choice. One, there is no control of what, or who, will put disguised poisons in their mouth and two, there may be secondary kills. Animals that then eat a dying poisoned animal. Cats are especially vulnerable… If your goal is to make a permanent dent in the population, then make the 'enemy' walk the plank. This is fondly called the 'bucket method' by exterminators. Fill a big plastic bucket ½ to 2/3 with water, set a plank up against the bucket, lay birdseed along the plank and then scatter some seed on the surface of the water. As the 'foe' munches its way up the plank, it eventually may try to reach the floating seeds and in it goes. Squirrels and chipmunks cannot swim. Sadly, voles can.

🌀 Add some spice to their lives. Cayenne pepper sprinkled on gardens being pulverized by voles, chipmunks and squirrels works, although you do need to reapply it after rain. Red pepper flakes last longer. I cracked up the first time I tried this. I watched a squirrel hop into the treated area, curiously sniff the ground, and then start jumping about like popping popcorn. Amusing. Cayenne pepper also works to change a male dog's marking habits. It drove me nuts to watch this guy walk his dog by our house and allow the dog to lift its leg on one of my perennial gardens. So one day I sprinkled a whole bunch of red cayenne pepper on that end of the garden. The next day when the dog came by for his 'usual', he sniffed the spot, started to do his 'leg lift' and froze. The dog started snorting, sneezing and shaking his head back and forth. No long term damage done, and no further peeing on my garden.

🌀 Castor oil has received high marks for repelling moles. Molemax, manufactured by Bonide, is a spray used on lawns where mole activity has been sighted. In tests by Michigan State University, it was effective 26 out of 27 times. It is also supposed to shoo voles as well. Bonide also sells Mole and Vole Repellent that is a granular, time-released castor oil product that protects lawns for up to two months. I was amused to read about a gadget, MoleMover, that sends out chatter replicating a mole's alarm and distress call to warn each other of danger. It won't kill the mole, just relocate it to your neighbor's yard. If you are curious or just want to have it as a conversation piece in your yard, check out www.exhart.com. They also sell Go Pher-It that 'communicates' with voles and gophers. Who thinks of these things?

🌀 There are many organic repellents on the market to deter little furry foes. Ro-pel, Bobbex-R, Shake-Away and Critter-Ridder are a few. This tactic is most effective if you keep switching the products so they don't get used to any one. Keep 'em guessing.

🌀 Fencing does work for voles. Protect plantings with small ¼" hardwire mesh dug into the ground at least 12" and then 12" to 15" above the ground. You can also use this around trees to protect them from eating the bark.

Top Ten Solutions to Slugs and Snails

Slugs are gross. At least snails discreetly cover part of their slimy figures with shells. But both are beauty queens compared to iris borers. If you have never seen an iris borer, don't.

Slugs and snails enjoy partying at night. They come out under the cover of darkness and chew holes in leaves. Hosta is one of their favorites. They can also act like paper shredders and wreck havoc on foliage with less substance. And don't think they just hang out in shade. They love daylilies and other sun lovers too.

Another calling card of slugs and snails is the slimy mucus trail they leave behind. It's almost like a sci-fi movie. Thankfully the slime is good for something. It seems the mucus is a natural anesthetic. If you lick a slug long enough, your tongue will go numb. Years ago some Native Americans would 'swish' slugs in their mouths when they had a toothache. We're just not as creative anymore. Except for little boys……

If luck were on our side, deer mowing down our Hosta would vacuum up slugs too. I think deer just spit them out because they get caught in their teeth. So how can we naturally wage war on these slimers? There are a number of ways to get the upper hand.

🐌 Diatomaceous Earth can be cast on the ground around vulnerable plants. DE is the sharp-edged skeletal remains of microscopic creatures. Sharp is not an attribute well received by these soft-bodied creatures. Concern is one of the popular brands available. Please note that this Diatomaceous Earth is not the same as that used in swimming pools.

🐌 Iron phosphate is very effective. Sluggo or Escar-Go are popular products but there are less expensive brands such as Slug Magic. Just make sure iron phosphate is the active ingredient on the label. Iron phosphate granules won't harm children, pets or wildlife plus any that are not ingested breakdown into the soil and fertilize plants. Everyone wins except you know who.

🐌 Beer traps are always a spirited solution for slugs over 21. Pour stale beer into bowls and set them into the ground with the lip of the bowl just at soil level. Slugs slip into the brine and drown. Of course this approach assumes that you drink beer and that you don't 'drink to the last drop'. Personally, I can't stand sharing my beer with slugs. One of my patrons experienced an unusual 'side effect' of using beer. She said it did reduce the slug population but now squirrels were the problem. It turned out squirrels were knocking back the beer and stumbling around her yard drunk. I suggested non-alcoholic beer.

ℭ Copper stripping and bands are exciting. When slimers start over the copper, they receive an electrostatic shock. You can enclose a garden bed with strips of copper placed on the ground, or nail copper along the top edge of raised beds, or use copper tubing to circle individual plants.

ℭ Flat boards are hangouts for slugs. The board offers protection and a cool retreat during the day and a launching point to slip out for their evening feed. Every few days pick up the board and remove the 'treasures' underneath. Another angle is using halved grapefruits or oranges. After enjoying your citrus, take the remains out to the garden and place the fruit face down on the soil near 'attacked' plants. The slugs and snails will be drawn to this nutritious snack. After a few days, you'll have a bowl full of slimers than can be set out for foraging birds to enjoy.

ℭ Share your breakfast. Crush egg shells and place these sharp pieces around plants at risk. The shells will break down into the soil adding calcium, a little nitrogen and some trace minerals. Are you a coffee drinker? Coffee grinds have been shown to be effective for protecting plants. Caffeine must give slugs the jitters. A combo of 80% coffee grinds and 20% chewing tobacco (unchewed) has received even higher reviews.

ℭ Hand pick slugs and snails off leaves in the evening or early morning before they slip off to their daytime hideout. Depending on how desperate my son is for cash, I have paid him an agreed upon amount per slimer collected. The problem I have is counting his stash. One mother had a different way of entertaining her young kids. She loaded plastic squirt guns with salt water and had them go on a safari hunt for slugs. Once they found these prehistoric looking creatures, they would spray the slugs and delight in how they 'magically' shriveled and disappeared (slug bodies have a high percentage of water and the salt extracts it quickly).

ℭ Hosta with thicker leaves are too much work for slimers. The heavier substance leaves are harder for them to 'chew'. What 'slugs'. Most blue Hosta, as well as those with heavy puckering in their leaves, fall into this group.

ℭ Don't water at night. You are just making it easier for them to slide across wet leaves. Make them work for their food.

ℭ Ammonia and water will clean up problems. Use household ammonia and mix it with water. Some say at a rate of one part ammonia to seven parts water. Others go as strong as one to four. I recommend using the more diluted mixture first to spray on leaves before inching up the strength of 'Mr. Clean'.

CHAPTER NINE

Creature Comforts

Top Ten Characters of Nature

You're probably wondering why I included this list. I guess it's because I was fascinated by how parts of flowers, leaves, stems and other natural tidbits found in our gardens could be woven together to create magnificent creatures. I was enthralled by it and I hope you will be too. Daniele Ippoliti's delightful Characters of Nature appear on the pages throughout this book, as well as in my first book, *The Ultimate Flower Gardener's Top Ten Lists.* These Characters of Nature are fascinating, and even more so once you realize what they were made from.

Daniele is a gifted artist with a special love for photography and the outdoors. She has her degree in art education, printmaking, and photography. She was inspired to start her business, Character of Nature, in 2007 just after her Father's death. He told her a few months before he died, "The world needs your Characters." Her company is eco friendly, charitable, and whimsical. Her company honors and supports nature by using natural products such as paper products printed on earth sustainable papers with veggie based inks, organic and made in USA 100% cotton t –shirts, tote bags, and photographs. Her company gives charitable donations to several organizations who focus on earth friendly practices, education, and support children's natural growth, such as The Adirondack School of Northeastern NY, Waldorf School of Saratoga Springs, The Nature Conservancy, The SPD Foundation, Saratoga Plan, and The Unitarian Universalist Congregation of South Glens Falls. The Characters of Nature are created from bits and pieces of her nature photographs. She then adds quotes to capture their fun and whimsical personalities. Daniele now offers you the opportunity to create your own personal Character of Nature for your business or personal needs. To learn more about her business, products, services, and to receive her e-newsletter, visit her web site at www.characterofnature.net or call (518) 878-4837.

Here are ten Characters of Nature that have blessed the pages of my books, along with Daniele's description of each. Smile and be fascinated.

Ms. Attitude was the first character I created. She is the only one I added color to. Her skirt is made from a photograph of amazing cobwebs between the spindles of my porch, graced with wild frost. This was the magical day where the Characters came flooding into my head.

The Hero is an ordinary person, just like so many of us, who for one reason of another became a hero to someone. He reminds me of a farmer who creates wonderful food, which sustains us all. His buttons are mushrooms from Canada and his eyes are little berries from a tree in my neighborhood.

The Dancer is a really whimsical Character who reminds us to live life as if no one is watching. In every way express the joy and love in your heart always. Her body is made from an Echinacea flower, her legs are Christmas cactus, and her eye is a raindrop. She reminds me of my Mother who loves to dance and taught the fun of it when I was young.

The Hard Worker whimsically tells how hard work spotlights the character of people. His hat is a bird's nest, his beard is the inside of milkweed, and his legs are a rock sculpture I found on a hike in Canada. He reminds me of my Father who was a very hard worker and taught me that hard work is a gift, which others appreciate.

The Adirondack Man reminds us to climb mountains and get their good tidings. He is completely made with things found in the Adirondacks. His legs are made from pinecones, his feet are the seeds inside the pinecones, and his "Adirondack Life" book is made from birch bark.

The Adirondack Woman walks through a mountain stream reminding us that, whatever is fluid, soft and yielding will overcome whatever is rigid and hard. She is completely made of things found in the Adirondacks. Her skirt is birch bark, her eyes are acorns, and her body is a spider egg sack. The two Adirondack people make a great couple; together they make a wonderful gift for the nature couple you know.

The Goddess sits in a lotus pose holding a nest. It represents the precious life that grows in everyone's nest. She beckons us to live our lives so that when we die the world cries and we rejoice. Her head is made of Indian corn, her head band is moss, her nose is a heart-shaped rock, and her eyes are raindrops.

The Proper Friend expresses to us that no matter how many things we may have; it is friends who make us the wealthiest of all. Her body and head are made from parts of a gerbera daisy, her eyes are white daisies, and her lips are roses.

The Bitching Friend comes to us with a funny yet strong presence and message about how we only have as many friends as we can tolerate the bitching of. He is made of the root of a tree that toppled over, his whiskers are strands of hay grass, his eyebrow is a mushroom, and he is leaning up against a mushroom.

The Singer rejoices with the gift of music. She reminds us how being creative connects us to the divine and our sensual self. Her body is made of a geranium leaf, her hair is queen-Anne's lace, and her nose is a leaf.

I hope you enjoy discovering more about the Characters. Maybe you see yourself or someone you know in them.

Wishing Great Discoveries
Daniele Ippolti

INDEX